IMF Adjustment Programmes and Developing Economies

About the book

A core responsibility of the IMF is to provide loans to countries experiencing balance of payments problems. This financial assistance enables member countries to rebuild their international reserves, stabilize their currencies, pay for imports, and restore conditions for strong economic growth. Unlike development banks, the IMF does not lend for specific projects.

However, when a country borrows from the IMF, its government makes commitments on economic and financial policies. These policies are intended to resolve a country's balance of payments difficulties, contribute to sustainable economic growth and to enable the government to repay the Fund. Together, these policies constitute a member country's policy programme (conditionality).

Over the years, the most controversial aspect of the IMF's relationship with its members has been the conditionality—the terms on which the Fund's resources become available to its members. Hence, analysis of contents of the programmes and assessment of macroeconomic performance of developing countries under these programmes becomes interesting and important. This is the subject-matter of this book. Six countries, viz. Morocco, Ghana, Chile, Mexico, India, and Bangladesh have been included in this study which covers the period from 1975 to 2002.

Author's profile

Dr. O.S. Deol obtained his M.Phil. and Ph.D. degrees from the University of Delhi. He has more than 14 years of teaching and research experience. Specialising in international business and finance, Dr. Deol has attended numerous seminars and conferences at the national level. Presently, he is a Reader in Commerce, Shaheed Bhagat Singh College (Evening), University of Delhi.

IMF Adjustment Programmes and Developing Economies

A Cross-country Analysis

Morocco Ghana Chile Mexico
India Bangladesh

O.S. Deol

New Century Publications
New Delhi, India

New Century Publications
4800/24, Bharat Ram Road,
Ansari Road, Daryaganj,
New Delhi-110 002
Tel.: 23247798, 55396605
Telefax: 011-51017798
E-mail: indiatax@vsnl.com
www.newcenturypublications.com

Editorial office:
34, Gujranwala Town, Part-2,
Delhi - 110 009
Tel.: 27247805, 27464774

First Published 2005

ISBN: 81-7708-089-x

Published by New Century Publications and printed at Singhal Print Media, Delhi -110 007

PRINTED IN INDIA

Preface

A core responsibility of the IMF is to provide loans to countries experiencing balance of payments problems. This financial assistance enables member countries to rebuild their international reserves, stabilize their currencies, pay for imports, and restore conditions for strong economic growth. Unlike development banks, the IMF does not lend for specific projects.

However, when a country borrows from the IMF, its government makes commitments on economic and financial policies. These policies are intended to resolve a country's balance of payments difficulties, contribute to sustainable economic growth and to enable the government to repay the Fund. Together, these policies constitute a member country's policy programme (conditionality).

Over the years, the most controversial aspect of the IMF's relationship with its members has been the conditionality—the terms on which the Fund's resources become available to its members. Economists have opined differently on the effectiveness of the IMF-supported programmes. They have also criticized the contents of the programmes. Developing countries are also raising question regarding the IMF-supported programmes. Hence, analysis of contents of the programmes and assessment of macroeconomic performance of developing countries under these programmes becomes interesting and important. This is the subject-matter of this book.

Six countries, viz. Morocco, Ghana, Chile, Mexico, India, and Bangladesh have been included in this study which covers the period from 1975 to 2002.

The book is organised into 11 chapters. Besides, there are 6 appendices which give relevant information about the policies and programmes of IMF.

I take this opportunity to express my deep sense of gratitude to a number of colleagues who each helped me at various stages of the completion of this book. I am thankful to the staff of Ratan Tata Library, University of Delhi, Library of Indian Institute of

Foreign Trade, New Delhi, FICCI Library and United Nations Library, New Delhi, from where I got the study material.

My special thanks are due to my wife, Asha and my son, Shubhankar for their cooperation and moral support.

Delhi
April 17, 2005

O.S. Deol

Abbreviations

ADB: Asian Development Bank
BIDS: Bangladesh Institute for Development Studies
BN: Billion
C: Constant
CA/GDP: Current account as% of gross domestic product
CN: Consumption
Cs: Cedis
DCR: Domestic credit growth rate
Ds: Dirhams
DS: Domestic savings
EA: Extended Arrangement
EIU: Economic Intelligent Unit
ESAF: Enhanced Structural Adjustment Facility
FB/GDP: Overall fiscal balance as % of gross domestic product
Forex: Foreign exchange reserve
GDP: Gross domestic product
GOI: Government of India
Gr: Growth rate
INFR: Inflation rate
INV: Investment
M/GDP: Imports as % of gross domestic product
MN: Million
NA: Not applicable
NPC: Non programme countries
OB/GDP: Overall balance as % of gross domestic product
PRGF: Poverty Reduction and Growth Facility
Ps: Pesos
Pre: Pre programme year value
Pro: Programme year value
RGDP: Real gross domestic product
Rs: Rupees
SAF: Structural Adjustment Facility
SBA: Stand By Arrangement
SDRs: Special drawing rights

Tk: Taka
T: Time
X/G: Exports as % of gross domestic product
M/G: Imports as % of gross domestic product
Z: Objective variable
Δ: Change

Contents

1

Macroeconomic Performance of Developing Countries

IMF-supported programmes have frequently been criticized on one aspect or another. The effectiveness and design of these programmes bear a question mark. Regarding the performance and design of the programmes, economists are also divided. Some have argued that, at best the Fund programmes do little in the way of improving economic picture. While, others have gone as far as to say that programmes worsen the economic situation by inducing stagflation. It has also been argued that over-optimism embodied in targets i.e. terms of trade, exports and tax revenues was often a problem in programme design which eventually led to the prolonged use of the Fund resources. It has also been alleged that the programmes enhance the dependency of developing countries. There is at present little agreement in the profession about how to estimate the macroeconomic performance of programmes.

In such a scenario, the study of effectiveness of the IMF-supported programmes on developing countries becomes interesting and important. In the present study, an effort has been made in this regard. The present book has following two main objectives:

1. To assess the macroeconomic performance of developing countries under the Fund-supported programmes.
2. To estimate whether these programmes enhance the dependency of developing countries.

An attempt has been made to accomplish these objectives by:

- Comparing the macroeconomic performance of the programme country during programme and prior to the implementation of the programme.

- Comparing the macroeconomic performance of the programme country and that of countries that did not implement the IMF programmes.
- Analyzing the macroeconomic performance of the programme country on the basis of sign and magnitude of the programme dummy variable. To accomplish this aim, few explanatory variables and a programme dummy variable have been linked with the ultimate targets.
- Identifying the regions where the IMF-supported programmes have been more successful.
- Observing the foreign trade trend of the programme country during the programme years.

This study is based on case study of six developing countries viz. Mexico, Chile, Ghana, Morocco, Bangladesh and India. These countries were selected were selected to represent different regions i.e. two belonging to Latin America, two from Africa and two from Asia.

The study period extends from 1975 to 2002.The following were the reasons for the selection of the period:

1. In 1974, the Extended Fund Facility was established, which provides fund for longer period and in larger amount than that of Stand-By Arrangements (SBAs).
2. Until the mid 1970s, the typical conditions placed on the use of Fund's resources involved the policies that influenced the level and composition of aggregate demand (Monetarist Approach). In the mid 1970s, the monetarist approach gave way to a more structural, longer run approach.

The macroeconomic performance of the IMF-economic adjustment programmes supported by Stand-By Arrangements (SBAs), Extended Arrangements (EAs), Structural Adjustment Facilities (SAFs), Enhanced Structural Adjustment Facilities, and Poverty Reduction and Growth Facilities (PRGFs) have been examined.

Since it is theoretically difficult to link all the policy variables contained in a Fund programme to the ultimate targets i.e. balance of payments, inflation rate, growth, and others, the study used only three approaches mentioned below.

1. The before-after approach,
2. The with-without approach, and
3. The generalized evaluation approach.

In the before-after approach, the macroeconomic performance during the programme was compared with that prior to the programme.

In with-without approach, the macroeconomic performance of the programme country was compared with that of a control group i.e. non-oil-non-programme developing countries. Each year, control group was formed out of 73 non-oil developing countries.

In generalized evaluation approach, few explanatory variables and a dummy variable have been linked with the ultimate targets. The behaviour of the programme economy was observed on the basis of sign and magnitude of coefficient of programme dummy variable.

The actual versus target approach could not be employed because of unavailability of statistics on ultimate targets in the case of most of the countries that implemented the IMF-supported programmes. However, if information was available in the case of any economic programme the actual versus target approach has been employed.

The variables used in this study have been divided into two categories:

1. Variables assessing the performance of the economy i.e. target variables.
2. Policy variables, which are used in fulfilling the targets.

Consumption, investment, domestic savings, exports-imports ratio, current account balance, overall balance, real gross domestic product, inflation rate, and foreign exchange reserves growth rate have been included in the first category. Exchange rate, interest rate, fiscal deficit, money supply growth, and domestic credit expansion have been included in the second category. Two variables: exports as percentage of GDP and imports as percentage of GDP have been employed to observe the dependency effect of the IMF-supported programmes.

Statistics on investment, domestic savings, and gross domestic product (all in national currency units) were collected from *National Account Statistics: Main Aggregates and Detailed Tables*, series compiled by United Nations, and *International Financial Statistics* compiled by International Monetary Fund. Statistics on exports, imports, current account balance, overall balance, real GDP growth rare, inflation rate, interest rate, exchange rate, and foreign exchange reserves were obtained from the *International Financial Statistics* compiled by the IMF staff. Government finance statistics were collected from the IMF' s *Government Finance Statistics* (Year Books).The relevant data were also compiled from UN's *Statistical Year Book*, UN's *National Accounts: Analysis of Main Aggregates*, IMF' s *Occasional Papers*, IMF' s *World Economic Outlook*, Economic Commission For Africa's *Economic Report on Africa*, and UN's *Statistics For Latin America* (Year Books).

The relevant variables were computed using the data base described above. The same sources were used in the case of non-oil- non-programme countries (control group).

2

IMF: Structure and Working

The International Monetary Fund, also called the Fund was established by 44 nations in July 1944. It started functioning from March 1, 1947. International Monetary Fund has 184 members. The total of members' quota in the IMF, as on 28th February, 2005, was SDR 213.5 billion. The fundamental purposes and objectives of the Fund have been laid down in Article 1 of the Agreement. They are as given below:

1. To promote international monetary cooperation through a permanent institution which provides the machinery for consultation and collaboration on international monetary problems.
2. To facilitate the expansion and balanced growth of international trade and to contribute there by to the promotion and maintenance of high level of employment and real income and to the development of the prospective resources of all members as primary objective of the policy.
3. To promote exchange stability, to maintain orderly exchange arrangements among members and to avoid competitive exchange depreciations.
4. To assist in the development of a multilateral system of payments in respect of current transactions between members and in the elimination of foreign exchange restrictions which hamper the growth of world trade.
5. To give confidence to members by making the Fund's resources available to them under adequate safeguards, thus providing them with the opportunity to correct maladjustment in their balance of payments without resorting to measures destructive to national or international prosperity, and
6. In according with above, to shorten the duration and lessen the degree of disequilibrium in the international balance of payments of members.

Structure of the Fund

The structure of the Fund consists of a Board of Governors, an Executive Board, a Managing Director, a Council and staff with its head quarters in Washington, USA. The ad hoc and standing committees are appointed by the Board of Governors and the Executive Board. The Board of Governors and the Executive Board are decision making organs of the Fund. They exercise powers and take decisions that are binding on members and the Fund. The Board of Governors is at the top in the structure of the Fund. It is composed of one Governor and one Alternative Governor appointed by each member.

The Board of Governors meets annually in which the details of the Fund activities for the previous year are presented. The annual meeting also takes a few decisions with regard to the policies of the Fund. Special meetings can be arranged by any of the five members having 25% of the voting rights. As a matter of practice, the majority of decision making powers of the Board of Governors have been delegated to the Executive Board such as decisions on access by the members to the Fund's resources, decisions on charges and remuneration, and the review of consultations between the Fund and its members.

The Executive Board has 24 members. Five Executive Directors are appointed by the five members (USA, UK, Germany, France, and Japan) having largest quotas. 19 Executive Directors are elected at interval of two years by the remaining members according to constituencies on a roughly geographical basis. There is a Managing Director of the Fund who is elected by the Executive Board.

The Executive Board is the most powerful organ of the Fund and exercises vast powers conferred on it by the Articles of Agreement and delegated by to it by the Board of Governors. Its powers relate to all Fund activities, including its regulatory, supervisory and financing activities. The Executive Board is in continuous session. Besides acting as the chairman of the Executive Board, the Managing Director is the head of the Fund staff and is responsible for its organization, appointments and dismissals.

Quota and Voting Power

Each member of the Fund has a quota, which is now expressed in SDRs. The member's quota determines its subscription to the Fund and its share in allocations of SDRs and also affects the member's voting power and maximum access to the financial resources of the Fund.

The initial quotas of the participants at the Bretton Woods conference were related to- but not rigidly governed- formulae that included national income, gold and dollar balances, average imports, the variability of exports, and the ratio of exports to national income. The formulae used as a basis for determining the quotas of original members was .

Quota = (0.02Y +0.05R +0.10M +0.10V) (1 +X/Y)

Where Y: national income in 1940;

R: gold and dollar balances on July 1, 1943;

M: average imports during 1934-1938;

V: maximum variation in exports during 1934-1948;

X: average exports during 1934-1938.

The formulae was later on revised and modified on different occasions. At the time of formation of the Fund each member was required to pay 24 percent of its quota in gold or 10 percent of its net official holdings of US dollars whichever is less. The remaining 75 percent of the quota was to be paid in the country's own currency. The practice of keeping gold with the Fund was discontinued in April 1978 and the Fund was de-linked from the gold since then. Now a country is allowed to the value of its currency and quota in term of the Special Drawing Rights (SDRs).

The Articles of Agreement provide for both general and specific adjustment in member's quota. The Board of Governors is required, at intervals not exceeding more than five years to conduct a general review of quotas and propose any adjustment that it believes appropriate. The present position of quota and voting power of member countries is given in Table 2.1.

Table 2.1: Members, Quota and Voting Power
As on February 28th, 2005

Member	Quota		Votes	
	SDRs (millions)	%age	Number	%age
Afghanistan	161.9	0.08	1869	0.09
Albania	48.7	0.02	737	0.03
Algeria	1254.7	0.59	12797	0.59
Angola	286.3	0.13	3113	0.14
Antigua &Barbuda	13.5	0.01	385	0.02
Argentina	2117.1	0.99	21421	0.99
Armenia	92.0	0.04	1170	0.05
Australia	3236.4	1.52	32614	1.52
Austria	1872.3	0.88	18973	0.87
Azerbaijan	160.9	0.08	1859	0.09
Bahamas	130.3	0.06	1553	0.07
Bahrain	135.0	0.06	1600	0.07
Bangladesh	533.3	0.25	5583	0.26
Barbados	67.5	0.03	925	0.04
Belarus	386.4	0.18	4114	0.19
Belgium	4605.2	2.16	46302	2.13
Belize	18.8	0.01	438	0.02
Benin	61.9	0.03	869	0.04
Bhutan	6.3	0.003	313	0.1
Bolivia	171.5	0.08	1965	0.09
Bosnia and Herzegovina	169.1	0.08	1941	0.09
Botswana	63.0	0.03	880	0.04
Brazil	3036.1	1.43	30611	1.41
Brunei	215.2	0.10	2402	0.11
Bulgaria	640.2	0.30	6652	0.31
Burkina Faso	60.2	0.03	852	0.04
Burundi	77.0	0.04	1020	0.05

Contd...

Cambodia	87.5	0.04	1125	0.05
Cameroon	185.7	0.09	2107	0.05
Canada	6369.2	2.99	63942	2.95
Cape Verde	9.6	0.005	346	0.02
Central African Republic	55.7	0.03	807	0.04
Chad	56.0	0.03	810	0.04
Chile	856.1	0.40	8811	0.41
China	6369.2	2.99	63942	2.95
Colombia	774.0	0.36	7990	0.37
Comoros	8.9	0.004	339	0.02
Congo, Demo Republic of	533.0	0.25	5580	0.26
Congo, Republic of	84.6	0.04	1096	0.05
Costa Rica	164.1	0.08	1891	0.09
Cote d`Ivoire	325.2	0.15	3502	0.16
Croatia	365.1	0.17	3901	0.18
Cyprus	139.6	0.07	3901	0.18
Czech Republic	819.3	0.39	8443	0.39
Denmark	1642.8	0.77	16678	0.77
Djibouti	15.9	0.01	409	0.02
Dominica	8.2	0.004	332	0.02
Dominican Republic	218.9	0.10	2439	0.11
Ecuador	302.3	0.14	3273	0.15
Egypt	943.7	0.44	9687	0.45
El Salvador	171.3	0.08	1963	0.09
Equatorial Guinea	32.6	0.02	576	0.03
Eritrea	15.9	0.01	409	0.02
Estonia	65.2	0.03	902	0.04
Ethiopia	133.7	0.06	1587	0.07
Fiji	70.3	0.03	953	0.04
Finland	1263.8	0.59	12888	0.59

Contd...

France	10738.5	5.05	107635	4.96
Gabon	154.3	0.07	1793	0.08
Gambia, The	31.1	0.01	561	0.03
Georgia	150.3	0.07	1753	0.08
Germany	13008.3	6.11	130332	6.01
Ghana	369.0	0.17	3940	0.18
Greece	823.0	0.39	8480	0.39
Grenada	11.7	0.01	367	0.02
Guatemala	210.2	0.10	2352	0.11
Guinea	107.1	0.05	1321	0.06
Guinea-Bissau	14.2	0.01	392	0.02
Guyana	90.9	0.04	1159	0.05
Haiti	81.9	0.04	1069	0.05
Honduras	129.5	0.06	1545	0.07
Hungary	1038.4	0.49	10634	0.49
Iceland	117.6	0.06	1426	0.07
India	4158.2	1.95	41832	1.93
Indonesia	2079.3	0.98	21043	0.97
Iran	1497.2	0.70	15222	0.70
Iraq	1188.4	0.56	12134	0.56
Ireland	838.4	0.39	8634	0.40
Israel	928.2	0.44	9532	0.44
Italy	7055.5	3.32	70805	3.26
Jamaica	273.5	0.13	2985	0.14
Japan	13312.8	6.26	133378	6.15
Jordan	170.5	0.08	1955	0.09
Kazakhstan	365.7	0.17	3907	0.18
Kenya	271.4	0.13	2964	0.14
Kiribati	5.6	0.003	306	0.01
Korea	1633.1	0.77	16586	0.76
Kuwait	1381.1	0.65	14061	0.65
Kyrgyz Republic	88.8	0..4	1138	0.05
Lao P D R	52.9	0.02	779	0.04
Latvia	126.8	0.06	1518	0.07

Contd...

Lebanon	203.0	0.10	2280	0.11
Lesotho	34.9	0.02	599	0.03
Liberia	71.3	0.03	0	0
Libya	1123.7	0.53	11487	0.53
Lithuania	144.2	0.07	1692	0.08
Luxembourg	279.1	0.13	3041	0.14
Macedonia	68.9	0.03	939	0.04
Madagascar	122.2	0.06	1472	0.07
Malawi	69.4	0.03	944	0.04
Malaysia	1486.6	0.70	15116	0.70
Maldives	8.2	0.004	332	0.02
Mali	93.3	0.04	1183	0.05
Malta	102.0	0.05	1270	0.06
Marshall Islands	3.5	0.002	285	0.01
Mauritania	64.4	0.03	894	0.04
Mauritius	101.6	0.05	1266	0.06
Mexico	2585.8	1.22	26108	1.20
Micronesia	5.1	0.002	301	0.01
Moldova	123.2	0.06	1482	0.07
Mongolia	51.1	0.02	761	0.04
Morocco	588.2	0.28	6132	0.28
Mozambique	113.6	0.05	1386	0.06
Myanmar	258.4	0.12	2834	0.13
Namibia	136.5	0.06	1615	0.07
Nepal	71.3	0.03	963	0.04
Netherlands	5162.4	2.43	51874	2.39
New Zealand	894.6	0.42	9196	0.42
Nicaragua	130.0	0.06	1550	0.07
Niger	65.8	0.03	908	0.04
Nigeria	1753.2	0.82	17782	0.82
Norway	1671.7	0.79	16967	0.78
Oman	194.0	0.09	2190	0.10
Pakistan	1033.7	0.49	10587	0.49
Palau	3.1	0.001	281	0.01

Contd...

Panama	206.6	0.10	2316	0.11
Papua New Guinea	131.6	0.06	1566	0.07
Paraguay	99.9	0.05	1249	0.06
Peru	638.4	0.30	6634	0.31
Philippines	879.9	0.41	9049	0.42
Poland	1369.0	0.64	13940	0.64
Portugal	867.4	0.41	8924	0.41
Qatar	263.8	0.12	2888	0.13
Romania	1030.2	0.48	10552	0.49
Russian Federation	5945.4	2.79	59704	2.75
Rwanda	80.1	0.04	1051	0.05
St. Kitts and Nevis	8.9	0.004	333	0.02
St. Lucia	15.3	0.01	403	0.02
St. Vincent and Grenadines	8.3	0.004	333	0.02
Samoa	11.6	0.01	366	0.02
San Marino	17.0	0.01	420	0.02
Sao Tome Principe	7.4	0.003	324	0.01
Saudi Arabia	6985.5	3.28	70105	3.21
Senegal	161.8	0.08	1868	0.09
Serbia and Montenegro	467.7	0.22	4927	0.23
Seychelles	8.8	0.004	338	0.02
Sierra Leone	103.7	0.05	1287	0.06
Singapore	862.5	0.41	8875	0.41
Slovak Republic	357.5	0.17	3825	0.18
Slovenia	231.7	0.11	2567	0.12
Solomon Islands	10.4	0.005	354	0.02
Somalia	44.2	0.02	692	0.03
South Africa	1868.5	0.88	18935	0.87
Spain	3058.9	1.43	30739	1.42
Sri Lanka	413.4	0.19	4384	0.20

Contd...

Sudan	169.7	0.08	1947	0.09
Suriname	92.1	0.04	1171	0.05
Swaziland	50.7	0.02	757	0.03
Sweden	2395.5	1.13	24205	1.12
Switzerland	3458.5	1.63	34865	1.61
Syrian Arab Republic	293.6	0.14	3186	0.15
Tajikistan	87.0	0.04	1120	0.05
Tanzania	198.9	0.09	2239	0.10
Thailand	1081.9	0.51	11069	0.51
Timor-Leste	8.2	0.004	332	0.02
Togo	73.4	0.03	984	0.05
Tonga	6.9	0.003	319	0.01
Trinidad and Tobago	335.6	0.16	3606	0.17
Tunisia	286.5	0.13	3115	0.14
Turkey	964.0	0.45	9890	0.46
Turkmenistan	75.2	0.04	1002	0.05
Uganda	180.5	0.08	2055	0.09
Ukraine	1372.0	0.64	13970	0.64
United Arab Emirates	611.7	0.29	6367	0.29
United Kingdom	10738.5	5.05	107635	4.96
United states	37149.3	17.46	371743	17.14
Uruguay	306.5	0.14	3315	0.15
Uzbekistan	275.6	0.13	3006	0.14
Vanuatu	17.0	0.01	420	0.02
Venezuela	2659.1	1.25	26841	1.24
Vietnam	329.1	0.15	3541	0.16
Yemen	243.5	0.11	2685	0.12
Zambia	489.1	0.23	5141	0.24
Zimbabwe	353.4	0.17	0	0
Totals	213478.4	100	2176037	100

Source: IMF- *International Financial Statistics*

Financing Sources

The IMF derives its resources from:

1. Resources in the general resource account, which may be used to provide balance of payment financing to all members and are obtained from both members' subscriptions and the IMF borrowing;
2. Resources in the Special Disbursement Account, which are used for concessional balance of payments assistance to low income developing countries and are obtained from the reflow of Trust Fund Resources (originally derived from the proceeds of the sale of a part of the IMF's gold holdings); and
3. Resources in the Poverty Reduction and Growth Facility Trust, which are derived from members' loan and donations, used by the Fund as trustee, for concessional balance of payments assistance to low income developing members.

The rules governing access to the Fund's general resources – that is, its holdings of currencies of member countries and SDRs, as well as borrowed resources- apply uniformly to all members. Access to these resources is determined primarily by the member's balance of payments need and the strength of its adjustment policies and may be permitted to limits that are defined in relation to member's quota. However, under the IMF's Articles of Agreement, the IMF may allow members access to its general resources in excess of these limits in exceptional circumstances.

General resources are used to finance stand-by and extended arrangements, as well as special facilities that are open to all members, including the compensatory financing facility, supplemental reserve facility, and emergency assistance.

Facilities

The IMF's financial resources are made available to its members under a variety of facilities and policies, which differ mainly in the type of balance of payments needs they address; the degree of conditionality attached to them, access limit to resources, and the cost to the borrower. These facilities have been listed in Table 2.2.

Table 2.2: The Facilities: General Terms

Facility	Year of Origin	Charges	Obligation schedule (years)	Expectation schedule (years)	Instalments
Stand by Arrangement	1952	Basic rate plus surcharge	3¼-5	2¼-4	Quarterly
Extended Fund Facility	1974	Basic rate plus surcharge	4½-10	4½-7	Semiannual
Compensatory Financing Facility	1963	Basic rate	3¼-5	2¼-4	Quarterly
Emergency Assistance	1962	Basic rate	3¼-5	N/A	Quarterly
Supplemental Reserve Facility	1997	Basic rate plus surcharge	2½-3	2-2¼	Semiannual
Poverty Reduction and Growth Facility	1999	0.5 percent per annum	5½-10	N/A	Semiannual

Note: The basic rate of charge is linked directly to the SDR interest rate by a coefficient that is fixed in each financial year.

Source: *IMF-Survey*

Reserve Tranche

A member has reserve tranche position in the Fund to the extent that its quota exceeds the IMF's holdings of its currency in the general resources account, excluding holdings arising out of purchases made by the member under all policies on the use of the Fund's general resources. A member may purchase up to the full amount of its reserve tranche at any time, subject only to the requirement of balance of payment need. A reserve tranche purchase does not constitute a use of IMF credit and is not subject to charges or to an expectation or obligation to repurchase.

Credit Tranches

The credit tranche policy is the IMF's basic policy on the use of its general resources. Credit is made available in four tranches, each equivalent to 25 percent of a country's quota. Members may request stand-by arrangement above this limit in context of other policies.

A first credit tranche purchase raises the IMF's holdings of the purchasing member's currency in the credit tranches to no more than 25 percent of quota. Generally, a member may request use of IMF's resources in the first credit tranche if it demonstrates that it is making reasonable efforts to overcome its balance of payment difficulties. A member may also request use of the first credit tranche as part of a stand-by arrangement.

Subsequent purchases are made in the upper credit tranches. A member may use the IMF's resources in the upper credit tranches if it adopts policies that provide appropriate grounds for expecting that the member's balance of payments difficulties will be resolved within a reasonable period. Use of upper credit tranche is almost always made under a stand-by or an extended arrangement.

Stand-by Arrangements

A stand-by arrangement, like an extended arrangement, assures the member that it will be able to make purchases from the IMF, up to a specified amount, during a given period, as long as it has observed the performance criteria and other terms specified in the arrangement. The length of stand-by arrangements has typically been between 12 and 18 months, but it may extend up to three years. Repurchases of credit tranche drawings financed with ordinary resources-that is, the IMF's holdings of member's currency and SDRs, rather than borrowed resources- are made three and quarter to five years after each purchase. The normal annual access limit is 100 percent of quota. The cumulative access in combination with Extended Fund Facility is up to 300 percent of quota.

Purchase of amounts available under a stand-by arrangement in the upper credit tranches or an extended arrangement are phased that is, they are made available in the instalments at specified intervals during the period of arrangement. The member's right to draw is subject to observance of performance criteria and other specified conditions. These criteria typically cover credit policy, government or public sector borrowing requirements, and policies on trade and payments restrictions.

Performance criteria allow the member and the IMF to assess the member's progress in carrying out policies during a stand-by (or an extended) arrangement and they signal the need for possible corrective policies. When the performance criteria have not been observed, further purchases are permitted only after the IMF and the member reach understandings-following consultations and Executive Board action-for resumption of purchases.

Extended Fund Facility

Under the extended fund facility (EFF), which was established in 1974, the IMF may provide assistance to its members to enable them to meet their balance of payments need for longer periods and in larger amounts in relation to quotas than under the credit tranche policies.

A member that requests an extended arrangement is expected to present a programme to outlining the objectives and policies for the whole period of arrangement, and to present each year a detailed statement of policies and measures that it will follow in the next twelve months.

The normal annual access limit is 100 percent of quota. The cumulative access limit in combination with Stand-By Arrangement is 300 percent. The length of extended arrangement is normally 3 years, although it may be extended to 4 years, at the request of member. Repurchases of drawings of ordinary resources under the EFF are made four and half to ten years after each purchase.

Compensatory Financing Facility

Compensatory financing under the Compensatory Financing Facility (CFF) helps countries meet shortfall in their exports receipts and or excesses in the cost of their cereal imports. Through an appropriate blend of additional financing and adjustment, this helps countries facing adverse external shocks that are beyond their control to maintain the momentum of adjustment programmes.

Compensatory financing was first introduced in 1963 to provide financial assistance to members experiencing- for reasons largely beyond their control- balance of payments problems resulting from temporary declines exports earnings below their medium term trend, particularly as a result of fluctuations in commodity prices. Initially, compensatory financing covered only merchandise export earnings, but the range of exports covered has expanded over the years. In 1979, the facility was broadened to include shortfalls in receipts from two categories of services: tourism and workers' remittances. In 1981, a new element was added to the facility to allow compensation for countries faced with an excessive rise in the cost of their imports of cereal products.

In December 1990, as a part of the IMF's policy adaptations in the light of events in the Middle East, the Executive Board further widened the range of services eligible for compensatory financing to cover most services, including earnings from pipelines, canal transit fees, shipping, transportation, construction and insurance. At the same time, the Board allowed quicker access to compensatory credit by permitting the members to use estimated, rather than actual, data for the entire shortfall year to calculate the earning shortfall. The maximum access limit is 45 percent of quota for each element- export shortfall and excess cereal import costs. The combined limit is 55 percent of quota.

Emergency Assistance

The IMF provides emergency assistance to countries that have experienced a natural disaster or are emerging form armed conflicts. The IMF provides its members quick, medium term assistance in case of balance of payments difficulties related to natural disasters. In 1995, a new element was added to this facility to allow assistance in case of armed conflict. The Fund provides quick, medium term assistance to member countries with balance of payments difficulties related to the aftermath of civil unrest or international armed conflict. The member country is expected to make reasonable efforts to overcome balance of payments difficulties. The focus will be on institutional and administrative capacity building to pave the way toward an upper credit tranche arrangement or an arrangement under the Poverty Reduction and Growth Facility Trust.

Purchases are made in quarterly instalments and repurchases expected to be made three and a quarter to five years after the purchase. The normal access limit is 25 percent of quota, although up to an additional 25 percent can be made available in exceptional cases.

Supplemental Reserve Facility

This facility was introduced in 1997 to meet the need for very short–term financing on a large scale. The motivation for the supplemental reserve facility was the sudden loss of market confidence experienced by emerging market economies in the 1990s, which led to massive outflow of capital and required financing on a much larger scale than anything the IMF had previously been asked to provide. There is no access limit. This facility is available only when access under associated regular arrangement would otherwise exceed either annual or cumulative limit.

The conditions applicable in context of a regular arrangement are applicable in this facility too. The very purpose is to strengthen the policies to address the loss of market confidence. This facility is available for one year with front-loaded access with two or more purchases. Repayments are expected to be made two and a half to three years after the purchase.

Poverty Reduction and Growth Facility

In September 1999, the IMF established the Poverty Reduction and Growth Facility (PRGF), which replaced its Enhanced Structural Adjustment Facility (ESAF). The PRGF broadened the objective of the IMF's concessional lending to include a more explicit focus on poverty reduction in the context of a growth oriented strategy. Demand for PRGF resources has been high. In recent years, more than 60 countries have had PRGF Arrangements or have transformed ESAF Arrangements to include the new features of the PRGF.

The IMF and the World Bank support strategies that low income borrowing countries elaborate in a poverty reduction strategy paper (PRSP). These PRSPs are prepared through a participatory process that involves domestic stakeholders and external development partners. These PRSPs integrate macroeconomic, structural, and poverty reduction policies. The papers are then broadly endorsed by the IMF and the World Bank as providing a sound basis for concessional lending. Updated periodically (up to five years) with annual progress reports, PRSPs describe the country's macroeconomic, structural, and social policies and programmes over a horizon of three years or longer. PRSPs also specify the external financing needed to implement the strategy.

Since the preparation of PRSP is a lengthy process, the IMF and the World Bank has agreed to provide concessional assistance on the basis of interim PRSPs. These interim strategy papers summarize the current knowledge and analysis of a country's poverty situation, describe the existing poverty reduction policy, and the layout the process for producing a fully developed PRSP in a participatory fashion.

A member can request under this facility up to 140 percent of its quota, but this limit can be raised to 185 percent of quota in exceptional circumstances. The semi-annual (or occasionally quarterly) disbursements are contingent on the observance of performance criteria and completion reviews. Charges are low in this facility. Repurchases are expected to be made five and a half to ten years after the purchase.

3

IMF-Supported Programmes and Conditionalities

When the IMF provides financial support to a member country to help it resolve balance of payments problems, its support is conditional on the country's implementation of the policy adjustments and the reforms needed to correct the problems that gave rise to the balance of payments difficulties.

A country requesting financing from the IMF prepares a "Letter of Intent" outlining the authorities' policy intentions during the programme period. The IMF's financing is usually provided in instalments; each instalment is conditional on the country's meeting specific performance criteria that indicate whether the policies envisaged have been carried out.

Evolution of Conditionalities

Article number one of the Fund's charter calls on the IMF to make financial resources available to members on a temporary basis and with adequate safeguards to permit them to correct payments imbalances. In 1952, the principle of conditionality was implicitly incorporated into the Fund's lending policies.

A further development in the functioning of conditionality was the statement in the annual report of 1959 on general standard relating to the extension of credit. A minimal level of conditionality was associated with first credit tranche and progressively higher degree was expected for the second to fourth credit tranches.

A review of conditionality was undertaken by the Executive Board in 1968. The Fund decided to incorporate the practice of conditionality explicitly into its chapter. Prior to this date, the concept of conditionality had generally been referred to in a vague manner. Amendment to the Fund's article of agreement in 1968 ended this confusion by introducing, for the first time, a clear language which outlined the Fund's position with respect to conditionality.

Until the mid 1970s, the typical conditions placed on the use of Fund resources involved the policies that influenced the level and composition of aggregate demand. During this period excess demand was perceived as the most important cause of inflation, currency overvaluation and ultimately payment difficulties. The expeditious elimination of excess demand was viewed as an essential condition for restoring payments equilibrium. This position has been often been referred to as the monetarist approach.

The monetarist approach views excess demand as the root cause of inflation and exchange rate disequilibrium. Its goal is the rapid alleviation, typically in one year or less, of inflation and restoration of exchange rate equilibrium viz., policies that alter the size and composition of aggregate demand. Monetarist policies generally call for:

- Control of the money supply,
- Reduction of the government deficit,
- Exchange rate devaluation,
- Deregulation of prices,
- Reduction of consumer subsidies, and
- Elimination of tariff and non tariff barriers.

In mid 1970s, the monetarist approach gave way to a more structural longer run approach. The introduction of this new approach to payments adjustments was precipitated by the growing recognition, both within and outside the Fund, that payments imbalances could no longer be corrected within one year. In response to this recognition, the Fund increased its support for programmes that called for adjustment over longer period. In 1974, the Fund established the extended fund facility, which was designed to provide members with up to three years of financial support. In addition, the Fund decided in 1979 to allow stand-by arrangements to be extended up to three years. This development was accompanied by growing support for more comprehensive programmes designed to affect the balance of payments through change in demand as well as supply. These programmes continued to rely on the typical monetarist instruments, but in a more gradual manner. In addition, they called for more structural supply oriented policies such as reducing the size of public sector, channellising resources away from the public sector, creating financial intermediaries, promoting savings and discouraging the wasteful investment by increasing real interest rates.

Again, in 1978 the Fund began its review of conditionality that culminated in the 1979 Executive Board decision on new guidelines. Among the new features that met the some of the concern of developing countries were:

- The possibilities of SBAs of a longer term framework, and
- The acceptance by the Fund, in devising adjustment programmes, to pay due regard to the domestic social and political objectives, the economic priorities and the circumstances of members, including the cause of their balance of payments problems.

In June 1989, the Board conducted regular review of conditionality, leaving the 1979 guidelines on conditionality unchanged. In September 2002, the Board approved new conditionality guidelines. The new guidelines emphasize the need to focus conditionality on policies that are critical to achieving the macroeconomic objectives of IMF-supported programmes. They also aim to establish a clearer division of labour with other international institutions, especially the World Bank.

In the new guidelines, the IMF recognizes that building consensus on economic policies is the responsibilities of the authorities. The guidelines out line ways that the IMF can help ensure that policy programmes are adequately supported in the country and are likely to be implemented:

- IMF staff should undertake an effective dialogue on feasible policy options.
- IMF staff should be aware of political factors that are likely to influence the prospects for implementation and should

provide the Executive Board with candid assessment of ownership.

- IMF should be open to programmes that differ from the staff's preferred options, as long as the core objectives of the programmes are not compromised.
- IMF technical assistance should be directed toward the medium and long term and aim at building countries' capacity to formulate and implement policies.
- IMF can play supportive role in communicating with the public about economic policies; thus, IMF staff has, to an increasing extent, been engaging in dialogue with a wider range of governmental institutions, with civil society, and with media.
- Finally, if there is an inadequate level of ownership for a viable policy programme, the IMF should be cautious in providing financial support.

IMF-Supported Programmes

The conditionality associated with the use of Fund's resources requires the member to undertake a programme. This requirement is designed to ensure that the Fund's financial assistance supports the implementation of economic policies that give a substantial assurance that a viable balance of payments position will be attained within a reasonable period of time. This involves restoring a sustainable balance between the aggregate demand for, and the aggregate supply of resources in the economy. The Fund's approach to design the stabilization programmes has been characterized as monetarist and owed much to the framework proposed by Polak. The Fund programmes are in fact a complex package of policy measures geared to the particular circumstances of the country. The choice of policies and the nature of policy mix in programme result from negotiations between the country's authority and the Fund. Aside from monetary and exchange rate policies, a typical programme calls for fiscal measures, such as reduction in government expenditure and increase in taxation, increase in domestic interest rate and producer prices to the realistic levels, policies to raise investment and improve its efficiency, trade liberalization, and wage restraint. The various policy measures, generally contained in the Fund-supported programmes, have been grouped into five categories as given below.

IMF Adjustment Programmes

1. Monetary and Fiscal Policies

- Domestic credit expansion restraints
- Fiscal restraints

2. Structural Reforms

- Trade policies
  - ➢ Trade liberalization
  - ➢ Pricing reforms
  - ➢ Efficient allocation of resources
- Pricing policies
  - ➢ Raise producer prices to world level
  - ➢ Elimination of subsidies
- Public sector policies
  - ➢ Restraint on wages and salaries
  - ➢ Reduction/elimination of subsidies
  - ➢ Expenditure control mechanism
  - ➢ Downsizing
  - ➢ Recruitment control
- Financial policies
  - ➢ Increase in domestic interest rates
  - ➢ Measures to raise investment and its efficiency
  - ➢ Banking sector reforms
- Tax system
  - ➢ Global income tax
  - ➢ Reduction in personal ıncome tax
  - ➢ Income tax extension
  - ➢ Introduction of payroll and land taxes

3. Exchange Rate Reforms

- Devaluation
- Reunification

- Removal of exchange measures

4. External Debt Policies

- Market-based debt reduction schemes
- Rescheduling

5. Other Reforms

- Improvement in overall management
- Investment planning and implementation
- Shift of resources from public sector to private sector
- Making favourable conditions for increased foreign direct investment

Monetary and Fiscal Policies: To check aggregate demand the Fund relies primarily on monetary and fiscal restraints. It is argued that, with fixed exchange rate, an expansion of the money stock (domestic credit) in excess of the growth of money demand induces the public to dispose of surplus money by acquiring foreign goods and securities- a worsening of the balance of payments-leaving the long term values domestic output and prices unaffected. When exchange rates are fully flexible, a similar expansion in domestic credit results in an increase in the money supply, a proportional depreciation of the domestic currency and a corresponding rise in the domestic price level once again the equilibrium output is unaffected.

But the question is whether such a model is applicable to most developing countries where financial markets are under developed, interest rates are set below market clearing levels by government, a relatively free kerb market operates and foreign exchange control are in force.

A fall in the supply of credit to the private sector will reduce absorption through its wealth effect and cause borrowers to turn to kerb markets, pushing up interest rates there and causing interest sensitive component of aggregate demand to decline. The decline in aggregate demand will tend to improve the current account of the balance of payments and put downward pressure on inflation rate. Even though the changes in the money may be neutral in the long run, during the adjustment process the policy reduces capacity utilization and raise unemployment. The size and duration of the deflationary. effect will depend on, among other things, the stickiness of prices, wage setting behaviour, the degree of slackness of economy, and the interest sensitivity of investment decisions.

In context of fiscal policy, the direct effects of reduction in government expenditure are well known. Any reduction in government expenditure reduces the aggregate demand. There is much controversy, however, over the indirect effects of government purchases. The main thing is the extent to which the increase in purchases reduces or increases private expenditure, thus resulting in rise in total expenditure different from the original increases in government expenditure.

Finally, theoretical and empirical also support the proposition that in practice a reduction in the fiscal deficit tends to reduce aggregate demand. This improves the balance of payments and reduces inflationary pressures on the economy. For these reasons- reducing the claim on resources and monetary expansion- cutting the fiscal deficit becomes an essential, if not the most critical, element of an adjustment programme.

Structural Reforms: The general purpose of structural policies contained in Fund-supported programmes is how these can be helpful in achieving medium term external and internal balances in the economy. The main aim is the efficient allocation of resources in the economy, in other words, shifting resources away from inefficient uses. This process of resources shifting is generally impeded by institutional rigidities and other factors. The structural reforms have an important role in removing these rigidities and achieving a balance of payments' viability. These structural reforms lay the basis for durable and sustained economic growth. So, structural policies become complementary to the aggregate demand policies. The structural policy mix contained in Fund-supported programmes varies from country to country. But, the aim is to achieve a required transformation of the economy and address the deep rooted structural problems of the economy.

The policies included in a programme depend on the nature of the economy and the type of problems it faces. Generally, structural policies include measures to improve efficiency and resource allocation, as well as, policies to expand the production capacity of the economy. Important ones of these policies have been mentioned below:

Trade Policies: The Fund-supported trade policies include trade liberalization. The first step in liberalization process is to move from quantitative restrictions to tariffs. After price differentials have been established as the main instrument of protection, targets and time tables can be set for their reduction. The next step in the process is to lower effective tariff protection and reduce the tariff variation. The reduction schedule can be according to the circumstances of a particular country. The Fund has flexible approach in this context. The main aim is to make efficient allocation of resources. This will lead to strengthen the balance of payments position.

A number of studies have shown that countries with outward looking strategies have generally fared better in terms of growth, employment, and balance of payments than those following inward looking strategies. The outward looking strategies generally have a provision of incentives for domestic production to shift towards exporting or competing with imports. Artificial barriers to foreign trade cause inefficiencies in the economy. The relative success of these strategies has prompted considerable efforts to encourage developing countries to create incentives for production of tradable and to liberalize their trading system.

Pricing Policies: The Fund supported programmes call for price reforms, particularly in agriculture sector. In developing countries, authorities usually fix the prices of agriculture commodities at levels below those prevailing in world markets to stabilize producer prices and income and subsidies the food consumption of urban population. When this policy results in severe distortions in producer prices or in wide ranging subsidization, it can have a powerful effect on the level and allocation of agriculture production and on consumption. Given the importance of the agriculture sector in many developing countries, inappropriate producer pricing policies can have a direct impact on the achievement of macroeconomic stability and a sustainable balance of payments.

It is argued that raising prices to world levels would be beneficial on both the production and fiscal front. Empirical evidence suggests that higher producer prices will help in increasing output, particularly in longer run. The first step in price reform process can be to set prices at the world level and then adopt a procedure for maintaining the relationship between domestic and world prices.

Public Sector Policies: The Fund prescribes restraint on wages and salaries of public sector employees. The Fund also recommends freeze/decrease in the number of new appointments. The policies call for liquidating public enterprises and making profit-oriented those which remain in public domain. In addition to these policies, reduction/abolition of subsidies and a shift in budget priorities are also prescribed to make resources available for more efficient use. Programme countries are asked for improved expenditure control mechanism, i.e. to reduce public sector expenditure. Improvement in investment planning and its implementation are also a part of the fund policy measures.

The basic purpose of these policy measures is to reduce the aggregate demand and to increase aggregate supply by stimulating efficient allocation of resources.

Financial Policies: The reforms give due importance to the financial sector in mobilizing resources to enhance investment and growth. But, there are certain impediments in the efficient functioning of the financial system in developing countries. The authorities control the financial system and regulate the nominal interest rates. These control and regulations, with inflation, led to negative real interest rates. Finally, real financial savings grow less rapidly than the real economy leading to disintermediation, especially through the parallel markets or capital flight. This type of process restricts the availability of credit through the financial system and thereby inhibits the level and inefficiency of investment. The available credit is largely allocated to big firms and state enterprises and the credit for small firms and households is rationed to a large extent. Ultimately, uneconomic project are often taken at the cost of efficient one.

The Fund to eliminate these problems calls for a rise in nominal interest rates leading to positive real interest rates and reducing wasteful investment, and for policies to make the financial system more efficient. The authorities should assure the investors that they will get the real returns that are competitive with those abroad. This assurance is essential in promoting balance of payments, increasing foreign investment and preventing capital flight.

But, there must be strong coordination between the above prescribed policies improving the financial system and other measures in a programme. Inappropriate combination of policies can disrupt the financial system- through the emergence of very high real interest rates and the collapse of banking system- that is undergoing structural reforms. To avoid high fluctuations in the flow of fund in and out of the financial system, the fiscal position must remain under control. Interest rate policy should be in coordination with the exchange rate policy to ensure that capital flows do not destabilize the financial system. Proper liberalization may also require other changes- the legal protection of property rights, changes in bank supervision procedures, expansion of private domestic banks, eased entry of foreign banks, creation of an efficient capital market, and reforms in public financial institutions.

Tax System: Fund's policies call for income tax extension, i.e. increasing the base. A reduction in personal income tax is also prescribed. It also calls for a schedule for changes in income tax system on the lines of global income tax pattern. The measures also include the introduction of payroll tax (social security contribution). The programme country is expected to improve arrear collection mechanism. Other measures include: introduction/raising of land taxes, extending the coverage of export duties, and surcharges on personal income tax.

Exchange Rate Reforms: Generally, the need for adjustment programmes arises from a chronic imbalance in the external sector, for which the obvious solution is to reduce imports or stimulate exports to eliminate the exhaustion of external capital sources. The intuitively obvious solution to this type of imbalance is to adjust relative prices so that imports are more dear or exports more profitable, or both. In this regard, an adjustment in exchange rate is a measure which has favourable effects on both aspects. The devaluation decreases the price in domestic currency terms of traded goods and consequently direct domestic resources to import substitution and export promotion. The argument for devaluation is particularly appealing in view of price and wage rigidities which normally prevail in markets, limiting the scope for absolute price decreases in the normal price of non traded goods. In these circumstances, the only practical option of securing sufficient adjustment in the traded/ non traded goods price ratio is often an upward adjustment of the price of traded goods. But, the success of the action will depend on sufficient monetary restraint to prevent the erosion of the devaluation induced by change in price relatives by subsequent increases in the prices of non traded goods.

Exchange rate reforms have been a common feature of Fund supported programmes. In most cases, actions favoured on exchange rate were more frequent adjustment of the exchange rate while , where multiple exchange rates existed, the reunification of exchange rates was an important aim. In some cases the exchange rate strategy was mentioned through a target on net foreign assets. Generally, exchange rate reforms involve policies and measures that eliminate the need for the exchange restrictions and facilitate their removal during the reform process. In some cases, actions called for the removal of exchange and other taxes on international transactions consistent with the position of the Fund that all taxes on international transactions must be applied outside the exchange system.

Objection against exchange rate action is that devaluation will reduce domestic resources available to the economy and will precipitate a cost push spiral that will ultimately leave the economy in a worse position than before. The other issues are those of relative elasticities of the import and export markets and the quality of exports which must be offered to satisfy import demands. These are legitimate concerns, but devaluation helps in easing the excess demand for foreign exchange and also improves the administrative efficiency of the economy. An economy which is chronically short of foreign exchange often develops a complex system of exchange controls to allocate the scarce resources in the absence of a market mechanism, with importation of some goods strictly controlled or imposition of waiting periods before they can be imported. Consequently, import licensing becomes difficult to obtain, and often the exchange system is subjected to special tax and export bonus scheme. The devaluation permits the public and private sector resources used in these activities to be reduced and the accompanying rules to be simplified, with a consequent freeing of resources for more productive uses. Moreover, greater use of the price mechanism reduces arbitrariness in the allocation of foreign exchange and improves the allocation of the economy's resources. This is of course particularly valid for those economies where the export sector has greater potential for growth than non -export sector.

Devaluation will have an additional effect on residents' wealth abroad. Normally those holding capital abroad are better off than those holding domestic capital. Clearly this distributional impact will affect the assessment of devaluation, of course, little can be done about it unless the authorities can force repatriation of foreign assets or can find an effective way of identifying and taxing the capital gains made on wealth held abroad. It should also be noted, however, that when returns to the capital are artificially reduced to protect labours' income, capital will normally emigrate, harming the growth.

External Debt Policies: For countries that find themselves in a debt crisis situation the Fund has undertaken a number of steps: providing additional financing from its own resources, facilitating rescheduling of the existing stock of debt, encouraging additional lending from both official and private sources, and participating in market based debt reduction schemes. All these efforts are made with the idea of eventually having these countries return to normal borrowing relationship. In general, external debt policies in Fund supported programmes are aimed at easing the liquidity problem of countries and helping them maintain their long term growth path.

It is suggested that a country can and should borrow from abroad as long as the proceeds from such loans produce a return to cover the cost of borrowing. In that case the borrower is increasing his capacity with the aid of foreign savings. Fund's external debt policies have been guided with this principle. Borrowing now to finance spending should be matched by repayments to be made in the future. This rule defines the limits to foreign borrowing from the demand side, and therefore the degree of adjustment that needs to be undertaken.

The assessment of appropriate level of borrowing is possible in theory, but in practice it is nearly impossible task. One has to resort to indicators such as debt service or debt to GNP ratios to provide some clues. The equilibrium level of such ratios will vary from country to country and for a given country over time, so that one can not be too confident about the information of these type of indicators. Perhaps the importance of these indicators is that they give the warning of when debt might grow explosively. A sharp increase in the debt service ratio may trigger a more thorough look at the debt situation to see whether the country is using foreign borrowing efficiently.

There are certain disinvestment effects of foreign debt. In addition to credit rationing effect on investment, foreign debt may affect investment through what has come to be known as the 'debt overhang' channel. The debt overhang disincentive to investment can arise in a situation in which a debtor country benefits very little from the return to any additional investment because of debt service obligations. When a country is unable to service its debt in full, actual payments are determined by some negotiation process between the debtor country and the creditor, the amount of debt payments usually becomes linked to the economic performance of the country. The debtor country may need to increase taxation of various sources of income, and this has the consequences that at least a part of return of investment will go to creditors rather than to the investor. The uncertain outlook and the prospects of taxation necessary to service the debt weaken the incentives to invest in the domestic economy. Similarly, by reducing the necessary domestic political support, the debt overhang is also likely to discourage government's efforts to undertake an adjustment programme. The rationale for voluntary debt reduction is based on the supposition that the disincentive effect of foreign debt may be so strong that a reduction in the debt stock would generate a strong improvement in the debtor's economy.

Other Reforms: In addition to above mentioned policies, the Fund recommends creating good conditions for increased foreign direct investment inflows. Efforts should be made to improve overall management of the economy. The resources should be diverted from public sector to private sector to get more efficient utilisation. Investment should be planned and the wasteful investment has to be curtailed.

Select common features of the Fund-supported programmes are given in Appendix A3 below.

Appendix-A3

Select features of the Fund-supported adjustment programmes.

I Monetary and Financial policies

1. Limit on credit expansion ceilings on

- Net domestic assets or total bank credit
- Bank credit to central government
- Bank credit to public sector
- Separate ceiling on bank credit to parastates

2. Reduction in the rate of growth of liquidity
3. Interest rate reform
4. Adequate share of credit to private sector
5. Measures to mobilize domestic savings

- Interest rate increases

- Reform of the financial system

6. Targets on net foreign resources
7. Improvement in regulatory framework for banking system
8. Others (selective credit allocation)

II Public Sector Policies

1. Restraint on central government current expenditures

- Wages and salaries
  - Freezing or reduction of government employee numbers
  - Freezing, reduction, or postponement of wage increases
  - Changes in the employment policy
  - Limit on salary indexation
- Goods and services
  - Improvement in overall expenditure controls
  - Cumulative monthly or quarterly ceilings on expenditures
  - Reduction in appropriation for specific expenditures
- Transfer and subsidies
  - Reduction in subsidies (food, petroleum, and fertilizers)
  - Reduction in other subsidies
  - Curtailment of current transfers to non-financial public enterprises
  - Control of state enterprises operation expenditures
- Capital expenditures and net lending
  - Curtailment of investment (real terms, nominal terms)
  - Limit or delay on new investment or new projects
  - Improvement of investment programmes
  - Reduction in domestically financed investment
- Expenditure administration
  - Improve expenditure control mechanism
  - Others (shift in budgetary priorities)

2. Tax System

- Income taxes
  - Move from scheduler to global income tax
  - Reduction of personal income tax
  - Surcharge in personal income tax
  - Income tax reform or extension
  - Increase in payroll tax or social security contribution

- ➢ Arrears
- • Corporate tax
- ➢ Income tax surcharge
- ➢ Collection tax arrears
- ➢ Shorter lag for corporate tax payment
- ➢ Modification or reduction of income tax or profit tax
- • Tax on property
- ➢ Introduce or raise land taxes
- ➢ Introduce or raise urban property taxes
- ➢ Other property taxes
- • Domestic taxes on goods and services
- ➢ Raise excise taxes
- ➢ Increase tax on petroleum products
- ➢ Raise or modify sales tax
- ➢ Temporary selected tax reduction
- ➢ Raise taxes on other domestic goods and services
- • Import duties
- ➢ General or selected increase in custom duties
- ➢ Increase in petroleum import taxes
- ➢ Reduction or elimination of selected import duties
- ➢ Tariff reform
- ➢ Import duty surcharge
- • Export duties
- ➢ Increase in rates
- ➢ Extension of coverage
- ➢ Export compensation scheme
- ➢ Others (reform or reduction)
- • Other taxes and non-taxes
- ➢ Tariffs, fees, charges etc.
- ➢ Others
- • Improve or reform tax administration

3. Non-financial public enterprises (NPEs)

- • Improvement in NPEs performance
- ➢ Improve prices structure
- ➢ Partial or total privatization
- • Improve overall management and control

4. Overall budget
- Reduction of deficit as percentage of GDP
- Reduction in domestic arrears
5. Selling or liquidating state enterprises
6. Those remained in public domain making them profit oriented

III External Debt Policies

1. Control of level and maturity of external debt
- Public and publicity guaranteed debt
- Public sector debt
2. Other debt management policies
- Debt relief/'rescheduling
- Others (arrears, reserves, preferential rate, etc.)

IV Exchange and Trade Policies

1. Liberalization and reform of exchange rate
- Frequently adjusted exchange rate
- Gradual unification of exchange rate
- Others
2. Liberalization and reform of trade system
- Rationalization of import system
- Export promotion measures
3. Standard clauses and others

V Wages and Salaries

1. Partial or general wage restraint policies
2. Wage guidelines or wage reform policies
3. Flexible pricing system
4. Reduction in price or cost distortions
5. Review or increase sector prices (agriculture, industry, etc)
6. Increase energy prices
7. Review price control system

VI Other Structural Adjustment Policies

1. Development and re3structuring of a sub sector
2. Improvement in overall management
3. Shift of resources from public to private
4. Investment planning and execution procedure
5. Creating conducive conditions for increased FDI inflows
6. Others

4

IMF Development Programmes: Global Review

Although there have been a number of studies on the IMF-supported programmes, but one can not say with certainty whether the programmes have worked well or not. Some researchers have argued, that at best the Fund programmes do little in the improving the economic picture. While others have gone as far as to say that programmes worsen the situation by inducing stagflation. Providing a clear cut statement in this regard turns out to be no easy task. There is at present little agreement in the profession either about how to estimate the macro economic effects of the programmes or about what impact past programmes have actually had on the principal macroeconomic variables the Fund typically is concerned with.

Since it is theoretically and empirically difficult to link all the policy instruments of Fund-supported programmes to the ultimate targets of balance of payments, inflation, and growth, most studies have attempted to assess the effects of the overall policy package. In this type of approach, the precise nature of underlying economic relationships and the specific policies adopted are not made explicit, and attention is directed solely at determining whether programmes have been effective in some sense in achieving the broad macroeconomic objectives for which they were formulated. Cross country studies of stand-by and extended arrangements have been undertaken periodically within the Fund (Khan and Knight 1981, 1985, Donovan 1981, 1982; etc.) and also by writers outside the Fund looking at various aspects of adjustment programmes. Although, there have also been case studies examining the individual country experiences, at present the literature is dominated by cross country analysis.

The literature suggests that four distinctive approaches have been applied to the evaluation of Fund supported programmes:

1. The before-after approach, which compares macroeconomic performance during a programme and performance prior to the programme,
2. The with-without approach, which compares macroeconomic performance in countries with programmes and performance in a 'control group' of countries without programmes,
3. The actual versus target approach, which compares actual macroeconomic performance under the programme and the performance specified in its targets, and
4. The comparison of simulation approach, which compares the simulated macroeconomic performance of Fund programme type policies and simulated performance with some other set of policies.

Various Studies

Reichmann and Stillson (1978): Reichmann, T.M., and Stillson, R.T. used before-after approach in their study in 1978. They examined a total of 79 Fund-supported programmes implemented during 1963-1972 and compared the behaviour of the balance of payments, inflation and growth. Using nonparametric tests (Mann-Whitney U test), they found that there was a significant improvement in the balance of payments in only about one fourth of all programmes. Of the 29 programmes involving countries with high inflation during the programme period, the rate of inflation fell in 6 to 11 programmes for which there was a notable deceleration in the rate of domestic credit expansion, in the 9 programmes involving devaluation, and there were 5 in which inflation was higher . In 40 percent of programmes the growth rate declined after the inception of the programmes relative to the previous two years' average rate of growth, but at the same time growth rate was higher in 47 percent of the programmes.

Reichmann (1978): Reichmann studied 21 programmes for 18 countries that were under programmes during 1973-1975 and compared the outcomes to targets for the balance of payments, inflation, and growth. He found that the balance of payments targets were met or exceeded in nearly two third of programmes. The targets for inflation were, however, exceeded in over half the programmes, greater success was achieved in the case of growth rate, with 62 percent of programmes meeting the targets.

Connors (1979): The before-after approach was employed by Connors who examined a total of 31 programmes in 23 countries during the 1973-1977. He compared periods of one year before and after the programmes. Using a nonparametric rank test, Connors concluded that Fund programmes had no desirable effects on the ultimate targets- growth and inflation, and current account deficit- or on important intermediate targets, such as the ratio of the fiscal deficit to gross domestic product.

Donovan (1981): Donovan employed with-without approach in his study in 1981.The control group of countries without programme was taken to consist of all non-oil developing, and the comparisons were carried out over one year and three year time horizons. His study covered 12 programmes (for 12 countries) implemented during 1970-1976. He found that the improvement in the rate of growth of exports was consistently higher for programme countries than for all non-oil developing countries. The increase in the rate of inflation for programme countries was about half that of the control group during the first year, although it rose when three year comparisons were made, it was nevertheless well below the average increase in the rate of inflation of a non-oil developing countries. The outcome for growth not clear-cut. In one year comparisons, there was a sharp improvement in growth in programme countries relative to control group, but in three year comparisons growth in programme countries fell more than it did in non-programme countries.

Donovan (1982): In 1982, Donovan extended the sample of programmes to 78 covering the period 1971-1980, and the same analysis as in the 1981 study was undertaken. He found that the balance of payments and current account positions of programme countries improved in relation to the control group in both the one year and three year comparisons. The increase in inflation in programme countries was about half that of non-oil developing countries in one year comparisons and fell to one third in three year comparisons. However, in contrast to 1981 study, the rate of growth of real GDP fell by more than the average decline experienced by non-oil developing countries in the one year comparisons, but by less in the three year comparisons.

Killick (1984): Killick attempted to capture the effects of lags by comparing the behaviour of various macroeconomic variables a year before the programme with the behaviour both one and two years after the programmes. Killick employed nonparametric tests (Mann-Whitney U test, and Wilcoxen rank test) to gauge the effects of 38 programmes covering 24 countries during the period 1974-1979. The simple before-after approach was used. Variables studied included growth, inflation, current account and basic balance of payments, change in international reserves, change in money supply and change in domestic credit. In contrast to other studies, Killick found that the balance of payments and current account deteriorated irrespective of time period over which the comparison was made. However, the difference between the pre programme and post programme values of those variables was not statistically significant. Inflation was reduced, but the effect on growth was ambiguous.

Zulu and Nsouli (1985): Zulu and Nsouli constructed before-after measures of programme effects in their study of 35 programmes implemented during 1980-1981 for 22 African countries. They found that growth was lower or the same in the year after the programme in about 60 percent of cases. For the current account and inflation targets, the split was even-with as many programmes showing an improvement in current account and inflation as those showing worsening or no change.

Goldstein and Montiel (1984): Goldstein and Monteil discovered the ways to modify with-without approach to reduce some of the biases. They employed the generalized evaluation estimator to a sample of 68 programmes for 58 countries implemented during 1974-1981. The variables employed were: the ratio of the overall balance of payments to nominal GNP, the ratio of the current account of the balance of payments to nominal

GNP, the rate of inflation and the rate of growth of real domestic product. They found that programme countries systematically demonstrated weaker performance- that is higher inflation, lower growth, and larger current account and balance of payments deficits than non-programme countries in the pre-programme period. After adjusting these differences in performances and taking into account the effects of policy instruments on targets, Goldstein and Monteil used regression analysis to estimate the programme effects. The following two interesting results were drawn from the study:

1. There was no statistically significant effect of programmes on the current account and balance of payments, on the rate of inflation and on the growth of real GDP;
2. The estimated programme effects under the generalized evaluation were quite different from those obtained with the standard with-without estimator. The latter indicated an improvement in current account, a sight worsening of the balance of payments, a reduction in inflation and a rise in growth rate associated with programmes. When the generalized evaluation estimator was used, the improvement in current account ratio disappeared, the deterioration in the balance of payments ratio was magnified and favourable outcomes for inflation and growth were reduced.

Gylfason (1987): Gylfason employed a version of with-without approach in his study of 32 programmes for 14 countries during 1977-1979.The control group included the developing countries that had experienced the balance of payments difficulties during 1975-1977, and nonparametric tests were used to determine if the behaviour of the macroeconomic variables for programme countries over a three year period was significantly different from that of control group. First, there was an improvement in balance of payments in programme countries relative to the outcomes in the control group. Second, inflation in programme countries did not fall, but rather remained approximately the same as the average inflation in the control group. Third, the growth rate was not significantly affected by programmes.

Pastor (1987): Pastor used before-after, and with-without approaches to have an overview of the IMF programmes for 18 Latin American countries. The variables included balance of payments measures, inflation rate and dependency measures, and finally, indicators of labour's share of income. The data covered the time period 1965-1981, longer than that of any published study. The country set for each year was broken into program and nonprogrammer groups to examine the relative performance of the programme group. The significance of the difference between the two groups for each year was determined by using both parametric and nonparametric techniques. The main findings were: (1) programme countries did experience significant balance of payments improvements, but this may be mostly due to significant capital account improvement, (2) in contrast to IMF goals, Fund programmes in Latin America seem to be associated with accelerating inflation, (3) Fund programmes had mixed impact on growth rate; and (4) Fund programmes were more significantly and consistently associated with decline in wage share.

Khan and Knight (1981): Khan and Knight constructed a dynamic model and estimated its parameters on a pooled cross section, time series sample of 29 developing countries. For each country, eight observations were obtained on the relevant variables. The basic purpose of the model was to allow output, prices, international reserves, money, and government budget policies to be determined simultaneously. The model contained nine equations, of which six were behavioural.

They then estimated the hypothetical effects of a stabilization programme that pursued an external balance target using policies that figure prominently in Fund supported programmes – namely, domestic credit restraints and reduction in government expenditure. The simulation experiments revealed that such a programme produced a sharp price deflation in the first year, followed by a temporary burst of inflation as prices rose back to their equilibrium level. Output, however, contracted sharply in the first year, rose temporarily above its full employment level, approaching that equilibrium level gradually over a period of several years.

Khan and Knight (1885): In a further study, Khan and Knight extended their simulation analysis to a comparison of alternative policies. Specially, they compared the results for the balance of payments, inflation, and real GDP growth of a package of demand management policies with a combined package of demand management and structural policies. The demand management policies improved balance of payments almost immediately, but at the cost of a temporary higher rate of inflation and a short run reduction in growth. The simulation of combined packaged revealed that structural policies could help to partially offset any short term adverse effect on growth that might result from demand restraint as well as the inflationary consequences of devaluation. Furthermore, the longer run effects of Fund type policies on the balance of payments, inflation and growth were more favourable than the short run effects.

Loxley (1984): Loxley employed the before-after and with-without approaches to a group of 32 developing countries that implemented Fund-supported programmes during 1971-1982. He found that the programme countries did no better, on average, in terms of current account, balance of payments and real output growth relative to other non programme developing countries. The improvement was statistically significant only in the case of inflation, and then only in three year comparisons.

Beveridge and Kelly (1980): Beveridge and Kelly examined the fiscal contents of all 105 programmes supported by Fund that were approved during 1969-1978. Their focus was on intermediate targets- domestic credit expansion, government revenues and expenditures, and deficit financing- rather than on the final macroeconomic objectives. They showed that almost all programmes contained government revenue and expenditure targets, and that both actual expenditures and revenues tended to differ from these forecasts. A shortfall in revenues occurred in about 40 percent of the cases, while expenditures were above projected values in nearly 60 percent of programmes. Consequently, the overall fiscal targets were achieved in about half of the programmes, as were the domestic credit ceilings. Authorities were more successful in meeting domestic nonblank financing limits than foreign financing limits.

M.S. Khan (1990): Khan employed before-after and with-without approaches, and generalized evaluation estimator to a large number of programmes for 69 developing countries implemented during 1973-1988. The empirical analysis indicated that in the short run the programmes had led to an improvement in the current account and the balance of payments, a lowering of inflation, and a decline in growth. In longer run the positive effects of programmes on the external balance and inflation were strengthened, and the adverse effect on growth was reduced. There was also evidence of a positive link between macroeconomic stability and economic growth.

Khosrow (1993): In1993, Khosrow Doroodian developed three models that examined relationship between relevant macroeconomic variables and the IMF's instrumental tools. The important variables were: the real output growth, the inflation rate, and the current account balance. To provide some empirical foundation for the analysis, the effects of such programmes were illustrated through analysis. The analysis covered 43 countries, of which 27 were programme countries that used IMF financial resources during 1977-83.The statistical values showed that the IMF adjustment, in general improved the inflation rate moderately and the current account balance significantly. These policies, however, did not have much impact on the level of economy. The changes in real interest rate had significant impact on the behaviour of key macroeconomic variables. The second important variable was the unanticipated growth in domestic credit. The variation in this variable generally led the programme country toward the desired goal. Fiscal policy and currency devaluation were next in terms of their effectiveness.

On the basis of analysis of the above mentioned studies, the following important points can be drawn:

1. Almost all studies have been cross country studies. Thus, the programmes had been successful in a particular region or in a particular country, can not be inferred from the above studies.
2. The performance of policy variables has not been taken into account, and nothing can be inferred about individual programmes.
3. Only few variables (generally four i.e. overall balance of payments, current account balance, inflation rate, and real output growth) have been employed to judge the success or failure of the programmes. Other important variables such as investment, consumption, domestic savings, terms of trade, trade balance, and foreign exchange reserves growth have generally been ignored while testing the performance of the programmes.
4. Different methods of evaluation have been employed by different writers. Their mathematical tests also differ. Some writers used parametric tests, while others used nonparametric tests. A few writers made comparison for three year figures, and majority employed one year comparisons. Their control groups also differ. Some writers used all developing countries as control group, some used all non-oil developing countries, while a few used a control group of non-oil developing countries that did not implement the Fund supported programmes.
5. Except a few studies, the time period has been shorter.
6. All studies revealed different results. The reasons might be: different methods of evaluation, time periods, techniques, variables and control groups.

Methodology

To have a better look of assessment of the Fund-supported programmes, this study took the following points into consideration.

1. The countries representing different regions have been included (i.e. two African, two Latin American and two Asian). It will be helpful in inferring, to some extent, the effectiveness of the programmes in different regions.
2. The number of macroeconomic variables has been extended. Equal weight was assigned to all macroeconomic variables employed to judge the macroeconomic performance of the Fund supported programmes.
3. The behaviour of policy instruments has also been observed. Whether the full amount was drawn or not has been made clear in case of every programme.
4. Three methods-namely, the before-after, with-without, and the generalized evaluation approaches have been employed. But, wherever information was available target approach has also been employed. Because, the countries implemented programmes almost continuously, so three year comparisons were not so meaningful. Thus only one year comparisons have been made. The performance of individual programmes has also been assessed.
5. The time period of the study has been longer. It is since the inception of Extended Fund Facility (EFF), i e. 1975.
6. The assessment of the Fund's programmes supported by Structural Adjustment Facility (SAF), Enhanced Structural Adjustment Facility (ESAF) and Poverty Reduction and Growth Facility (PRGF) has also been made.

Approaches

Since it is theoretically and empirically difficult to link all the policy instruments contained in a Fund programme to the ultimate targets i.e. balance of payments, inflation, growth and others, the study used only three approaches mentioned below:

1. The before-after approach,
2. The with-without approach, and
3. The generalized evaluation approach

The actual versus target approach could not be employed because of unavailability of statistics on ultimate targets in most of the cases. But, wherever information was available target approach has also been employed. In the before-after approach, as mentioned earlier, the macroeconomic performance during the programme was compared with that prior to implementation of programme.

In with-without approach, a 'control group' was formed out of 73 non-oil developing countries.Every year, these countries were divided into two sets. First, those implemented IMF adjustment programmes, and second, those did not implement the programmes. The second set was used as 'control group' for that particular year. The macroeconomic performance of the programme country was compared with that of 'control group' i.e. non-oil non-programme developing countries.

In generalized evaluation approach, one needs to identify the relevant reduced form relationships that link main policy instruments and the programme dummy variable to policy targets. The purpose of this approach, in this study, is to show how the economy performed during the programme years. No attempt has been made to link all policy instruments with the ultimate targets. But only main policy instruments have been used in the model. During the programme year dummy variable was assigned with (1) number, otherwise (0). Finally, the effect of the programme on the economy has been assessed on the basis of sign and magnitude of coefficient of dummy variable. Since, the multiple regression gives a good fit for the whole period i.e. 1975-2002 in this study, inferences have been made regarding the macroeconomic performance of the programme country during the programme years on the basis of coefficient of dummy variable.

The following model was employed in the case of gross domestic product, investment and consumption.

$$Z = m_1 X + m_2 D + b$$

Where, Z is objective variable, X is relevant independent variable, D is dummy variable and b is constant. For gross domestic product, investment was employed as independent variable. Gross domestic product was employed as independent variable in the case of investment and domestic savings.

For real GDP growth, inflation rate, exports as percentage of imports, current account balance as percentage of GDP, overall balance of payments as percentage of GDP, the under mentioned model was employed:

$$Z = m_1 Z_{-1} + m_2 FB + m_3 DCR + m_4 T + m_5 D + b$$

Where, Z is objective variable, FB fiscal position (overall balance as % of GDP), DCR is domestic credit growth rate, T is time, D is dummy variable and b is constant.

In assessing the overall macroeconomic performance of the programmes equal weight was assign to all the macroeconomic variables.

Programme Period and Programme Year

When a country signs an arrangement with the Fund, the period for which programme is to be implemented is usually prescribed by the IMF. The year during which the Fund programme was to be implemented has been called programme year. If the programme period was not published, the period of arrangement has been considered as the period of programme implementation. Where the period of programme implementation covered more than one calendar/fiscal year, the years covering the said period have been treated as separate programme years. If a programme was implemented for less than one year, but more than six months, that year was treated as programme year. Each programme year has been assumed supported by a separate stand by arrangement (SBA).

In absolute test, for SBAs the comparison has been made between the year prior to the programme year and the programme year. Consequitive SBAs have treated as separate agreements; in practice, this means that in case of two consequitive SBAs, the post programme value for the first SBAs has been used as the pre-programme value for the second SBAs. Extended arrangements, Structural Adjustment Facility arrangements, Enhanced Structural Adjustment Facility arrangements and Poverty Reduction and Growth Facility arrangements have been treated as sets of consequitive SBAs.

The similar procedures have been adopted in case of with - without approach and the generalized evaluation approach.

Test Statistics

In assessing an adjustment programme, in the case of both approaches i.e. before-after approach and with-without approach, the number of macroeconomic variables having better performance has been compared with that of having poor performance. The following criteria have been employed to determine the performance of a programme.

Poor Performance: If the total number of variables having better performance was less than that of having poor performance.

Same Performance: If the total number of variables having better performance was equal to that of having poor performance.

Better Performance: If the total number of variables having better performance was more than that of having poor performance.

To determine the macroeconomic performance of a variable for all programmes, in case of before-after and with-without approaches, the total number of programme years method has been employed, that is, the total number of programme years having better performance has been compared with that of having poor performance and the above mentioned criteria have been employed.

The second method to test the performance of a variable for all the programmes, in both the before-after and with-without approaches, has been the difference between the means method. The paired t-test for difference of means was employed to determine the significance of difference between programme and non-programme countries' performances as well as between pre-programme and programme years' performances of a programme country.

The t-test for paired observations works as follows: For example, Ghana implemented the Fund-supported programmes during 1979, 1983, 1984, 1985, 1986, 1987, 1988, 1989, 1990, 1995, 1996, 1997, 1999, 2000 and 2001. This means that there will be 15 pre-programme year observations and 15 programme year observations for every variable. Let us take example of real GDP growth rate (Table 4.1).

Table 4.1

Programme year (1)	Pre-programme year (2)	Programme year value (3)	d, (3)-(2) (4)	d^2 (5)
1979	8.5	-3.2	-11.7	136.89
1983	-7.2	0.7	7.9	62.41
1984	0.7	2.6	1.9	3.61
1985	2.6	5.1	2.5	6.25
1986	5.1	5.2	0.1	0.01
1987	5.2	4.8	-0.4	0.16
1988	4.8	5.6	0.8	0.64
1989	5.6	5.1	-0.5	0.25
1990	5.1	3.3	-1.8	3.24
1995	3.3	4.0	0.7	0.49
1996	4.0	4.6	0.6	0.36
1997	4.6	4.2	-0.4	0.16
1999	4.7	4.4	-0.3	0.09
2000	4.4	3.7	-0.7	0.49
2001	3.7	4.2	0.5	0.25
			$\sum d = -0.8$	$\sum d^2 = 167.41$

The test statistics employed is the student's t-test. After putting all the values in the above equation, we get t-value equivalent to 0.017. The critical value of t is more than the computed value; so we can with the help of sign and magnitude of $\bar{d}/n$ say that real GDP growth rate declined after the implementation of the programmes , although statistically insignificantly.

In the case of generalized evaluation approach, multiple regression technique was used to see the programme the programme effects. Since, all equations were of reduced form we could employ the ordinary least squares regression for their estimation without introducing bias. Inferences regarding the programme effects were drawn on the basis of sign and magnitude of coefficient of programme dummy variable. Since, multiple regression gave a good fit for the whole period i.e. 1975-2002, its results were supposed to be stronger and different from those obtained by the first two approaches viz. the before-after and with-without approaches.

To determine the macroeconomic performance of a country for all programme years the number of variables having better performance has been compared with that of having poor performance.

Variables

The variables employed in this study have been divided into two categories viz. (i) variables assessing the performance of the economy i.e. target variables and (ii) variables, which are used in fulfilling the targets i.e. instrumental variables. The variables included in the former category are: consumption, investment, domestic savings, current account balance, overall balance of payments, exports- imports ratio, real GDP growth, inflation rate and foreign exchange reserves' growth. While exchange rate, interest rate, money supply, domestic credit expansion and fiscal balance have been included in the latter category. Two variables- exports as percentage of GDP and imports as percentage of GDP have been used to assess the dependency effect of programmes.

Consumption: For economic development, especially in case of developing countries- where domestic savings-GDP ratio is low, the savings must be raised through increased mobilization of domestic resources curtailing consumption and improving the domestic growth. The absolute reduction in consumption is not favourable for economic development of a country. The favourable thing is that the rate of growth of consumption must be lower than that of output (Table 4.2).

Table 4.2: Non-oil Developing Countries to Form Control Group

Afghanistan	Guatemala	Niger
Argentina	Guyana	Pakistan
Bangladesh	Haiti	Panama
Bolivia	Honduras	Paraguay
Brazil	India	Peru
Burundi	Israel	Philippines
Cameroon	Jamaica	Rwanda
Central African Republic	Jordan	Senegal
Chad	Kenya	Sierra Leone
Chile	Korea	Singapore
China	Lebanon	Somalia
Colombia	Macedonia	South Africa
Congo, Republic of	Madagascar	Sri Lanka
Costa Rica	Malawi	Sudan
Cote d` Ivoire	Malaysia	Syria
Cyprus	Mali	Tanzania
Dominican Republic	Malta	Thailand
Ecuador	Mauritania	Togo
Egypt	Mauritius	Trinidad and Tobago
El Salvador	Mexico	Tunisia
Ethiopia	Morocco	Turkey
Gabon	Myanmar	Uganda
Gambia	Nepal	Uruguay
Ghana	Nicaragua	Zambia

To accomplish this objective, the movements of 'consumption as percentage of GDP' have been observed. The increase in the amount of this variable meant that the consumption rose faster than GDP which is not favourable. On the other side, decrease in the amount of this variable meant that consumption grew slower than GDP, which is favourable for a developing economy.

Investment: Investment leads to an increase in the level of income and production by increasing the production capacity. In other words, increase in investment tends to raise the growth rate of economy. To fulfil this aim, the trend of 'investment as percentage of GDP' has been observed. Increase in the amount of this variable has been assumed as favourable to the economy. On the other hand, decrease in the amount of this variable meant an unfavourable effect on the economy. In generalized evaluation method, investment has been treated income elastic.

Domestic Savings: The supply of savings is an important consideration that determines the growth rate of an economy. The poor countries hardly save about 5 percent of their income. It is the increased savings which augment the supply of capital in the economy. In this study, the variable employed for this purpose is 'gross domestic savings as percentage of GDP'. Increase in the amount of variable was treated favourable to the growth of an economy, while decrease in the amount of this variable meant unfavourable one. In generalized evaluation method, domestic savings were supposed as a function of GDP.

Overall Balance of Payments: The major objective of adjustment programmes is to obtain a sustainable balance of payments position. Secondly, payments disequilibria affect economic performance adversely. Thus, analysis in this study presents information on the balance of payments behaviour. The 'overall balance of payments as percentage of GDP' has been employed to accomplish this aim. Overall balance equals the current account plus direct investment, portfolio investment, and other capital not included elsewhere, and net errors and omissions. Thus figure excludes reserves, exceptional financing, and liabilities constituting foreign authorities' reserves.

Current Account Balance: We can assess the performance of overall balance on the basis current account performance. In other words, we can found out whether improvement in overall balance owed to the current account or the capital account. To accomplish this aim 'current account balance as percentage of GDP' variable has been employed.

Exports as Percentage of Imports: For developing countries, which already experience balance of payments problem, the rate of growth of exports should be more than that of imports. For this purpose, the behaviour of exports-imports ratio has been observed. It is a version of trade account. The trade deficit also has adverse effects on economy. As the ratio increases, it has favourable effect on the economy; otherwise adverse.

Change in Consumer Prices: There fairly solid evidence of an inverse relationship between inflation and real economic growth. The Fund generally argues that its programmes tend to reduce the rate of inflation or at least the rate at which it increases. In testing inflation, inflation rates based on the consumer price index have been examined.

Real GDP Growth: An increase in the real GDP growth rate has been assumed as a favourable effect on the economy, otherwise unfavourable. In case of the with-without approach, more increase in real GDP growth rate of programme country than that of control group has been considered as better performance. On the other hand, more decrease as poor performance.

Foreign Exchange Reserves Growth Rate: The increase in the growth rate of foreign exchange reserves has been considered as a favourable effect on the economy, though this assumption can be disputed.

Exports as Percentage of GDP: To test the dependency effect, the movements of 'exports as percentage of GDP' have been observed. Increase in the amount of this variable has been assumed as an enhancement of dependency of the economy (Table 4.3).

Table 4.3: Control Group: Change in Economic Indicators

Year	ΔCN/ GDP	ΔINV/ GDP	ΔDS/GDP	ΔX/M	ΔCA/ GDP	ΔOB/ GDP	ΔRGDP Gr	ΔINFR	ΔX/GDP	ΔM/GDP
1975	3.3	1.0	-3.3	-13.1	-3.0	-1.4	-2.9	-0.1	-4.2	-1.2
1976	-1.0	-0.1	1.0	8.6	0.9	0.2	2.1	-6.0	0.8	-0.9
1977	0.1	0.6	-0.1	-0.8	-0.5	0.6	-1.1	2.2	0.3	0.8
1978	1.1	0.6	-1.1	-5.5	-2.1	-0.7	0.7	-3.7	-1.1	0.1
1979	-0.6	-0.1	0.6	10.8	0.8	-1.0	-0.1	4.8	1.4	0.4
1980	0.8	0.7	-0.8	-11.3	-2.3	-1.6	1.7	1.3	0.6	2.7
1981	1.0	0.6	-1.0	-4.7	-2.6	-0.4	-1.0	1.8	-2.3	-0.9
1982	2.7	-0.4	-2.7	0.7	-0.4	-2.1	-4.3	0.1	-2.4	-2.5
1983	-0.3	-2.3	0.3	4.3	0.4	-1.2	-0.3	3.8	-1.8	-3.2
1984	-0.4	-1.3	0.4	4.9	1.9	1.3	1.0	11.1	0.6	-1.4
1985	0.3	-1.2	-0.3	-0.6	-0.8	-0.5	1.3	5.6	-1.0	-1.0
1986	0.5	-0.2	-0.5	-6.2	0.0	0.3	0.2	-7.6	-1.0	-1.3
1987	-0.3	1.0	0.3	-2.1	-0.8	0.0	1.0	4.8	0.6	1.6
1988	0.0	0.2	0.0	0.2	0.8	-0.5	-2.5	2.4	1.6	1.5
1989	-0.6	0.6	0.6	8.8	0.0	0.5	-0.8	4.5	1.1	0.9
1990	0.4	0.3	-0.4	-4.7	-0.8	-0.4	1.4	2.4	-0.6	1.9
1991	1.3	0.0	-1.3	0.0	0.0	0.2	0.0	0.6	-0.6	-0.1

Contd...

1992	0.9	-0.2	-0.9	-1.9	-0.1	-0.3	0.9	-2.3	-0.9	-0.7
1993	0.1	0.4	-0.1	-6.8	-1.0	0.6	-1.1	0.0	0.0	0.7
1994	-1.7	0.5	1.7	1.3	0.6	0.1	0.8	5.1	1.4	1.0
1995	-0.2	-0.1	0.2	0.3	0.0	-0.6	-0.5	-3.6	1.0	0.6
1996	0.2	-0.1	-0.2	-1.3	-0.3	0.6	-0.3	-2.3	-0.8	-0.9
1997	-0.3	-0.2	0.3	1.3	0.1	-0.6	-0.6	-0.8	-0.3	-0.1
1998	0.5	0.1	-0.5	-1.2	0.7	-0.6	-0.3	-0.8	1.8	-0.3
1999	0.1	-1.3	-0.1	6.1	0.1	0.2	-0.6	-3.2	-0.6	-1.0
2000	-0.9	0.1	0.9	1.4	-0.9	-0.5	1.4	-1.3	1.7	2.5
2001	1.6	-0.2	-1.6	-0.9	0.7	1.3	-1.7	0.2	-1.4	-1.4
2002	-0.2	-0.2	0.2	1.3	0.8	-0.5	0.1	-0.1	0.9	0.6

Imports as Percentage of GDP: This variable has also been employed to assess the dependency effect of the Fund supported programmes. Increase in the magnitude of this variable has been assumed as an enhancement of dependency or openness of the economy.

Exchange Rate: The movements of exchange rate of domestic currency of the programme country have been observed to see the effects of devaluation on the economy, particularly in the case of current account balance. This variable has been employed as an instrumental variable.

Interest Rate: This is an instrumental variable. The movements of it have also been observed.

Money Supply: The trend of money supply has been studied. This variable is generally includes in Fund-supported programmes as an instrumental variable.

Domestic Credit: Domestic credit control is used as an instrument to control inflation. The movements of it have also been studied.

Overall Budget Surplus/Deficit: The IMF programme contains a cut in fiscal deficit as an instrument to check inflation and improve the both –external and internal balances.

5

Morocco: External Sector Improvement

Morocco gained independence from France and Spain in 1956 and became a member of the Fund in April 1958. Its principal industries include phosphate, mining and processing, tourism, food processing, textiles, and fishing.

The sudden increase in the prices of phosphate in 1974 led to unbalanced growth of Moroccan economy. As the main beneficiary of the revenue surplus, the government embarked on an ambitious spending programme. As a result, prices increased faster for non tradable than tradable goods, and production switched from export to domestic demand. When the export boom abruptly ended in 1976, with a 47 per cent falloff phosphate prices, the government was not able to cut spending. The resulting budget deficit amounted to 17.6 per cent of GDP, and a drastic reallocation of resources was called for.

After 1976, fiscal revenues remained at practically the same level as current expenditure, so that public capital expenditures were financed by borrowing from abroad. In 1978, a government strategy included a civil servants' wage freeze, rise in tax rates and a cut in public investment. But, several exogenous factors interrupted the application of strategy in 1979; the second oil shock, bad crop due to drought; and social uprising.

Faced with large internal and external imbalances stemming from the expansionary policies pursued in 1970s, Morocco adopted a series of Fund supported adjustment programmes during 1980s (Table 5.1). The Moroccan authorities also - with the assistance of World Bank- have implemented a series of structural reforms in key sectors of the economy, including agriculture, education, and public enterprises.

Table 5.1: Morocco: Lending arrangements with the IMF, 1975-2002

(Amount expressed in millions of SDRs)

Facility	Date of arrangement	Date of expiration	Amount approved	Balance not drawn	Programme years	Remarks
EA	16.10.1980	15.10.1983	810.0	663.0	1980	Replaced by EA 1981
EA	09.03.1981	31.10.1983	817.1	681.0	1981	Receded
SBA	26.04.1982	25.04.1983	281.3	0	1982	
SBA	16.09.1983	15.03.1985	300.0	0	1983,1984	
SBA	12.09.1985	28.02.1987	200.0	190.0	1985,1986	Programme implemented
SBA	16.12.1986	15.04.1988	230.0	0	1987	
SBA	30.08.1988	31.12.1989	210.0	0	1988,1989	
SBA	20.07.1990	31.03.1991	100.0	52.0	1990	
SBA	31.01.1992	31.03.1993	92.0	73.6	1992	

Source: IMF Survey, various issues.

1980 Adjustment Programme

The Fund approved a three year extended arrangement for the government of Morocco authorizing purchases up to equivalent of SDR 810 million on 16 Oct, 1980. This arrangement supported a three year programme which addressed itself to both the demand and supply sides of the economy, and attempted to implement a set of consistent wage, fiscal, monetary and external debt policies with the objective of increasing domestic savings, reorienting the restructure of demand and containing the inflation. A reduction of food subsidies was also part of this. However, this led to a 50 per cent increase in food prices and violent riots in Casablanca in the spring of 1981. In addition, the external environment and weather were unfavourable (drought,. and revaluation of US$).The stabilization programme was cancelled in 1982.

The macroeconomic performance of 1980 economic programme may be summarized as:

- The Moroccan economy did not perform better than that in 1979, and
- The Moroccan economy out performed the 'control group' i.e. non-programme non-oil developing countries.

1981 Adjustment Programme

The Fund approved a request by the government of Morocco for an extended arrangement over the period through October 1983 authorizing up to SDR 817 million, in support of the economic and financial programme on March 9, 1981. This arrangement replaced an extended arrangement approved by the Fund in October 1980. The economic programme for 1981 was framed in the context of the medium term programme adopted in 1980 and built upon the strategy which had been implemented since mid 1980. The programme aimed at achieving a rate of growth of GDP of 4.5 per cent, limiting the rate of inflation and reducing current account budget deficits. To achieve these objectives, the authorities intended to emphasize directly productive projects in their development programme, initiated a reform of public enterprises, introduced tax reform measures and liberalized the exchange and trade system. Monetary and credit policies were designed to be consistent with the aims of the economic programme.

The macroeconomic performance of the programme can been summarized as follows: (a) the Moroccan economy showed very poor absolute performance; (b) the Moroccan economy fared very poor as compared to the 'control group' and (c) all the targets established in the programme could not be achieved.

1982 Adjustment Programme

In April 1982, an extended arrangement approved by the Fund in Oct 1980 was cancelled at the request of Moroccan government's request. At the same time, the Fund approved a stand-by arrangement in support of the government's economic and financial programme for 1982. The programme combined short term stabilization policies with a continuation of structural adjustment efforts. The programme aimed at a growth rate of 4 per cent in 1982, a reduction in the current account deficit to 10 per cent of GDP from 12.5 per cent and containing the rate of inflation below 12.5 per cent. The programme relied upon improving the viability of public enterprises, reforming the tax system, conserving the energy and expanding domestic energy production, promoting exports and further liberalizing the trade system. Sharp reduction of transitory deficit to 8.2 per cent of GDP was planned, through a combination of revenue raising measures, expenditure restraints and more effective management of the treasury accounts. Credit expansion was to be restrained.

The following conclusions can be drawn regarding the performance of Moroccan economy in 1982: (a) the economy had batter macroeconomic performance than that of 1981; (b) Moroccan economy performed better than the 'control group' and (c) Only two targets viz., real GDP growth and inflation were met. Current account deficit and fiscal deficit targets could not be achieved (Tables 5.2, 5.3, 5.4 and 5.5).

Table 5.2: Morocco: Programme Effects: Before-After Approach

(The difference between means method)

Variable		Programme Years												Effect	t-value
		1980	1981	1982	1983	1984	1985	1986	1987	1988	1989	1990	1992		
CN/ GDP	Pre	87.1	87.0	89.1	86.8	86.7	88.1	85.2	86.9	87.4	83.0	84.4	85.2	+	0.675
	Pro	87.0	89.1	86.8	86.7	88.1	85.2	86.9	87.4	83.0	84.4	79.8	86.8		
INV/ GDP	Pre	24.5	24.2	26.1	28.2	24.0	25.4	27.1	22.8	20.6	21.3	24.1	22.2	+	0.154
	Pro	24.2	26.1	28.2	24.0	25.4	27.1	22.8	20.6	21.3	24.1	25.7	22.3		
DS/ GDP	Pre	12.9	13.0	10.9	13.2	13.3	11.9	14.8	13.1	12.6	17.0	15.6	14.8	+	0.673
	Pro	13.0	10.9	13.2	13.3	11.9	14.8	13.1	12.6	17.0	15.6	20.2	13.2		
X/M	Pre	51.1	59.9	54.1	47.8	55.8	53.2	56.2	64.5	66.8	75.5	60.2	74.2	+	0.158
	Pro	59.9	54.1	47.8	55.8	53.2	56.2	64.5	66.8	75.5	60.2	62.7	67.0		
CA/ GDP	Pre	-9.5	-7.5	-12.1	-12.2	-6.4	-7.8	-6.9	-1.2	0.9	2.1	-3.5	-1.5	+	0.723
	Pro	-7.5	-12.1	-12.2	-6.4	-7.8	-6.9	-1.2	0.9	2.1	-3.5	-0.8	-1.5		
OB/ GDP	Pre	-0.7	-1.5	-2.8	-2.7	-1.6	-0.7	-0.4	2.0	2.0	1.2	0.0	3.4	+	0.879
	Pro	-1.5	-2.8	-2.7	-1.6	-0.7	-0.4	2.0	2.0	1.2	0.0	6.9	2.7		
INFR	Pre	8.3	9.4	12.5	10.5	6.2	12.4	7.7	8.7	2.7	2.4	3.1	8.0	+	0.289
	Pro	9.4	12.5	10.5	6.2	12.4	7.7	8.7	2.7	2.4	3.1	6.9	5.7		
RGDP Gr	Pre	4.5	3.4	-2.8	9.6	-0.6	4.3	6.3	8.4	-2.6	10.4	2.2	8.9	-	0.545
	Pro	3.4	-2.8	9.6	-0.6	4.3	6.3	8.4	-2.6	10.4	2.2	1.7	-4.0		
FOREX Gr	Pre	-10.8	-25.9	-42.7	-4.8	-51.2	-54.7	139	67.0	112	34.4	-10.8	43.0	+	0.672
	Pro	-25.9	-42.7	-4.8	-51.2	-54.7	139	67.0	112	34.4	-10.8	323	17.3		
Memorandum Items															
X/GDP	Pre	11.8	13.2	15.6	13.4	14.4	16.3	16.8	14.4	14.9	16.4	14.8	18.5	Pre<	0.651
	Pro	13.2	15.6	13.4	14.4	16.3	16.8	14.4	14.9	16.4	14.8	16.9	17.3	Pro	
M/GDP	Pre	23.0	22.1	28.8	28.0	25.8	30.7	29.9	22.4	22.3	21.7	24.5	24.9	Pre<	0.707
	Pro	22.1	28.8	28.0	25.8	30.7	29.9	22.4	22.3	21.7	24.5	27.0	25.8	Pro	

Notes: (1) + sign indicates better performance, - sign indicates poor performance and 0 indicates same performance.

Table 5.3: Morocco: Programme Effects: Before-After Approach

(Total number program years method)

Variable	Programme years												Performance (no. of years)		
	1980	1981	1982	1983	1984	1985	1986	1987	1988	1989	1990	1992	Better	Poor	Same
CN/GDP	+	-	+	+	-	+	-	-	+	-	+	-	6	6	0
INV/GDP	-	+	+	-	+	+	-	-	+	+	+	+	8	4	0
DS/GDP	+	-	+	+	-	+	-	-	+	-	+	-	6	6	0
X/M	+	-	-	+	-	+	+	+	+	-	+	-	7	5	0
CA/GDP	+	-	-	+	-	+	+	+	+	-	+	0	7	4	1
OB/GDP	-	-	+	+	+	+	+	0	-	-	+	-	6	5	1
RGDP Gr	-	-	+	-	+	+	+	-	+	-	-	-	5	7	0
INFR	-	-	+	+	-	+	-	+	+	-	-	+	6	6	0
FOREX Gr	-	-	+	-	-	+	-	+	-	-	+	-	4	8	0
No of variables with better performance	4	1	7	6	3	9	4	4	7	1	7	2	55 (50.9)		
No of variables with poor performance	5	8	2	3	6	0	5	4	2	8	2	6		51 (47.2)	
No of variables with same performance	0	0	0	0	0	0	0	1	0	0	0	1			2 (1.9)

Notes (1) + sign indicates better performance, - sign indicates poor performance and 0 indicates same performance.
(2)Figures in parenthesis are percentages.

Table 5.4: Morocco: Programme Effects: With-Without Approach

(The difference between means method)

Variable		Programme years												Effect	t-value
		1980	1981	1982	1983	1984	1985	1986	1987	1988	1989	1990	1992		
Δ CN /GDP	MR	-0.1	2.1	-2.3	-0.1	1.4	-2.9	1.7	0.5	-4.4	1.4	-4.6	1.6	+	1.247
	NPC	0.8	1.0	2.7	-0.3	-0.4	0.3	0.5	-0.3	0.0	-0.6	0.4	0.9		
Δ INV/ GDP	MR	-0.3	1.9	2.1	-4.2	1.4	1.7	-4.3	-2.2	0.7	2.8	1.6	0.1	+	0.441
	NPC	0.7	0.6	-0.4	-2.3	-1.3	-1.2	-0.2	1.0	0.2	0.6	0.3	-0.2		
Δ DS/ GDP	MR	0.1	-2.1	2.3	0.1	-1.4	2.9	-1.7	-0.5	4.4	-1.4	4.6	-1.6	+	1.247
	NPC	-0.8	-1.0	-2.7	0.3	0.4	-0.3	-0.5	0.3	0.0	0.6	-0.4	-0.9		
Δ X/M	MR	8.8	-5.8	-6.3	8.0	-2.6	3.0	8.3	2.3	8.7	-15.3	2.5	-7.2	+	0.561
	NPC	-11.3	-4.7	0.7	4.3	4.9	-0.6	-6.2	-2.1	0.2	8.8	-4.7	-1.9		
Δ CA/ GDP	MR	2.0	-4.6	-0.1	5.8	-1.4	0.9	5.7	2.1	1.2	-5.6	2.7	0.0	+	1.097
	NPC	-2.3	-2.6	-0.4	0.4	1.9	-0.8	0.0	-0.8	0.8	0.0	-0.8	-0.1		
OB/ GDP	MR	-0.8	-1.3	0.1	1.1	0.9	0.3	2.4	0.0	-0.8	-1.2	6.9	-0.7	+	1.439
	NPC	-1.6	-0.4	-2.1	-1.2	1.3	-0.5	0.3	0.0	-0.5	0.5	-0.4	-0.3		
ΔINFR	MR	1.1	3.1	-2.0	-4.3	6.2	-4.7	1.0	-6.0	-0.3	0.7	3.8	-2.3	+	1.662
	NPC	1.3	1.8	0.1	3.8	11.1	5.6	-7.6	4.8	2.4	4.5	2.4	-2.3		
Δ RGDP Gr	MR	-1.1	-6.2	12.4	-10.2	4.9	2.0	2.1	-11.0	13.0	-8.2	-0.5	-12.9	-	0.447
	NPC	1.7	-1.0	-4.3	-0.3	1.0	1.3	0.2	1.0	-2.5	-0.8	1.4	0.9		
Memorandum Items															
Δ X/ GDP	MR	1.4	2.4	-2.2	1.0	1.9	0.5	-2.4	0.5	1.5	-1.6	2.1	-1.2	MR> NPC	1.362
	NPC	0.6	-2.3	-2.4	-1.8	0.6	-1.0	-1.0	0.6	1.6	1.1	-0.6	-0.9		
ΔM/ GDP	MR	-0.9	6.7	-0.8	-2.2	4.9	-0.8	-7.5	-0.1	-0.6	2.8	2.5	0.9	MR> NPC	0.548
	NPC	2.7	-0.9	-2.5	-3.2	-1.4	-1.0	-1.3	1.6	1.5	0.9	1.9	-0.7		

Notes: (1) MR: Morocco and NPC: Non programme countries.

(2) + sign indicates better performance, - sign indicates poor performance and 0 indicates same performance.

Table 5.5: Morocco: Programme Effects: With-Without Approach

(Total number program years method)

Variable	Programme years												Performance (no. of years)		
	1980	1981	1982	1983	1984	1985	1986	1987	1988	1989	1990	1992	Better	Poor	Same
Δ CN/GDP	+	-	+	-	-	+	-	-	+	-	+	-	5	7	0
Δ INV/GDP	-	+	+	-	+	+	-	-	+	+	+	+	8	4	0
Δ DS/GDP	+	-	+	-	-	+	-	-	+	-	+	-	5	8	0
Δ X/M	+	-	-	+	-	+	+	+	+	-	+	-	7	5	0
ΔCA/GDP	+	-	+	+	-	+	+	+	+	-	+	+	9	3	0
ΔOB/GDP	+	-	+	+	-	+	+	0	-	-	+	-	6	5	1
ΔRGDP Gr	-	-	+	-	+	+	+	-	+	-	-	0	5	6	1
ΔINFR	+	-	+	+	+	+	-	+	+	+	-	-	8	4	0
No of variables with better performance	6	1	7	4	3	8	4	3	7	2	6	2	53 (55.2)		
No of variables with poor performance	2	7	1	4	5	0	4	4	1	6	2	5		41 (42.7)	
No of variables with same performance	0	0	0	0	0	0	0	1	0	0	0	1			2 (2.1)

Notes (1) + sign indicates better performance, - sign indicates poor performance and 0 indicates same performance.
(2)Figures in parenthesis are percentages.

1983-1984 Adjustment Programme

The Fund approved a stand-by arrangement for the government of Morocco, authorizing purchases up to the equivalent to SDR 300 million over the period to March 15, 1985, in support of the government's economic and financial programme for 1983-84 on Sept 1983. The primary objective of the programme was to contain the growth of consumption, and to maintain overall investment consistent with resource availability and a satisfactory rate of growth. The agreement with IMF included the following measures:

- reducing food subsidies,
- bringing the fiscal deficit down to 7 per cent of GDP,
- limiting public sector recruitment,
- slowing down the annual growth rate of domestic credit from 20 per cent to 15 per cent, and
- reducing the current account deficit through a series of devaluations.

The results in context of the performance of the programme have been summarized below:

- Moroccan economy had satisfactory performance in 1983, but it showed poor performance in 1984.
- Moroccan economy had same performance as that of the 'control group' in 1983, but it was out performed by the 'control group' in 1984.
- Only two intermediate targets i.e. fiscal deficit and domestic credit expansion could be met.
- Drought in the first half of 1984 reduced agriculture and hydroelectric production, and slowed down economic activity.

1985-1986 Adjustment Programme

The Fund approved a stand-by arrangement of SDR 200 million for the government of Morocco in support of an adjustment programme for 1985-86 on Sept 12, 1985. The programme aimed to achieve a sustainable external account position by 1988 and laid the foundation for the resumption of growth over the medium term. The programme aimed at reducing the current account deficit to 7.1 per cent of GDP in 1985 and to some 4-4.5 per cent in 1986, at improving the efficiency of production system- particularly in the area of investment planning and public enterprises, and at promoting a shift of resources to the external sector. The government intended to keep exchange and interest rate policies flexible during the adjustment period and to further expand the liberalization of imports. In addition, the government intended to reform the system of subsidies in order to reduce the burden on the budget.

The macroeconomic performance of the economy under the adjustment programme has been summarized below:

- Moroccan economy had better performance in 1985, but a poor performance in 1986.
- Moroccan economy showed better performance as compared to that of the "control group" in 1985, but the same performance as of the 'control group' in 1986.
- The current account targets were met.

1987 Adjustment Programme

In December 1986, the Fund approved another stand-by arrangement of SDR 230 million for the government of Morocco, in support of its economic adjustment programme for 1987. The programme was designed within a medium term framework that included fiscal and structural measures expected to achieve a major adjustment of Morocco's external imbalances, firmly establish a sustainable balance of payments and restore normal relations with external creditors. The programme aimed at maintaining a rate of growth of at least 3 per cent in 1987, keeping inflation on a downward trend, and further reducing the imbalances of the economy. To these ends, the fiscal deficit was expected to be reduced from about 6.6 per cent of GDP in 1986 to 4.3 per cent in 1987 on the strength of new revenue measures and continued expenditure restraint. Restraint in the growth of domestic credit were to be accompanied by positive real interest rates and together with restrictive budgetary policies and continued pursuit of a flexible exchange rate policy, were expected to allow for a reduction of the external current account deficit from about 1.7 per cent of GDP in 1986 to virtually equilibrium in 1987 and an increase in international reserves to the equivalent of almost one month of imports.

The following conclusions may be drawn regarding the 1987 adjustment programme:

- Moroccan economy revealed poor performance in 1987.
- Moroccan economy had poor performance as compared to that of the 'control group'.
- The current account deficit, inflation rate and fiscal deficit targets were met.

1988-1989 Adjustment Programme

The Fund approved a stand-by programme for Morocco, authorizing purchases up to the equivalent of SDR 210 million in support of the economic and financial programme for 1988-89 on August 30, 1988. The programme provided a continuation of the thrust of the adjustment policies of the last five years, while addressing the outstanding issues in the fiscal area and placing increased emphasis on policies to encourage the private sector. The authorities aimed for a further reduction in the fiscal deficit and improved expenditure control. Policies aimed at stimulating the private sector, included the promotion of exports and exploration of new export markets, the encouragement of foreign direct investment and further trade liberalization.

The result of programme performance has been summarized below:

- Moroccan economy performed better in 1988, but it had poor performance in1989.
- Moroccan economy out performed the 'control group' in 1988, but it was out performed by the 'control group' in 1989.

1990 Adjustment programme

In July 1990, the Fund approved a stand-by arrangement for Morocco authorizing purchases up to the equivalent of SDR 100 million to support the government's economic and financial programme for 1990. The 1990 programme aimed subsequently strengthening the adjustment efforts, especially in the fiscal area, in order to achieve both balance of payments viability by 1993 and acceleration in economic growth in an environment of financial stability. Economic growth was expected to be broadly based and to rise to an annual rate of 5 per cent in 1992-93, while inflation rate was expected to remain low. The external current account was projected to shift to equilibrium in 1993 and to a surplus subsequently.

Other essential elements of the medium term strategy were a new phase of public enterprise reform involving extensive privatization, reform of the financial system, and a further opening of the Moroccan economy to the rest of the world.

The macroeconomic performance of the economy under the programme has been summarized below:

- The economy performed better in 1990 as compared to 1989.
- During 1990, the economy performed better than the 'control group'.

1992 Adjustment Programme

In January 1992, the Fund approved a stand-by arrangement for Morocco authorizing purchases up to the equivalent of SDR 92 million in support of its economic and financial programme for the period January 1992 to March 1993. The authorities' programme for 1992 was consistent with their medium term strategy, which emphasized major structural reforms to promote investment and raise productivity while continuing efforts to strengthen budgetary position and reorient credit toward the private sector. The aim of the programme was to restore its capacity to undertake debt servicing in full and to achieve currency convertibility for current account transactions.

The 1992 programme aimed at a 4.0 per cent growth in real GDP, a reduction in the rate of inflation to 5.0 per cent, and a narrowing of the external current account deficit. To achieve these objectives, the government was implementing a series of revenue and expenditure measures to cut the overall budget deficit too.8

per cent of GDP in1992 from 3.1 per cent in1991, and to reduce reliance on domestic financing of the deficit. Monetary policy under the programme gave greater emphasis to the provision of credit to the private sector. The programme envisaged greater use of indirect monetary control instruments and improvements in the regulatory framework for banking system, with a view to foster the development of a modern and competitive financial sector. The authorities also intended to reduce trade barriers by restructuring the tariff system and eliminating the quantitative restrictions on imports. The public enterprise sector was being restructured through the privatization of a number of enterprises and the reform of others.

The macroeconomic performance of the programme has been summarized below:

- Moroccan economy had poor performance during 1992.
- Moroccan economy performed poor as compared to the 'control group'.
- All the targets established in the programme i.e. growth rate, inflation rate and current account deficit could not be achieved.

Macroeconomic Performance under Different Approaches

The macroeconomic performance of the Moroccan economy during the Fund-supported programmes under different approaches has been summarized below:

Before-After Approach: The following conclusions have been drawn regarding the macroeconomic performance of the Moroccan economy:

- When the 'total number of programme years' method was employed, four variables viz., investment as per cent of GDP, exports as per cent of imports, current account balance as per cent of GDP and overall balance of payment as per cent of GDP showed improvement during the programme period. Two variables, namely: real GDP growth and foreign exchange reserves growth rate revealed poor performance. Three variables i.e., inflation rate, consumption as per cent of

GDP and domestic savings as per cent of GDP had same performance. (Table 5.3)

- When the difference between means method was used eight variables viz., consumption as per cent of GDP, investment as per cent of GDP, domestic savings as per cent of GDP, exports as per cent of imports, current account balance as per cent of GDP, overall balance of GDP, inflation rate and foreign exchange reserves growth rate showed improvement during programme years, though the results were not statistically significant. One variable, namely- real GDP growth rate had poor, albeit not statistically significant, performance.(Table 5.2)
- The difference between means method showed that the dependency of the economy has been enhanced during the programme years, though the results were not statistically significant. (Table 5.2)

With-Without Approach: The following conclusions have been drawn in context of the macroeconomic performance of the Moroccan economy:

- According to the total number of programme years method, five variables- investment as per cent of GDP, exports as per cent of imports, current account balance as per cent of GDP, overall balance of payments as per cent of GDP, and inflation rate showed better performance of Moroccan economy in comparison of the 'control group'. Moroccan economy revealed poor performance as compared to the 'control group' in the case of three variables i.e., consumption as per cent of GDP, domestic savings as per cent of GDP, and real GDP growth rate. (Table 5.5)
- When the difference between means method was employed, seven variables i.e., consumption as per cent of GDP, investment as per cent of GDP, domestic savings as per cent of GDP, exports as per cent of imports, current account balance as per cent of GDP, overall balance as per cent of GDP, and inflation rate revealed better performance of the Moroccan economy as compared to that of the 'control

group'. But, disappointing result was found in the case of real output growth. However, all the results were not statistically significant. (Table 5.4)

- The dependency of Moroccan economy showed more increase as compared to the 'control group' during programme years. The results were again not statistically significant. (Table 5.4)

Generalized Evaluation Approach: The generalized evaluation approach revealed favourable effects of The Fund-supported programmes on four variables viz., investment, domestic savings, current account balance as percentage of GDP, and overall balance of payments as percentage of GDP. But, unfavourable effects on nominal GDP, exports as percentage of imports, inflation rate and real GDP growth rate were found (Table 5.6). However, there is the need of a lot of care and consideration of other things in assessing the economy's performance on the basis of this approach. (Table 5.6)

Overall Macroeconomic Performance

The followings points are noteworthy in context of the overall macroeconomic performance of Moroccan economy under the Fund supported programmes:

- A clear success was achieved in investment as proposition of output. Though the result was not statistically significant, most of the Fund supported programmes showed favourable effect on investment as proposition of GDP.
- Though there seems a little success in respect of consumption as proposition of gross domestic product, the performance was poor as compared to that of the 'control group'.
- There also seems ambiguity about the effect of the Fund supported programmes on domestic savings. Contradictory results were obtained by different approaches.

Table 5.6: Morocco: Programme Effects: Generalized Evaluation (1975-2002)

Z	C	GDP	INV	Z_{-1}	FB/G	DCR	T	D	R^2	F
GDP	- 4.108 (0.470)		4.518 (31.56)					- 7.653 (1.078)	0.98	592.2
INV	1.867 (0.120)	0.216 (31.56)*						1.199 (1.225)	0.98	579.1
DS	-0.330 (0.113)	0.1419 (3.186)*						1.001 (0.404)	0.89	100.5
X/M	50.655 (6.076)*			0.197 (2.074)*	1.181 (3.443)*	0.132 (1.372)	0.431 (2.119)*	-0.972 90.487)	0.86	26.2
CA/GDP	-1.432 (0.489)			0.275 (2.464)*	0.574 (3.178)*	-0.054 (1.054)	0.164 (1.551)	0.755 (0.747)	0.86	26.6
OB/GDP	5.975 (2.216)*			0.295 (1.784)*	0.320 (1.992)*	-0.109 (2.421)*	-0.181 (1.885)*	0.559 (0.623)	0.46	3.8
RGDP Gr	10.290 (1.976)*			-0.605 (3.564)*	0.043 (0.140)	0.001 (0.005)	-0.230 (1.233)	-1.579 (0.8820	0.44	3.4
INFR	6.405 (1.489)			0.113 (0.584)	-0.264 (1.429)	-0.017 (0.330)	-0.186 (1.254)	0.705 (0.678)	0.67	8.9

Note: (1) Figures in parenthesis are t-values.
(2) *sign indicates significant at 5% level of significance.

- A clear-cut picture emerged in context of external sector. Trade account deficit showed improvement during the programme periods, but the generalized evaluation approach refuted this result. On in depth analysis, the improvement in trade account was substantiated. Though there was improvement in exports as percentage of imports during programme period (1980- 1992), the improvement was much more during non programme period (1993- 2002), refer to Appendix 1. When regression equation was fitted for entire period (1975- 2002), the improvement in trade account balance during programme period was over shadowed by the improvement during non programme period, resulting in giving an impression of negative effect of the Fund supported programmes on trade account. Dummy variable showed positive effect, but not statistically significant, of the Fund supported programmes on trade account, when regression was fitted for 1975- 1992 period only. Due to these reasons, the explanation of generalized evaluation approach needs utmost care.
- The external current account balance as percentage of GDP revealed a remarkable success during programme years. All the three approaches supported this result. But, the result was not statistically significant.
- The overall balance of payments as percentage of GDP also showed noteworthy progress during programme years. All the three approaches gave the same result, though it was not statistically significant.
- A definite success was met in context of inflation rate during programme years. The inflation rate was brought down to an extent during programme years. This result was supported by all the three approaches. When performance of Moroccan economy- in context of inflation rate- was compared with the 'control group', the result was statistically significant at 10 per cent level of significance.

- No clear opinion could be immerged regarding the foreign exchange reserves growth rate. There was an utter failure on this aspect during initial programme years (1980- 1984).
- The disappointing results were found regarding real output growth. Not a single approach showed positive effect of the Fund supported programmes on real GDP growth rate concerning the Moroccan economy. Apart from the amount of growth, the variability in growth rate was also a matter of concern.
- As far as the fulfilment of established targets was concerned, a near majority of targets could be met.
- The programmes seem to have enhanced the dependency of the Moroccan economy, though the results were not statistically significant. But, the amount of increase in dependency of Moroccan economy was more than that of the 'control group'.
- As far as performance of intermediate variable was concerned, a remarkable success was shown by overall budget deficit as proposition of GDP. The overall budget deficit, which was equal to 9.7 per cent of GDP in 1980, declined gradually over the years and was brought down to 1.3 per cent in 1992.
- Another instrumental variable, which was implemented as per the Fund's formulae, was interest rate. The interest rate, which was 4.5 per cent in 1979 rose gradually over the years and reached at 9 per cent in 1990.
- There had been gradual depreciation of domestic currency against US dollar over the programme years.
- Money supply growth remained under control- usually in the range of 10 per cent to 16 per cent per annum- during programme period. Moroccan economy revealed better macroeconomic performance for six different years out of total twelve programme years.
- In sum, Moroccan economy showed satisfactory macroeconomic performance under the Fund supported programmes (Tables 5.7 and 5.8).

Table 5.7: Morocco: Programme Effects (summary)

Variable	Before-After Approach		With-Without Approach		Generalized Evaluation
	Difference between means method	Total number of programme years	Difference between means method	Total number of programme years	
CN/ GDP	+	0	+	-	
INV/GDP	+	+	+	+	N A
DS/GDP	+	0	+	-	N A
X/M	+	+	+	+	N A
CA/GDP	+	+	+	+	-
OB/GDP	+	+	+	+	+
RGDP Gr	-	-	-	-	+
INFR	+	0	+	+	-
FOREX Gr	+	-	N A	N A	-
GDP	N A	N A	N A	N A	N A
INV	N A	N A	N A	N A	-
DS	N A	N A	N A	N A	+
Total	8	4	7	5	+
Better	1	2	1	3	4
Poor	0	3	0	0	4
Same					0

Note: (1) + sign indicates better performance,-sign indicates poor performance and 0 indicates same performance.

Table 5.8: Morocco: Policy variables, (1975-2002)

Year	Exchange rate (Ds per U.S. $)	Interest rate (%)	Money supply (% change)	Domestic credit (% change)	Budget deficit (as % of GDP)
1975	4.18	---	55.4	24.0	-9.1
1976	4.42	---	18.2	20.2	-17.6
1977	4.33	---	19.5	21.9	-15.3
1978	3.89	4.5	17.3	23.8	-10.5
1979	3.74	4.5	13.9	13.2	-9.7
1980	4.33	4.9	11.9	17.7	-9.7
1981	5.33	6.0	16.3	18.3	-13.4
1982	6.27	6.4	11.1	18.4	-11.4
1983	8.06	6.5	17.5	19.7	-7.8
1984	9.55	6.5	10.3	8.6	-6.0
1985	9.62	8.0	18.1	14.3	-7.3
1986	8.72	8.5	15.8	11.1	-7.7
1987	7.80	8.5	9.7	7.1	-4.4
1988	8.21	8.5	14.8	8.8	-3.2
1989	8.12	---	11.5	10.2	-5.1
1990	8.04	9.0	14.6	2.4	-2.0
1991	8.15	9.0	16.8	19.0	-2.1
1992	9.05	---	9.2	10.9	-1.3
1993	9.65	---	7.9	8.5	-2.3
1994	8.96	10.0	10.1	11.1	-3.2
1995	8.47	---	7.0	14.6	-4.4
1996	8.80	---	6.5	6.0	-2.9
1997	9.71	---	11.1	49.2	-1.5
1998	9.26	13.5	10.8	8.5	-3.8

Contd...

1999	10.09	13.3	10.2	2.5	0.9
2000	10.62	13.3	8.4	12.8	-5.8
2001	11.56	13.3	14.0	-2.7	-2.6
2002	10.17	13.1	6.4	4.2	-4.3

Sources: Compiled and computed form *IMF-International Financial Statistics*, various issues, and *UN-National Accounts Statistics, Main Aggregates and detailed Tables*, various issues.

Conclusions

Moroccan economy implemented the Fund supported programmes for twelve different years spanning from 1980 to 1992. The economy showed improvement in investment as proposition of GDP during these years. The Fund supported programmes' effect on consumption and domestic savings, both as percentage of GDP, was not clear.

External sector showed clear cut improvement during programme years. Trade account improved during programme years. Noteworthy performance was revealed by both the current account balance and overall balance of payments. The both accounts had steady improvement under the Fund supported programmes.

A remarkable success was achieved in the case of inflation rate. There was almost continuous decline in inflation during program years. The effect on foreign exchange reserves growth rate was not much clear.

The only disappointing effect was found on real GDP growth. All the three approaches revealed poor performance of real output. In addition to decline in real GDP growth rate, there was much variation in the growth rate. It also seems that the Fund supported programmes enhanced the dependency of the Moroccan economy, albeit the results were not statistically significant.

Finally, the Moroccan economy revealed satisfactory performance under the Fund-supported programmes.

Appendix 5A: Morocco: Statistics on macroeconomic variables (1975-2002)

Year	CN/ GDP	INV/ GDP	DS/ GDP	X/M	CA/ GDP	OB/ GDP	INFR (%)	RGDP Gr	FOREX Gr (%)	X/ GDP	M/ GDP
1975	84.3	25.3	15.7	60.1	-5.7	-0.3	7.9	4.1	-10.4	17.2	28.6
1976	90.0	28.0	10.0	48.2	-14.8	-0.2	8.5	7.0	50.7	13.6	28.2
1977	84.5	34.1	15.5	40.7	-16.6	-0.1	12.6	6.5	8.8	11.8	28.9
1978	86.6	25.7	13.4	50.8	-10.0	-0.5	9.8	3.4	21.6	11.4	22.4
1979	87.1	24.5	12.9	51.1	-9.5	-0.7	8.3	4.5	-10.8	11.8	23.0
1980	87.0	24.2	13.0	49.9	-7.5	-1.5	9.4	3.4	-25.9	13.2	22.1
1981	89.1	26.1	10.9	54.1	-12.1	-2.8	12.5	-2.8	-42.7	15.6	28.8
1982	86.8	28.2	13.2	47.8	-12.2	-2.7	10.5	9.6	-4.8	13.4	28.0
1983	86.7	24.0	13.3	55.8	-6.4	-1.6	6.2	-0.6	-51.2	14.4	25.8
1984	88.1	25.4	11.9	53.2	-7.8	-0.7	12.4	4.3	-54.7	16.3	30.7
1985	85.2	27.1	14.8	56.2	-6.9	-0.4	7.7	6.3	139.6	16.8	29.9
1986	86.9	22.8	13.1	64.5	-1.2	2.0	8.7	8.4	67.0	14.4	22.4
1987	87.4	20.6	12.6	66.8	0.9	2.0	2.7	-2.6	111.9	14.9	22.3
1988	83.0	21.3	17.0	75.5	2.1	1.2	2.4	10.4	34.4	16.4	21.7
1989	84.4	24.1	15.6	60.2	-3.5	0.0	3.1	2.2	-10.8	14.8	24.5
1990	79.8	25.7	20.2	62.7	-0.8	6.9	6.9	1.7	323.2	16.9	27.0
1991	85.2	22.2	14.8	74.2	-1.5	3.4	8.0	8.9	43.0	18.5	24.9
1992	86.8	22.3	13.2	67.0	-1.5	27	5.7	-4.0	17.3	17.3	25.8
1993	86.3	22.7	13.7	70.5	-1.9	1.5	5.2	-1.0	3.3	18.0	25.5
1994	78.2	20.7	21.8	72.4	-2.4	1.6	5.1	10.4	19.6	18.3	25.3
1995	88.9	21.4	11.1	73.4	-3.9	-5.7	6.1	-6.6	-17.6	20.6	28.1
1996	88.0	19.3	12.0	75.8	-0.2	-2.2	3.0	12.4	6.0	22.8	30.1
1997	86.4	20.6	13.6	79.0	-0.5	-2.9	1.0	-2.2	5.5	20.8	26.3
1998	85.7	22.3	14.3	75.4	-0.4	-1.7	2.8	7.0	11.0	19.5	25.9

Contd...

1999	84.7	24.3	15.3	75.4	-0.5	-0.2	0.7	-0.7	25.4	21.9	29.1
2000	87.4	24.1	12.6	69.6	-1.5	-3.4	1.9	0.7	-16.3	22.2	31.8
2001	87.0	22.2	13.0	70.2	4.7	2.5	0.6	5.9	79.1	20.9	29.7
2002	86.6	22.9	13.4	71.9	4.1	-0.1	2.8	3.4	20.0	21.8	30.3

Sources: Compiled and computed form *IMF-International Financial Statistics*, various issues, and *UN-NationalAccounts Statistics, Main Aggregates and detailed Tables*, various issues.

6

Ghana: Poor Performance Despite Inflow of Capital

Ghana is a low income developing country, located on the West Coast of Africa. Ghana is well endowed with abroad range of natural resources, such as arable land, forests and sizable deposits of gold diamonds, bauxite, manganese, as well as a considerable potential for hydroelectric power. The economy had traditionally depended to a high degree on primary (agriculture as well as mineral) production and exports. Exports of cocoa, gold and timber account for the bulk of total merchandise exports. Agriculture production is concentrated in cocoa and staple food crops. Ghana ranks among the world's largest producers and exporters of cocoa.

During 1970s, inappropriate domestic policies and external shocks (droughts in 1975-77 and a marked decline the terms of trade) led to a severe worsening in economic and financial performance. Large fiscal deficits, financed primarily by borrowing from the domestic banking system, gave rise to a high rate of inflation and an increasingly overvalued exchange rate. Heavy government intervention in the economy through price, distribution, and import controls, as well as a massive expansion of the public sector through the establishment of a large number of state enterprises, exacerbated distortions in the economy and severely eroded incentives to produce, save, and invest. Shortage of foreign exchange and imported goods and distortions in the structure of relative prices led to a proliferation of parallel markets. As a consequence, the growth of output had come to a halt and then turned negative. The overall balance of payments deficit widened, giving a rise to depletion of gross official reserves and an accumulation of external payments arrears.

Started in 1979, Ghana had implemented a series of adjustment programmes supported by the IMF. The latest arrangement was approved by the Fund on 20th June 2003, for three years, under Poverty Reduction and Growth Facility (PRGF).

1979 Adjustment Programme

In the summer of 1978, the authorities began implementing stabilizing measures and in January 1979, Ghana obtained financial support by the Fund under a stand-by arrangement. The measures were designed to strengthen the balance of payments, to achieve a substantial reduction in inflation rate to correct cost price distortions, and thus lay the basis for sustained growth of production and exports. The measures included the tightening of fiscal and monetary policies and a more flexible exchange rate policy; and more appropriate policies relating to producer prices.

The macroeconomic performance of the programme has been summarized below:

- Ghanaian economy showed better macroeconomic performance in 1979.
- Ghanaian economy had better performance as compared to the 'control group'.

1983-1984 Adjustment programme

After a modest recovery in 1980, real output dipped again by about 2 percent and dropped further by 7 percent in 1982. The decline in output was compounded by the sharp drop in the world prices for all of Ghana's export products; particularly cocoa, which until 1980 accounted for two third of export receipts. Imports and other payments had subsequently cut down to levels comparable to declining exports while external payments arrears had accumulated (Table 6.1).

In 1983, the Fund approved SDR 238.5 million stand-by arrangement in support of the government's economic adjustment programme for 1983-1984. The economic programme was intended to be a major step in a sustained effort over the medium term to deal with the serious structural imbalance and to rehabilitate the Ghanaian economy. The measures focused on a

Table 6.1: Ghana: Lending Arrangements with IMF, 1975-2002

(Amount expressed in millions of SDRs)

Facility	Date of arrangement	Date of expiration	Amount approved	Balance not drawn	Programme years	remarks
SBA	10.01.1979	09.01.1980	53.0	21.0	1979	
SBA	03.08.1983	02.08.1984	238.5	0	1983,1984	
SBA	27.08.1984	31.12.1985	180..0	0	1985	
SBA	15.10.1986	14.10.1987	81.8	0	1986	
EA	06.11.1987	05.11.1990	245.4	147.9	1987	Replaced by ESAF 1988
SAF	06.11.1987	05.11.1990	129.9	89.0	1987	Replaced by ESAF 1988
PRGF	09.11.1988	05.03.1992	388.6	0	1988,1989,1990	
PRGF	30.06.1995	02.05.1999	164.4	27.4	1995,1996,1997	
PRGF	03.05.1999	30.11.2002	228.8	51.8	1999,2000,2001	

Source: IMF Survey, various issues.

substantial restructuring of prices in favour of productive sectors and exports, improving the financial position of the public sector, raising the volume of imports to promote the economy, and reducing external payments arrears. Together with the reforms of exchange rate system, these measures were expected to generate larger supplies for the market, in part by reabsorbing a substantial portion of the parallel economy into normal channels.

The following conclusions have been drawn regarding the performance of the 1983-84 adjustment programme.

- Ghanaian economy had poor macroeconomic performance in 1983, but it showed good performance in 1984.
- In 1983, the Ghanaian economy had poor performance in comparison of performance of the 'control group', while it had better performance in 1984.
- The drought of 1981-1983 was responsible for poor performance of the economy to a large extent.

1985 Adjustment Programme

The Fund approved another stand-by arrangement in support of the government's economic adjustment programme in August 1984, authorizing purchases up to SDR 180 million. This programme was designed to consolidate the stabilization achieved and set the stage for resumption of growth. It was formulated in cooperation with the World Bank and aimed at continued restructuring of relative prices in favour of producing sector and exports, reducing the underlying rate of inflation, and promoting the economic activity throughout the economy to achieve balance of payments viability over the medium term. In addition to maintaining exchange rate flexibility, continued efforts to reduce external payments arrears and controlling liquidity creations, the important policy actions for 1985 programme were in the area of pricing and interest rate policy. The authorities decided to allow sellers to fix their own prices at the wholesale and retail levels and adopted a formulae and a time table to achieve positive real interest rates by mid 1986. Fiscal policy during 1985 was expected to be geared toward supporting these objectives by limiting the size of the fiscal deficit.

The following conclusions have been drawn regarding the 1985 adjustment programme:

- Ghanaian economy had somewhat better macroeconomic performance in 1985.
- Ghanaian economy performed better than the 'control group'.
- The Fund claimed that its programme was successful (Tables 6.2, 6.3, 6.4 and 6.5).

1986 Adjustment programme

The Fund approved a standby arrangement for the government of Ghana, authorizing purchases up to SDR 82 million in support of economic and financial programme for 1986. The economic programme aimed at consolidating the progress made by the Ghanaian economy during 1983-85. The programme envisaged the implementation of a number of structural policies, particularly with regard to the exchange rate system, tax and expenditure control, the public enterprise sector, and the civil service. A foreign exchange auction system was just instituted with the objective of broadening the access to foreign exchange market and maintaining a more flexible exchange rate policy. A major objective of the programme was the recovery of cocoa production, which was critical to export growth. Monetary and credit policies under the programme were formulated with the objective of promoting economic activity in the production sector, while remaining consistent with attainment of the inflation and balance of payments targets.

According to an IMF publication, 'the difficulties in the policy implementation led to a weakening of overall economic performance by early 1986. To regain the momentum, fiscal policy was tightened, the foreign exchange system was further liberalized through the establishment of an auction market for foreign exchange, and import licensing system was freed. As a result, the macroeconomic objectives of the 1986 programme were realized.

Table 6.2: Ghana: Programme Effects: Before-after Approach

The difference between means method

Variable		Programme years															Effect	t-value
		1979	1983	1984	1985	1986	1987	1988	1989	1990	1995	1996	1997	1999	2000	2001		
CN/	Pre	94.3	96.2	96.7	93.3	92.4	92.3	91.8	89.3	94.0	88.3	88.2	88.1	88.0	89.0	99.0	-	0.699
GDP	Pro	93.6	96.7	93.3	92.4	92.3	91.8	89.3	94.0	96.4	88.2	88.1	92.1	89.0	99.0	94.0		
INV/	Pre	6.6	3.4	3.8	7.0	9.6	9.3	10.4	10.9	13.5	22.5	21.1	20.5	22.0	23.0	24.0	+	2.026*
GDP	Pro	6.4	3.8	7.0	9.6	9.3	10.4	10.9	13.5	12.3	21.1	20.5	23.6	23.0	24.0	24.0		
DS/	Pre	5.7	3.8	3.3	6.7	7.6	7.7	8.2	10.7	6.0	11.7	11.8	11.9	12.0	11.0	1.0 6.0	-	0.699
GDP	Pro	6.4	3.3	6.7	7.6	7.7	8.2	10.7	6.0	3.6	11.8	11.9	7.9	11.0	1.0			
X/M	Pre	110	124	88.0	91.0	84.4	110	98.9	111	80.0	78.3	84.8	80.5	69.8	60.8	69.9	-	0.971
	Pro	117	88.0	91.0	84.4	110	98.9	111	80.0	73.8	84.8	80.5	69.4	60.8	69.9	62.8		
CA/	Pre	-0.4	-0.3	-0.8	-0.5	-2.1	-0.8	-2.0	-1.3	-1.9	-4.7	-2.2	-4.7	-5.0	-11.6	-8.4	-	0.200
GDP	Pro	1.2	-0.8	-0.5	-2.1	-0.8	-2.0	-1.3	-1.9	-3.7	-2.2	-4.7	-8.0	-11.6	-8.4	-5.3		
OB/	Pre	-0.4	0.0	-0.8	0.5	0.2	-1.1	2.9	3.5	3.0	4.5	2.7	-0.4	0.3	-1.8	-3.7	-	0.372
GDP	Pro	0.4	-0.8	0.5	0.2	-1.1	2.9	3.5	3.0	1.7	2.7	-0.4	1.5	-1.8	-3.7	-2.3		
INFR	Pre	73.1	22.3	123	39.7	10.3	24.6	39.8	31.4	25.2	24.9	59.5	46.6	14.6	12.4	25.2	-	0.042
	Pro	54.4	123	39.7	10.3	24.6	39.8	31.4	25.2	37.3	59.5	46.6	27.9	12.4	25.2	32.9		
RGDP	Pre	8.5	-7.2	0.7	2.6	5.1	5.2	4.8	5.6	5.1	3.3	4.0	4.6	4.7	4.4	3.7	-	0.017
Gr	Pro	-3.2	0.7	2.6	5.1	5.2	4.8	5.6	5.1	3.1	4.0	4.6	4.2	4.4	3.7	4.2		
FOREX	Pre	94.3	-4.3	2.8	111	52.4	11.2	-64.9	23.3	46.6	43.8	20.7	19.7	-42.1	29.8	-39.0	-	0.564
Gr	Pro	2.4	2.8	111	52.4	11.2	-64.9	23.3	43.6	-32.5	20.7	19.7	-36.3	29.8	-39.0	27.2		
Memorandum Items																		
X/GDP	Pre	9.1	2.8	2.1	7.0	9.8	15.1	20.1	19.4	19.4	22.8	21.9	24.0	28.0	26.7	38.8	Pre<	3.130*
	Pro	9.7	2.1	7.0	9.8	15.1	20.1	19.4	19.4	18.0	21.9	24.0	29.5	26.7	38.8	35.2	Pro	
M/GDP	Pre	8.2	2.2	2.4	7.7	11.6	13.7	20.4	17.4	24.3	29.1	25.8	29.8	40.0	43.8	55.5	Pre<	2.956*
	Pro	8.3	2.4	7.7	11.6	13.7	20.4	17.4	24.3	24.4	25.8	29.8	42.4	43.8	55.5	56.0	Pro	

Notes: (1) +sign indicates better performance, -sign indicates poor performance and 0 indicates same performance.
(2) * sign indicates significant at 5% level of significance.

Table 6.3: Ghana: Programme Effects: Before-after Approach

Total number program years method

Variable	1979	1983	1984	1985	1986	1987	1988	1989
CN/GDP	+	-	+	+	+	+	+	-
INV/GDP	-	+	+	+	-	+	+	+
DS/GDP	+	-	+	+	+	+	+	-
X/M	+	-	+	-	+	-	+	-
CA/GDP	+	-	+	-	+	-	+	-
OB/GDP	+	-	+	-	-	+	+	-
RGDP Gr	-	+	+	+	+	-	+	-
INFR	+	-	+	+	-	-	+	+
FOREX Gr	-	+	+	-	-	-	+	+
No of variables with better performance	6	3	9	5	5	4	9	3
No of variables with poor performance	3	6	0	4	4	5	0	6
No of variables with same performance	0	0	0	0	0	0	0	0

Contd...

Variable	Performance (no. of years)									
	1990	1995	1996	1997	1999	2000	2001	Better	Poor	Same
CN/GDP	-	+	+	-	-	-	+	9	6	0
INV/GDP	-	-	-	+	+	+	0	9	5	1
DS/GDP	-	+	+	-	-	-	+	9	6	0
X/M	-	+	-	-	-	+	-	6	9	0
CA/GDP	-	+	-	-	-	+	+	7	8	0
OB/GDP	-	-	-	+	-	-	+	6	9	0
RGDP Gr	-	+	+	-	-	-	+	8	7	0
INFR	-	-	+	+	+	-	-	8	7	0
FOREX Gr	-	-	-	-	+	-	+	6	9	0
No of variables with better performance	0	5	4	3	3	3	6		68(50.4)	
No of variables with poor performance	9	4	5	6	6	6	2		66(48.9)	
No of variables with same performance	0	0	0	0	0	0	1		1(0.7)	

Notes (1) + sign indicates better performance, - sign indicates poor performance and 0 indicates same performance. (2) Figures in parenthesis are percentages.

Table 6.4: Ghana: Programme Effects: With-without Approach

The difference between means method

Variable		Programme years															Effect	t-value
		1979	1983	1984	1985	1986	1987	1988	1989	1990	1995	1996	1997	1999	2000	2001		
ΔCN/	GH	-0.7	0.5	-3.4	-0.9	-0.1	-0.5	-2.5	4.7	2.4	-0.1	-0.1	4.0	1.0	10.0	-5.0	-	0.630
GDP	NPC	-0.6	-0.3	-0.4	0.3	0.5	-0.3	0.0	-0.6	0.4	-0.2	0.2	-0.3	0.1	-0.9	1.6		
ΔINV/	GH	-0.2	0.4	3.2	2.6	-0.3	1.1	0.5	2.6	-1.2	-1.4	-0.6	3.1	1.0	1.0	0.0	+	2.253*
GDP	NPC	-0.1	-2.3	-1.3	-1.2	-0.2	1.0	0.2	0.6	0.3	-0.1	-0.1	-0.2	-1.3	0.1	-0.2		
ΔDS/	GH	0.7	-0.5	3.4	0.9 -	0.1	0.5	2.5	-4.7	-2.4	0.1	0.1	-4.0	-1.0	-10.0	5.0	-	0.630
GDP	NPC	0.6	0.3	0.4	0.3	-0.5	0.3	0.0	0.6	-0.4	0.2	-0.2	0.3	-0.1	0.9	-1.6		
ΔX/M	GH	6.3	-36	3.0	-6.6	25.8	-11.3	12.6	-31.5	-6.2	6.5	-4.3	-11.1	-9.0	9.1	-7.1	-	1.162
	NPC	10.8	4.3	4.9	-0.6	-6.2	-2.1	0.2	8.8	-4.7	0.3	-1.3	1.3	6.1	1.4	-0.9		
ΔCA/	GH	1.6	-0.5	0.3	-1.6 -	1.3	-1.2	0.7	-0.6	-1.8	2.5	-2.5	-3.3	-6.6	3.2	3.1	-	0.654
GDP	NPC	0.8	0.4	1.9	0.8	0.0	-0.8	0.8	0.0	-0.8	0.0	-0.3	0.1	0.1	-0.9	0.7		
ΔOB/	GH	0.8	-0.8	1.3	-0.3	-1.3	4.0	0.6	-0.5	-1.3	-1.8	-3.1	1.9	-2.1	-1.9	1.4	-	0.141
GDP	NPC	-1.0	-1.2	1.3	-0.5	0.3	0.0	-0.5	0.5	-0.4	-0.6	0.6	-0.6	0.2	-0.5	1.3		
ΔINFR	GH	-19	100	-84	-29	14.3	15.2	-8.4	-6.2	12.1	24.6	-12.9	-18.7	-2.2	12.8	7.7	+	0.093
	NPC	4.8	3.8	11.1	5.6	-7.6	4.8	2.4	4.5	2.4	-3.6	-2.3	-0.8	-3.2	-1.3	0.2		
Δ GDP	GH	-11.7	7.9	1.9	2.5	0.1	-0.4	0.8	-0.5	-1.8	0.7	0.6	-0.4	-0.3	-0.7	0.5	-	0.042
Gr	NPC	-0.1	-0.3	1.0	1.3	0.2	1.0	-2.5	-0.8	1.4	-0.5	-0.3	-0.6	-0.6	1.4	-1.7		
Memorandum Items																		
Δ X/	GH	0.6	-0.7	4.9	2.8	5.3	5.0	-0.7	0.0	-1.4	-0.9	2.1	5.5	-1.3	12.1	-3.6	GH>N	2.528*
GDP	NPC	1.4	-1.8	0.6	-1.0	-1.0	0.6	1.6	1.1	-0.6	1.0	-0.8	-0.3	-0.6	1.7	-1.4	PC	
Δ M/	GH	0.1	0.2	5.3	3.9	2.1	6.7	-3.0	6.9	0.1	-3.3	4.0	12.6	3.8	11.7	0.5	GH>N	2.651*
GDP	NPC	0.4	-3.2	-1.4	-1.0	-1.3	1.6	1.5	0.9	1.9	0.6	-0.9	-0.1	-1.0	2.5	-1.4	PC	

Notes: (1) GH: Ghana and NPC: Non Programme Countries

(2) + sign indicates better performance, - sign indicates poor performance and 0 indicates same performance.

(3) * sign indicates significant at 5% level of significance.

Table 6.5: Ghana: Program Effects: With-without Approach

Total number programme years method

Variable	1979	1983	1984	1985	1986	1987	1988	1989
ΔC/G	+	-	+	+	+	+	+	-
ΔINV/G	-	+	+	+	-	+	+	+
ΔDS/G	+	-	+	+	+	+	+	-
ΔX/M	-	-	-	-	+	-	+	-
ΔCA/G	+	-	-	-	+	-	-	-
ΔOB/G	+	+	0	+	-	+	+	-
ΔRGGr	-	+	+	+	-	-	+	+
ΔINFR	+	-	+	+	-	-	+	+
No of variables with better performance	5	3	5	6	4	4	7	3
No of variables with poor performance	3	5	2	2	4	4	1	5
No of variables with same performance	0	0	1	0	0	0	0	0

Contd....

Variable	Performance (no. of years)									
	1990	1995	1996	1997	1999	2000	2001	Better	Poor	Same
ΔC/G	-	-	+	-	-	-	+	8	7	0
ΔINV/G	-	-	-	+	+	+	+	10	5	0
ΔDS/G	-	-	+	-	-	-	+	8	7	0
ΔX/M	-	+	-	-	-	+	-	4	11	0
ΔCA/G	-	+	-	-	-	+	+	5	10	0
ΔOB/G	-	-	-	+	-	-	+	7	7	1
ΔRGGr	-	+	+	-	+	-	+	9	6	0
ΔINFR	-	-	+	+	-	-	-	7	8	0
No of variables with better performance	0	3	4	3	2	3	6		58(48.3)	
No of variables with poor performance	8	5	4	5	6	5	2		61(50.9)	
No of variables with same performance	0	0	0	0	0	0	0		1(0.8)	

Notes (1) + sign indicates better performance, - sign indicates poor performance and 0 indicates same performance. (2) Figures in parenthesis are percentages.

The macroeconomic performance of the programme has been summarized below:

- Ghanaian economy performed slightly better in1986.
- The macroeconomic performance of the Ghanaian economy was same as that of the 'control group'.

1987 Adjustment Programme

During the second half of 1980s, the Ghanaian government was seeking to consolidate the gains it had achieved since 1983. The Fund was supporting macroeconomic and structural adjustment measures to be implemented during 1987-90 with an SDR 245 million extended fund facility and an SDR 130 million structural adjustment facility. The basic objectives of the programme for 1987-90 were:

- To achieve an annual growth rate of real GDP on the average of 5 percent.
- To reduce the average annual rate of inflation to 8 percent in 1990.
- To generate significant overall balance of payments surpluses that would become consistent with the elimination of Ghana's balance of payments arrears.

To attain these objectives, the Ghanaian authorities decided to pursue a broad range of structural and financial policies. With the continuation of prudent fiscal and monetary policies it was decided to improve incentives for efficient production, exports, and imports substitution through the continuation of a flexible exchange rate policy, exchange and trade liberalization, and remunerative agriculture produce prices. Investment for rehabilitation and restructuring of production capacity, infrastructure and social services was to be raised. Measures were to be implemented to encourage savings and an efficient allocation of resources through market determined interest rates and broadened of the range of financial instruments. The state enterprise sector was to be reformed. Fiscal policy was decided to mobilize additional revenues to support rehabilitation and other high priority investment. The overall budget deficit was to be held to about to 3 percent of GDP in both 1987 and 1988.The fiscal measures and prospective financing flows were expected to permit a significant reduction in net bank credit to the government, which was to allow credit to private sector to rise broadly in line with projected growth in nominal GDP.

The summarized macroeconomic performance under the 1987 programme has been given below:

- Ghanaian economy had poor macroeconomic performance in 1987.
- The macroeconomic performance of the Ghanaian economy was same as that of the 'control group'.
- The real GDP growth and inflation rate targets could not be met.

1988-1990 Adjustment Programme

On November 10 1988, the Fund approved a three year arrangement for Ghana authorizing purchases up to SDR 368 million under the enhanced structural adjustment facility (ESAF). The ESAF replaced the then under operation three year extended arrangement and an arrangement under the SAF. Though no explicit reason was cited by the Fund for this replacement, but in a publication it was cited 'under the ESAF arrangement, Ghana would be able to draw larger amount on more concessional terms and repayment conditions, given the county's heavy debt burden'. The programme provided for a continuing and strengthening of the reform efforts, with a view to sustaining the growth momentum of economy and achieving a viable external payments position over the medium term. The programme also addressed in a systematic manner the needs of poor and most vulnerable group in Ghana. To attain these objectives, the programme involved not only a reinforcement of the judicious macroeconomic policies pursued in the past years but also an acceleration of structural reforms, a strengthening of the institutional framework and the implementation of a broadly based economic development strategy.

The summarized macroeconomic performance under the 1988-90 programme is give below:

- Ghanaian economy had good performance in 1988, but it revealed very poor performance during1989-90.
- In 1988, the Ghanaian economy had better performance as compared to the 'control group', but it had relatively poor performance during 1989-90.

1995-1997 Adjustment Programme

In 1992, Ghana encountered serious difficulties in implementing additional economic reforms in the run-up to the first multi party elections under the new system. Consequently the reforms slipped off the track, and strong price and balance of payments pressures re-emerged. The Fund, on July 3, 1995 approved a series of loans for Ghana over the next three years under the enhanced structural adjustment facility (ESAF) totalling the equivalent of SDR 164.4 million in support of the 1995-1997 economic adjustment programme.

The economic programme for 1995-97 aimed to accelerate the real GDP growth to 5.0 percent in 1995, to 5.0 percent in 1996, and to 5.5 percent in1997, while reducing inflation rate to 19.5 percent in 1995, to 8.0 percent in 1996 and to 5 percent in 1997. The external current account deficit was projected to be down to 3.7 percent of GDP in 1995, to 3.4 percent of GDP in 1996 and to 2.7 of GDP percent in 1997. Ghana's programme aimed at improving the environment for private savings and investment by pursuing sound financial policies consistent with reducing the inflation rate and maintaining a stable exchange rate. The structural policies were directed at providing a supporting environment to private sector initiative and foreign investment through curtailing public sector involvement in the economy.

Ghana's medium term fiscal strategy was geared to generating additional domestic savings to help meet the programme's investment and external current account objectives. The overall budget balance, excluding divestiture receipts, was expected to move from a deficit of 2.9 percent of GDP in 1994 to a surplus of

1.3 percent by 1997. The government also planned to restructure its budgetary outlays to fund improvements in the country's economic infrastructure and the provision of better education and health services. To bring inflation firmly under control, broad money supply growth was to be reduced sharply. Monetary restraint was to be accompanied by a flexible exchange and interest rate policy aimed at protecting Ghana's external competitiveness and foreign exchange reserve position.

The structural reform strategy focused on deregulation of the cocoa and petroleum sectors, and expanding the privatization programme. Privatization policy aimed at selling or liquidating a large number of the major state enterprises and was to be expanded to cover banks and public utilities. The financial operations of state enterprises that remained in the public domain were being strengthened and placed on a profit making. No government or central bank financial support, including loan guarantees, were to be provided to these enterprises, which were to be dependent on their internal sources or private capital markets to cover their financial needs.

The macroeconomic performance under the 1995-97 programme has been summarized below:

- Ghanaian economy performed little bit better in 1995, but it showed poor performance during 1996-97.
- Ghanaian economy had poor macroeconomic performance as compared to that of the 'control group' during 1995-97.
- Not even a single established target (real GDP growth rate, inflation rate and current account deficit) was met.
- The programme was not successful.

1999-2001 Adjustment Programme

On May3, 1999, the IMF approved a three year loan for Ghana under the enhanced structural adjustment facility (ESAF), equivalent to SDR 155 million to support the economic reform programme for 1999-2001. The main objectives of the programme were to consolidate the achievements already made in macroeconomic stability and accelerate the pace of structural reform. The real GDP growth was projected to increase to 5.5 percent in 1999, to 6 percent in 2000 and again to 6 percent in 2001. The government intended to bring inflation rate down to 10 percent in 1999, to 6.4 percent in 2000 and to 5 percent in 2001.The programme aimed at reducing external current account deficit to 2.9 percent of GDP in 1999, to 2.5 percent of GDP in 2000 and 2.4 percent of GDP in 2001. To achieve these objectives, domestic budget financing was to be limited to about 2.8 percent of GDP in 1999.

Ghana intended to take significant steps to liberalize the cocoa and energy sector, accelerate the divestiture of state enterprises, and strengthening the banking system. Public sector reforms were to be carried out to limit the scope of government to core areas, in particular, agriculture, the social sectors and basic infrastructure.

Ghana's economic programme emphasized on education and health, since the government believed the level of growth required to reduce poverty was difficult to achieve without significant increase in labour productivity. Expenditure programmes were designed for education and health and were implemented with donor support.

The following conclusions were drawn regarding the programme:

- Ghanaian economy had poor macroeconomic performance during 1999-2000, but showed an improvement in 2001.
- Ghanaian economy had performed poor as compared to the 'control group' during 1999-2000, but it performed better in 2001.
- The established targets i.e. real GDP growth rate, inflation rate and current account deficit were not met.
- The programme was not successful.

Macroeconomic Performance under Different Approaches

The macroeconomic performance of the Ghanaian economy according to different approaches has been summarized below:

Before-After Approach: The following conclusions have been drawn regarding the macroeconomic performance of the Ghanaian economy during programme years.

- When the 'total number of programme years' method was employed, five variables viz., consumption as percentage of GDP, investment as percentage of GDP, domestic savings as percentage of GDP, real GDP growth rate and inflation rate showed better performance of the Ghanaian economy during programme years. While, four variables viz., exports as percentage of imports, current account balance as percentage of GDP, overall balance of payments as percentage of GDP and foreign exchange reserves growth rate revealed poor performance. (Table 6.3)
- According to the difference between means method, only one variable- investment as proposition of GDP- showed statistically significant and better performance of the Ghanaian economy during programme years. Eight variables viz., consumption as percentage of GDP, domestic savings as percentage of GDP, exports as percentage of imports, current account balance as percentage of GDP, overall balance as percentage of GDP, inflation rate and foreign exchange reserves growth rate revealed poor performance. (Table 6.2)
- The Fund supported programmes enhanced the dependency of the Ghanaian economy. The results were statistically significant at 5 percent level of significance. (Table 6.2)

With-Without Approach: The following conclusions have been drawn regarding the macroeconomic performance of the Ghanaian economy under the Fund supported programmes.

- According to the total number of programme years method, four variables viz., consumption as percentage of GDP, investment as percentage of GDP, domestic savings as percentage of GDP and real GDP growth rate showed better performance of the Ghanaian economy in comparison of the 'control group'. While, three variables namely, exports as percentage of imports, current account balance as percentage of GDP and inflation rate showed relatively poor performance of the Ghanaian economy. (Table 6.5)

- The Ghanaian economy showed poor performance in the case of six variables viz., consumption as percentage of GDP, domestic savings as percentage of GDP, exports as percentage of imports, current account balance as percentage of GDP, overall balance of payments as percentage of GDP and real GDP growth rate, as compared to the 'control group', according to the difference between means method. Only two variables- investment as percentage of GDP and inflation rate showed better performance of the Ghanaian economy. (Table 6.4)
- There was more increase in the dependency of the Ghanaian economy as compared to that of the 'control group'. The results were statistically significant at 5 percent level of significance. (Table 6.4)

Generalized Evaluation Approach: When generalized evaluation approach was employed, three variables, namely- exports as percentage of imports, nominal GDP and real GDP growth rate showed positive effects of the Fund supported programmes on the Ghanaian economy. While, five variables viz., domestic savings, investment, current account as percentage of GDP, overall balance of payments as percentage of GDP and inflation rate revealed negative effects of the Fund supported programmes. (Tables 6.6 and 6.7)

Overall Macroeconomic Performance

The important points in the context of macroeconomic performance of the Ghanaian economy under the Fund supported programmes have been mentioned below:

- The substantial improvement was found in investment, as percentage of GDP, during programme years. The results were statistically significant at 5 percent level of significance.
- Very disappointing results were obtained in context of domestic savings as proposition of GDP. Domestic savings as percentage of GDP remained around about 6 percent during

Table 6.6: Ghana: Programme Effects: Generalized Evaluation (1975-2002)

Z	C	GDP	INV	Z_{-1}	FB/G	DCR	T	D	R^2	F
GDP	352.5 (2.348)*		4.177 (91.8)*					100.0 (0.483)	0.99	4613.1
INV	-82.59 (2.294)*	0.238 (91.8)*						-20.086 (0.404)	0.99	4599.9
DS	133.4 (1.038)	0.062 (6.70)*						-83.786 (0.473)	0.66	23.7
X/M	102.0 (4.129)*			0.156 (0.725)	0.259 (0.453)	-0.144 (1.516)	-1.574 (3.172)*	2.7138 (0.492)	0.66	8.4
CA/GDP	2.696 (1.783)*			0.288 (1.196)	0.071 (0.601)	-0.032 (1.684)	0.207 (2.085)*	-0.211 (0.203)	0.57	5.9
OB/GDP	3.922 (4.309)*			-0.115 (0.783)	0.378 (5.094)*	-0.017 (1.580)	-0.040 (1.165)	-0.897 (1.546)	0.60	6.6
RGDP Gr	-3.626 (1.556)			0.135 (0.655)	0.163 (0.891)	0.060 (1.929)*	0.253 (2.483)*	0.392 (0.249)	0.45	3.6
INFR	41.371 (2.039)*			-0.011 (0.061)	-1.526 (1.184)	0.391 (1.812)*	-1.887 (2.568)*	8.216 0.731)	0.43	3.3

Note: (1) Figures in parenthesis are t-values.
(2) *sign indicates significant at 5% level of significance.

Table 6.7: Ghana: Programme Effects, (summary)

Variable	Before-After Approach		With-Without Approach		Generalized Evaluation
	Difference between means method	Total number of programme years	Difference between means method	Total number of programme years	
CN/ GDP	-	+	-	+	N A
INV/GDP	+*	+	+	+*	N A
DS/GDP	-	+	-	+	N A
X/M	-	-	-	-	+
CA/GDP	-	-	-	-	-
OB/GDP	-	-	-	0	-
RGDP Gr	-	+	-	+	+
INFR	-	+	+	-	-
FOREX Gr	-	-	N A	N A	N A
GDP	N A	N A	N A	N A	+
INV	N A	N A	N A	N A	-
DS	N A	N A	N A	N A	-
Total	1	5	2 6	4	3 5
Better	8	4	0	3	0
Poor	0	0		1	
Same					

Note: (1) + sign indicates better performance,-sign indicates poor performance and 0 sign indicates same performance.
(2) * sign indicates significance at 5% level of significance.

most of the programme years. There was a big gap between domestic savings and investment levels both as proposition of GDP (refer to Appendix 6A).

- The level of consumption in relation to output remained quite high during programme years, resulting in low level of domestic savings as percentage of GDP. There was utmost need to reduce consumption as proposition of GDP.
- Even after implementation of the Fund supported programmes for 15 years, external sector's position deteriorated instead of improvement. Trade account deficit as percentage of GDP widened over the programme years.
- The external current account position became worse from bad during programmes. The current account deficit, which was equal to 0.4 percent of GDP in 1979, widened steadily over the years and during the last two programmes- the 1995-1997 and 1999-2001 programmes- it was in the range of 4.7 % - 11.6 % of GDP.
- The overall balance of payments as percentage of GDP revealed poor performance during programme years. It showed surplus during 1984-1995, but thereafter a gradual deterioration in its position and ultimately a deficit equal to 3.7 percent in 2000.The deterioration in overall balance of payments much less than those of current account and trade account. This might be due to increased capital inflows induced by the IMF's 'seal of approval'.
- Disappointing results were also found in the case of inflation rate. The inflation rate was 33 percent in 2001. There was utmost need to do important to reduce the inflation.
- Though the established targets were not met, the real output growth rate did not give much disappointment. The volatility in growth rate was reduced to a large extent, albeit there was a little bit decline in the growth rate of real output during programme years.
- Foreign exchange reserves' growth rate declined during the programmes.
- Only few targets were met.

- The Fund supported programmes led to enhance the openness of the Ghanaian economy. There was more increase in the dependency of the Ghanaian economy as compared to that of the 'control group'. The results were statistically significant at 5 percent level of significance.
- As far as the performance of intermediary variables is concerned, results were not up to expectations. The overall budget deficit, which was brought down and was under control till 1991, showed huge deficits from 1998 onward.
- During the programmes, there was rapid growth in money supply. This rapid growth of money supply in combination of high inflation rate hurt the economic performance of the economy in recent years.
- The domestic credit expansion also showed sudden increase in on a number of occasions. But, as compared to money supply growth, domestic credit expansion was much lower during programme years.
- There was heavy depreciation of domestic currency against US dollar during programme years, but it also failed in improving the external sector position.
- The interest rates were increased on certain occasions during the programme years. In 1998 and 1999, interest rates were reduced.
- According to the before-after approach, seven programme years showed a little improvement in the economy out of fifteen years.
- In sum, the Fund supported programmes failed in improving the macroeconomic position of the Ghanaian economy. Though, the non strict implementation of instrumental variables might be responsible for it to an extent (Table 6.8).

Conclusions

Ghana implemented the Fund supported programmes for fifteen different years spanning from 1979- 2001. Only one variable – investment as percentage of GDP- showed a

Table 6.8: Ghana: Policy Variables, (1975-2002)

Year	Exchange rate (Cs per U.S. $)	Interest rate (%)	Money supply (% change)	Domestic credit (% change)	Budget deficit (as % of GDP)
1975	1.2	---	40.0	23.1	-8.0
1976	1.2	---	35.7	50.0	-11.9
1977	1.2	---	57.9	58.3	-12.5
1978	2.8	11.5	70.0	71.1	-11.8
1979	2.8	11.5	13.7	13.8	-7.3
1980	2.8	11.5	34.5	28.4	-5.0
1981	2.8	11.5	53.8	63.2	-8.1
1982	2.8	11.5	23.3	17.4	-6.0
1983	30.0	11.5	39.9	78.0	-2.7
1984	50.0	15.0	54.1	50.3	-1.8
1985	60.0	15.8	46.4	59.8	-2.2
1986	90.0	17.0	47.7	53.0	0.0
1987	176.1	17.6	53.6	72.3	0.5
1988	229.9	16.5	46.2	-4.4	0.4
1989	303.0	---	54.2	24.0	0.7
1990	344.8	33.0	13.4	4.1	0.2
1991	390.6	20.0	14.0	82.5	1.5
1992	520.8	30.0	53.1	25.2	-4.8
1993	819.6	35.0	85.8	43.4	-2.4
1994	1052.0	33.0	9.7	15.8	-2.1
1995	1449.3	45.0	43.7	52.9	0.9
1996	1754.4	45.0	38.9	42.2	-2.9
1997	2272.7	45.0	43.8	72.9	-2.1
1998	2325.6	37.0	17.4	18.0	-6.0

Contd...

1999	3535.1	27.0	14.7	57.5	-8.2
2000	7047.6	27.0	69.2	59.4	-9.7
2001	7321.9	27.0	31.6	18.9	-9.0
2002	8438.8	24.5	48.8	22.8	-6.0

Sources: Compiled and computed form *IMF-International Financial Statistics*, various issues, *UN-National Accounts Statistics, Main Aggregates and detailed Tables*, various issues, and Economic Commission for Africa- *Economic Report on Africa, 2003*.

statistically significant improvement during the programme years. Very disappointing results were shown by both the consumption and domestic savings. Consumption accounted generally for more than 90 percent of output, leaving a little portion for domestic savings. Increase in investment was largely due to inflow of foreign resources, especially after 1990, resulting in worsening external account position.

The external sector had very poor performance during the programme years. The situation became worse from bad in the case of all the three accounts i.e. trade account, current account and overall balance of payments. Overall balance of payments showed a surplus for few years i.e. 1987- 1995, but there was no improvement in current account during this period. This indicates that the temporary improvement in overall balance of payments was due to increased capital inflows induced by the IMF's 'seal of approval' and not due to current account or trade account.

Another disappointment was due to no improvement seen in inflation rate. The inflation rate remained high – though there was no further substantial increase- during programme years. An achievement was in context of volatility in real output growth. Real GDP growth rate became less volatile during programme years, but there was a little decline in real GDP growth rate on average basis. The Fund supported programmes led to enhance the dependency of the Ghanaian economy. The results were statistically significant at 5 percent level of significance.

Finally, the Fund supported programmes failed in improving the macroeconomic economic situation in Ghana. Even there was deterioration in the economic position of the Ghanaian economy under last two programmes- 1995-1997 and 1999-2001 programmes.

Appendix 6A: Ghana: Statistics on Macroeconomic Variables (1975-2002)

Year	CN/ GDP	INV/ GDP	DS/ GDP	X/M	CA/ GDP	OB/ GDP	INFR (%)	RGDP Gr	FOREX Gr (%)	X/GDP	M/GDP
1975	86.8	13.2	13.2	100.9	0.4	2.3	29.8	-12.9	148.2	17.6	17.4
1976	92.3	9.2	7.7	98.6	-1.3	-2.4	56.1	-3.5	-27.6	14.7	14.9
1977	89.3	9.8	10.7	88.7	-0.8	-0.1	116.5	2.3	62.3	10.4	11.7
1978	94.3	6.6	5.7	110.5	-0.4	-0.4	73.1	8.5	94.3	9.1	8.2
1979	93.6	6.4	6.4	116.8	1.2	0.4	54.4	-3.2	2.4	9.7	8.3
1980	95.1	5.6	4.9	111.3	0.2	-0.2	50.1	0.0	-33.5	8.1	7.2
1981	96.1	4.6	3.9	96.3	-1.6	-1.1	116.5	-1.8	-19.7	4.0	4.2
1982	96.2	3.4	3.8	123.8	-0.3	0.0	22.3	-7.2	-4.3	2.8	2.2
1983	96.7	3.8	3.3	88.0	-0.8	-0.8	122.9	0.7	2.8	2.1	2.4
1984	93.3	7.0	6.7	91.0	-0.5	0.5	39.7	2.6	111.4	7.0	7.7
1985	92.4	9.6	7.6	84.4	-2.1	0.2	10.3	5.1	52.4	9.8	11.6
1986	92.3	9.3	7.7	110.2	-0.8	-1.1	24.6	5.2	11.2	15.1	13.7
1987	92.8	10.4	8.2	98.9	-2.0	2.9	39.8	4.8	-64.9	20.1	20.4
1988	89.3	10.9	10.7	111.5	-1.3	3.5	31.4	5.6	23.3	19.4	17.4
1989	94.0	13.5	6.0	80.0	-1.9	3.0	25.2	5.1	43.6	19.4	24.3
1990	96.4	12.3	3.6	73.8	-3.7	1.7	37.3	3.3	-32.5	18.0	24.4
1991	78.8	13.1	21.2	75.6	-3.8	2.0	18.0	5.3	150.9	15.0	19.8
1992	97.7	13.7	2.3	67.7	-5.9	-1.6	10.1	3.9	-45.7	15.4	22.7
1993	93.3	23.7	6.7	61.5	-9.4	0.6	25.0	5.3	32.1	17.9	29.2
1994	88.4	22.5	11.6	78.3	-4.7	4.5	24.9	3.3	43.8	22.8	29.1
1995	88.2	21.1	11.8	84.8	-2.2	2.7	59.5	4.0	20.7	21.9	25.8
1996	88.1	20.5	11.9	80.5	-4.7	-0.4	46.6	4.6	19.7	24.0	29.8
1997	92.1	23.6	7.9	69.4	-8.0	1.5	27.9	4.2	-36.3	29.5	42.4
1998	88.0	22.0	12.0	69.8	-5.0	0.3	14.6	4.7	-42.1	20.0	28.7

Contd...

1999	89.0	23.0	11.0	60.8	-11.6	-1.5	12.4	4.4	29.8	23.3	38.0
2000	99.0	24.0	1.0	69.9	-8.4	-4.0	25.2	3.7	-39.0	24.0	38.0
2001	94.0	24.0	6.0	62.8	-5.3	-2.0	32.9	4.2	27.2	30.4	48.4
2002	---	---	---	74.4	0.5	1.9	14.8	4.5	82.3	31.6	42.5

Sources: Compiled and computed form *IMF-International Financial Statistics*, various issues, *UN-National Accounts Statistics, Main Aggregates and detailed Tables*, various issues, and *UN-National Accounts: Analysis of Main Aggregates*, 2001, *UN- Statistical Yearbook*, 48th Edition, and *IMF- World Economic Outlook*, Sept. 2004.

7

Chile: Strong Macroeconomic Fundamentals

The republic of Chile is located on the Pacific Coast of South America. It is a long, narrow country, stretching about 2700 miles and averaging only about 110 miles in width. Despite its size, it is one of the lowest population densities in Latin America. This is due to fact that over 70 percent of its continental territory is characterized by desert, mountain, or some other geographical feature that makes human habitation impossible.

Industries constitute about 80 percent of the total gross domestic product, of which agriculture only for about 10 percent. Industrial supplies and machinery account for about 60 percent of imports, and food imports accounts only for about 5 percent of imports, while fuels for about 15 percent. Agricultural products account for about 15 percent of exports, while manufacturing sector accounts for about 75 percent of exports.

During 1971 and 1972 the Chilean economy faced hyper inflation and deep recession. The Chilean authority coming to power in 1973 sought to correct a serious balance of payments deficit, bring inflation under control, and create the basis for rapid rate of growth. Their medium term strategy placed major emphasis on expanding the role of market forces in the economy. Accordingly, fiscal and monetary policies were accompanied. Other measures included dismantling of price control, the lowering of trade barriers, and pursuit of exchange and interest rate policies. By mid 1973, extremely serious internal and external imbalances had emerged. In1974, an economic programme supported by the Fund, was implemented.

The summary of the Fund supported programmes, implemented by the Chilean authorities is given in Table 7.1.

Table 7.1: Chile: Lending Arrangements with IMF, 1975-2002

(Amount expressed in millions of SDRs)

Facility	Date of arrangement	Date of expiration	Amount approved	Balance not drawn	Programme years	remarks
SBA	10.03.1975	18.03.1976	79.0	59.0	1975	Programme implemented
SBA	10.01.1983	09.01.1985	500.0	0	1983,1984	
EA	15.08.1985	14.08.1988	750.0	0	1985,1986,1987,1988	
SBA	08.11.1989	07.11.1990	64.0	0	1989,1990	

Source: IMF Survey, various issues.

1975 Adjustment Programme

In 1975, the Fund approved another stand-by arrangement for Chile authorizing purchases equivalent to SDR 79 million in support of an economic and financial programme for 1975. The programme included the measures to reduce the rate of inflation and contain the balance of payments deficits. To achieve the goal of reducing inflation and keeping the balance of payments deficit at a manageable level, the authorities planned to pursue an adequate exchange rate policy and tighten fiscal and credit policies. The authorities planned to continue their efforts to achieve a better allocation of resources and improve the public enterprises' financial position by the implementation of a price policy involving a free system of price determination for most goods and services and the avoidance of subsidies on items subject to control. To contain demand pressure, the government was implementing a major tax reform, including a number of new economic measures, and proposed to observe a greater austerity in spending. The authorities planned to maintain the degree of exchange and trade liberalization achieved so far despite the some what unfavourable prospects for Chile's terms of trade in 1975.

The macroeconomic performance of the economy under the 1975 adjustment programme has been summarized below:

- Chilean economy had poor performance in 1975.
- The 'control group' out performed the Chile in 1975.

During 1975-79, the Chilean economy had a favourable performance largely attributed by the realistic policies in the external sector and by a favourable international environment. By 1976, the non financial sector showed an overall surplus, which was expanded to the equivalent to 4.7 percent of GDP in 1979.

Under otherwise favourable economic conditions and with the intention of reducing inflation from persistent level of about 30 percent to world level, the authorities abandoned their previous exchange rate policy of frequent and small adjustments and fixed the exchange rate at Ch $39 = US $1. During 1980-81, the combined effect of exchange rate fixed against the US dollar, indexed wages, and the appreciation of the US dollar led to a significant real effective appreciation of the Peso. As a result, imports boomed and economic growth was concentrated in non traded goods. The current account deficit increased from $1.2 billion in 1979 to $ 4.7 billion in 1981. By the end of 1981, the Chilean economy was characterized by high level of external debt and of private domestic debt in dollars; with attendant debt service burdens. In these circumstances, the financial system began to accumulate a high proportion of nonperforming debt.

While Chile's private sector and financial system began to encounter solvency problems in 1981, the price of copper dropped to an average of $ 0.79 per pound from an average of $ 1.00 in 1980. The continued decline in the price of copper and the increasing reluctant of foreign commercial banks to lend the countries in Latin America brought about major strains on Chile's balance of payments. In addition, rising government expenditure for welfare and unemployment benefits resulted in a shift from a small surplus in the overall finances of the non financial public sector in 1981 to a deficit equivalent to 3.4 percent of GDP in 1982. Faced with these difficulties, in mid 1982 the authorities devalued Peso and started to pursue strict demand management policies. The external current account deficit was cut sharply – mainly as result of a decline in imports- though the value of exports stagnated because of a decline in the prices of Chile's main export commodities. The external adjustment was accompanied by a steep decline in economic activity and high unemployment. Real GDP fell by more than 14 percent in 1982 and national unemployment reached as high as 24 percent.

Building on the policies initiated in mid 1982, the authorities developed an economic programme for 1983-84 aimed at continuing external adjustment, reducing inflation and restoring the conditions for economic growth.

1983-1984 Adjustment Programme

In January 1983, the Fund approved a stand-by arrangement for Chile authorizing purchases equivalent to SDR 500 million in support of an economic programme for 1983-84. The aim of the programme was to establish the basis for economic recovery within a framework of a satisfactory balance of payments and gradual reduction in rate of inflation. The programme was built upon the basic economic strategy of the government, i.e. to promote adjustment and economic growth by relying upon market forces and price incentives to guide resource allocation within the economy.

The restoration of competitiveness through a major depreciation of peso during 1982 and the adoption of a flexible exchange rate regime were consistent with the basic strategy. Real GDP was projected to increase by 4 percent in 1983 and somewhat more in 1984. The rate of price increase, which was about 40 percent in the second half of 1982, was projected to slowdown to 25 percent in 1983. For 1984, a further reduction was projected.

The following conclusions have been drawn regarding the 1983-84 economic adjustment programme:

- Chilean economy had better macroeconomic performance during 1983-84.
- Chilean economy had somewhat better macroeconomic performance than that of 'control group'.
- Though the real GDP growth and inflation rate targets could not be met, the performance was very close to the established targets.

But, the IMF claimed in a publication that the objectives of the economic programme for 1983-84 were broadly achieved. It stated that 'shortly after the programme was approved, a financial crisis erupted in Chile, and authorities intervened and liquidated a number of financial institutions. Foreign banks reacted by halting lending to Chile, and net international reserves declined sharply. In the face of theses difficulties, the authorities took additional strong corrective actions and were able to stabilize the financial system and return to the path of economic progress during the second half of 1983' (Tables 7.2, 7.3, 7.4, 7.5).

Table 7.2: Chile: Programme Effects: Before-after approach

The difference between means method

Variable		Programme years									Effect	t-value
		1975	1983	1984	1985	1986	1987	1988	1989	1990		
CN/GDP	Pre	78.3	90.6	87.4	87.4	83.5	81.6	79.0	75.8	76.0	+	0.251
	Pro	88.7	87.4	87.4	83.5	81.6	79.0	75.8	76.0	76.9		
INV/GDP	Pre	21.7	11.3	9.8	13.6	13.7	14.6	16.9	17.0	20.3	+	0.128
	Pro	14.1	9.8	13.6	13.7	14.6	16.9	17.0	20.3	20.2		
DS/GDP	Pre	21.7	9.4	12.6	12.6	16.5	18.4	21.0	24.2	24.0	+	0.251
	Pro	11.3	12.6	12.6	16.5	18.4	21.0	24.2	24.0	23.1		
X/M	Pre	130	105	139	115	139	135	131	146	124	-	0.013
	Pro	116	139	115	139	135	131	146	124	118		
CA/GDP	Pre	-2.6	-9.5	-5.7	-11.0	-8.8	-7.1	-4.3	-0.8	-3.0	+	0.226
	Pro	-6.8	-5.7	-11.0	-8.8	-7.1	-4.3	-0.8	-3.0	-3.0		
OB/GDP	Pre	-5.9	-5.6	-21.7	-10.8	-16.3	-16.7	-10.1	-3.8	1.7	+	0.458
	Pro	-8.4	-21.7	-10.8	-16.3	-16.7	-10.1	-3.8	1.7	8.4		
INFR	Pre	504	9.9	27.3	19.9	30.7	19.5	19.9	14.7	17.0	+	0.854
	Pro	375	27.3	19.9	30.7	19.5	19.9	14.7	17.0	26.0		
RGDP Gr	Pre	1.0	-14.1	-0.7	6.4	2.5	5.6	5.7	7.4	10.0	+	0.095
	Pro	-12.9	-0.7	6.4	2.5	5.6	5.7	7.4	10.0	2.1		
FOREX Gr	Pre	---	-44.9	18.2	12.8	6.8	-4.0	4.7	26.5	15.7	+	1.666
	Pro	29.8	18.2	12.8	6.8	-4.0	4.7	26.5	15.7	68.3		
Memorandum Items												
X/GDP	Pre	22.4	15.2	19.4	19.1	23.9	24.9	27.6	31.9	31.8	Pre<	1.825*
	Pro	21.5	19.4	19.1	23.9	24.9	27.6	31.9	31.8	29.9	Pro	
M/GDP	Pre	17.3	14.5	13.9	16.6	17.1	18.4	21.1	21.9	25.6	Pre<	2.760*
	Pro	18.5	13.9	16.6	17.1	18.4	21.1	21.9	25.6	25.3	Pro	

Notes: (1) + sign indicates better performance, - sign indicates poor performance and 0 indicates same performance. (2) The * sign means significant at 5% level of significance.

Table 7.3: Chile: Programme Effects: Before-after approach

Total number program years method

Variable	Programme years									Performance (no. of years)		
	1975	1983	1984	1985	1986	1987	1988	1989	1990	Better	Poor	Same
CN/GDP	-	+	0	+	+	+	+	-	-	5	3	1
INV/GDP	-	-	+	+	+	+	+	+	-	6	3	0
DS/GDP	-	+	0	+	+	+	+	-	-	5	3	1
X/M	-	+	-	+	-	-	+	-	-	3	6	0
CA/GDP	-	+	-	+	+	+	+	-	0	5	3	1
OB/GDP	-	-	+	-	-	+	+	+	+	5	4	0
RGDP Gr	-	+	+	-	+	+	+	+	-	6	3	0
INFR	+	-	+	-	+	-	+	-	-	4	5	0
FOREX Gr	+	+	-	-	-	+	+	-	+	5	4	0
No of variables with better performance	2	6	4	5	6	7	9	3	2	44(54.3)		
No of variables with poor performance	7	3	3	4	3	2	0	6	6	34(42.0)		
No of variables with same performance	0	0	2	0	0	0	0	0	1	3(3.7)		

Notes (1) + sign indicates better performance, (-) sign indicates poor performance and (0) indicates same performance. (2)Figures in parenthesis are percentages.

Table 7.4: Chile: Programme Effects: With-without approach

The difference between means method

Variable		Programme years									Effect	t-value
		1975	1983	1984	1985	1986	1987	1988	1989	1990		
ΔCN/GDP	CH	10.4	-3.2	0.0	-3.9	-1.9	-2.6	-3.2	0.2	0.9	+	0.602
	NPC	3.3	-0.3	-0.4	0.3	0.5	-0.3	0.0	-0.6	0.4		
ΔINV/GDP	CH	-7.6	-1.5	3.8	0.1	0.9	2.3	0.1	3.3	-0.1	+	0.286
	NPC	1.0	-2.3	-1.3	-1.2	-0.2	1.0	0.2	0.6	0.3		
ΔDS/GDP	CH	-10.4	3.2	0.0	3.9	1.9	2.6	3.2	-0.2	-0.9	+	0.602
	NPC	-3.3	0.3	0.4	-0.3	-0.5	0.3	0.0	0.6	-0.4		
ΔX/M	CH	-13.8	34.2	-24.7	24.8	-4.0	-4.6	15.1	-21.6	-6.2	+	0.122
	NPC	-13.1	4.3	4.9	-0.6	-6.2	-2.1	0.2	8.8	-4.7		
ΔCA/GDP	CH	-4.2	3.8	-5.3	2.2	1.7	2.8	3.5	-2.2	0.0	+	0.434
	NPC	-3.0	0.4	1.9	-0.8	0.0	-0.8	0.8	0.0	-0.0		
ΔOB/GDP	CH	-2.5	-16.1	10.9	-5.5	-0.4	6.6	6.3	5.5	6.7	+	0.573
	NPC	-1.4	-1.2	1.3	-0.5	0.3	0.0	-0.5	0.5	-0.4		
ΔINFR	CH	-130	17.4	-7.4	10.8	-11.2	0.4	-5.2	2.3	9.0	+	1.071
	NPC	-0.1	3.8	11.1	5.6	-7.6	4.8	2.4	4.5	2.4		
ΔRGDP Gr	CH	-13.9	13.4	7.1	-3.9	3.1	0.1	1.7	2.6	-7.9	+	0.165
	NPC	-2.9	-0.3	1.0	1.3	0.2	1.0	-2.5	-0.8	1.4		
Memorandum Items												
ΔX/GDP	CH	-0.9	4.2	-0.3	4.8	1.0	2.7	4.3	-0.1	-1.9	CH>NPC	2.213*
	NPC	-4.2	-1.8	0.6	-1.0	-1.0	0.6	1.6	1.1	-0.6		
ΔM/GDP	CH	1.2	-0.6	2.7	0.5	1.3	2.7	0.8	3.7	-0.3	CH>NPC	2.494*
	NPC	-1.2	-3.2	-1.4	-1.0	-1.3	1.6	1.5	0.9	1.9		

Notes: (1) CH: Chile and NPC: Non Programme Countries. (2) + sign indicates better performance, - sign indicates poor performance and 0 indicates same performance. (3) The * sign means significant at 5% level of significance.

Table 7.5: Chile: Programme Effects: With-without approach

Total number program years method

Variable	Programme years									Performance	(no. of years)	
	1975	1983	1984	1985	1986	1987	1988	1989	1990	Better	Poor	Same
ΔCN/GDP	-	+	-	+	+	+	+	-	-	5	4	0
ΔINV/GDP	-	+	+	+	+	+	-	+	-	6	3	0
ΔDS/GDP	-	+	-	+	+	+	+	-	-	5	4	0
ΔX/M	-	+	-	+	+	-	+	-	-	4	5	0
ΔCA/GDP	-	+	-	+	+	+	+	-	+	6	3	0
ΔOB/GDP	-	-	+	-	-	+	+	+	+	5	4	0
ΔRGDP Gr	-	+	+	-	+	-	+	+	-	5	4	0
ΔINFR	+	-	+	-	+	+	+	+	-	6	3	0
No of variables with better performance	1	6	4	5	7	6	7	4	2	42 (58.3)		
No of variables with poor performance	7	2	4	3	1	2	1	4	6		30 (41.7)	
No of variables with same performance	0	0	0	0	0	0	0	0	0			0 (0.0)

Notes (1) + sign indicates better performance, (-) sign indicates poor performance and (0) indicates same performance. (2) Figures in parenthesis are percentages.

1985-1988 Adjustment Programme

On August15, 1985 the Fund approved a three year extended arrangement; which was later extended by one year in 1988, for the government of Chile authorizing purchases equivalent to DSR750 million in support of its economic programme for 1985-1988.The principle element of the programme were:

- External policies designed to support diversification and expansion of exports as well as import substitution, mainly through appropriate exchange and tariff policies.
- A reduction in overall budget deficit, accompanied by a significant increase in public sector savings.
- Monetary and fiscal policies designed to limit the growth of domestic demand, reduce inflation, and help ensure the achievement of external objectives.
- A policy of wage restraint to foster employment and help protect external competitiveness.
- Control of new foreign borrowing to reduce over the time the ratio of external debt to gross domestic product.

Under the programme, the external current account deficit was projected to decline from about 10.5 percent of GDP in 1984 to 4.5 percent in 1987. The overall public sector deficit, which stood at 4.8 percent of GDP in 1984, was to be virtually eliminated by 1987. Demand management involved the pursuit of a prudent monetary policy, consistent with the objectives- i.e. balance of payments and gradual reduction of inflation rate to about 15 percent by 1987. The following conclusions have been inferred regarding the 1985-88 economic programme:

- Chilean economy showed good macroeconomic performance during 1985-88.
- Chilean economy had better macroeconomic performance as compared to the 'control group'.
- Almost all targets were achieved.

1989-1990 Adjustment Programme

In November 1989, the Fund approved a one year stand-by arrangement in first credit trenche for the government of Chile authorizing purchases up to equivalent of SDR 64 million in support of its economic and financial programme for 1989-90. The authorities' economic and financial programme maintained medium term framework, policies and objectives developed under the extended fund facility (EFF) 1985. The goals were: to expand exports, continue to strengthen domestic savings and investment, and improve balance of payments position with a view to maintaining output growth of 4-5 percent a year.

The performance of the 1989-90 programme has been summarized below:

- Chilean economy had poor macroeconomic performance during 1989-90.
- The 'control group' showed better performance than the Chilean economy during 1989-90.

Macroeconomic Performance Under Different Approaches

The macroeconomic performance of the Chilean economy–as per different approaches- has been summarized below:

Before-After Approach: The following conclusions have been drawn in context of Macroeconomic performance of the Chilean economy during programme years:

- When the total number of programme years method was employed, seven variables- consumption as percentage of GDP, domestic savings as percentage of GDP, investment as percentage of GDP, current account as percentage of GDP, overall balance of payments as percentage of GDP, real output growth rate and foreign exchange reserves growth rate- showed better performance of the Chilean economy during programme years. Only two variables viz., trade balance account and inflation rate revealed poor performance of the economy. (Table 7.3)
- According to the difference between means method, the Chilean economy showed some improvement in the case of eight variables viz., consumption as percentage of GDP, investment as percentage of GDP, domestic savings as percentage of GDP, current account balance as percentage of

GDP, overall balance of payments as percentage of GDP, real GDP growth rate, inflation rate and foreign exchange reserves growth rate, albeit the results were not statistically significant. Only one variable- trade account- had poor performance during programme years, though it still revealed trade surplus. (Table 7.2)

- During the implementation of the Fund supported programmes, the dependency of the Chilean economy was increased. The results were statistically significant at 5 percent level of significance.

With-Without Approach: The macroeconomic performance of the Chilean economy during programme years has been presented below:

- According to the total number of programme years method, the Chilean economy performed better than the 'control group' during the programme years in the case of seven variables viz., consumption as percentage of GDP, investment as percentage of GDP, domestic savings as percentage of GDP, current account balance as percentage of GDP, overall balance of payments as percentage of GDP, inflation rate and real output growth rate. While, only one variable- exports as percentage of imports revealed poor performance. In fact, trade account (exports as percentage imports) still showed surplus, but in small quantum.
- When the difference between means method was employed, all the variables- consumption as percentage of GDP, investment as percentage of GDP, domestic savings as percentage of GDP, trade account balance, current account balance as percentage of GDP, overall balance as percentage of GDP, real output growth rate and inflation rate showed better performance of the Chilean economy as compared to that of the 'control group'.
- During the implementation of the Fund supported programmes, the openness of the Chilean economy increased more than that of the 'control group'. These results were statistically significant at 5 percent level of significance.

Generalized Evaluation Approach: The generalized evaluation approach showed unfavourable effects of the Fund supported programmes on five variables viz., investment, domestic savings, current account balance as percentage of GDP, overall balance of payments as percentage GDP and inflation rate-though the effects were not statistically significant. Three variables showed favourable effects of the Fund-supported programmes (Tables 7.6 and 7.7). As mentioned earlier too, there is utmost need of care in explaining the results of the generalized evaluation approach. A due analysis of economic trends revealed that there was an improvement in the economic position during the programme years, but the period after the implementation – 1991 onward- showed more improvement in all the variables except real GDP growth rate and exports as percentage of imports (refer to Appendix 7A and Table 7.2). When regression analysis was fitted for the entire period (1975- 2002), the improvement during the programme years was overshadowed by the improvement in the non programme years (i.e. 1991 onward) and ultimately programme dummy variable showed unfavourable effects on macroeconomic variables except real GDP growth and trade account balance. The results became more favourable when regression was fitted for period 1975-1990.

Overall Macroeconomic Performance

The following important conclusions have been drawn regarding the macroeconomic performance of the Chilean economy during the implementation of the Fund supported programmes:

- Consumption as percentage of GDP showed positive effects of the Fund-supported programmes on the Chilean economy, though the results were not statistically significant.
- Domestic savings as percentage of GDP rose steadily during programme years, albeit the results were not statistically significant.
- Investment as percentage of GDP also revealed improvement during the implementation of the Fund supported

Table 7.6: Chile: Programme Effects: Generalized Evaluation (1975-2002)

Z	C	GDP	INV	Z_{-1}	FB/GDP	DCR	T	D	R^2	F
GDP	49.959 (0.085)		4.329 (42.04)*					876.466 (1.144)	0.99	1128.5
INV	48.366 (0.363)	0.228 (42.05)*						-250.146 (1.444)	0.99	1162.3
DS	-18.648 (0.349)	0.242 (111.2)*						-96.951 (1.393)	0.99	7196.2
X/M	82.155 (0.789)			0.155 (0.196)	-1.963 (1.198)	-0.004 (0.089)	0.308 (0.650)	22.648 (2.393)*	0.58	5.7
CA/GDP	-5.808 (1.935)*			0.338 (1.575)	0.047 (0.123)	0.005 (0.452)	0.179 (1.486)	-0.1284 (0.080)	0.53	3.8
OB/GDP	-2.829 (0.834)			0.229 (1.053)	1.647 (2.623)*	0.005 (0.313)	0.108 (0.655)	-3.977 (1.238)	0.64	7.5
RGDP Gr	7.364 (2.445)*			-0.028 (0.131)	1.174 (1.848)*	-0.045 (2.953)*	-0.098 (0.601)	0.657 (0.266)	0.45	3.4
INFR	-25.751 (5.028)*			0.411 (9.908)*	3.091 (3.583)*	0.409 (6.869)*	0.883 (3.526)*	20.331 (5.253)*	0.99	533.9

Note: (1) Figures in parenthesis are t-values. (2) *sign indicates significant at 5% level of significance.

Table 7.7: Chile: Programme Effects (summary)

Variable	Before-After Approach		With-Without Approach		Generalized Evaluation
	Difference between means method	Total number of programme years	Difference between means method	Total number of programme years	
CN/ GDP	+	+	+	+	N A
INV/GDP	+	+	+	+	N A
DS/GDP	+	+	+	+	N A
X/M	-	-	+	-	+*
CA/GDP	+	+	+	+	-
OB/GDP	+	+	+	+	-
RGDP Gr	+	+	+	+	+
INFR	+	-	+	+	-*
FOREX Gr	+	+	N A	N A	N A
GDP	N A	N A	N A	N A	+
INV	N A	N A	N A	N A	-
DS	N A	N A	N A	N A	-
Total	8	7	8	7	3
Better	1	2	0	1	5
Poor	0	0	0	0	0
Same					

Note: (1) + sign indicates better performance,-sign indicates poor performance and 0 sign indicates same performance. (2) * sign indicates significance at 5% level of significance.

programmes. Investment continuously rose in proposition of GDP during programme years, though the results were not statistically significant.

- The external sector also revealed better performance during the programme years. The trade account surplus-exports as percentage of imports- declined during the programme years, but still showed surplus in the account.
- The current account deficit as percentage of GDP declined to a large extent during the programme years. The current account deficit, which was equal to 9.5 percent of GDP in 1982, was brought down to 3 percent in 1990.
- The overall balance of payments revealed steadily improvement. The overall balance of payments account, which showed a deficit equal to 21.7 percent of GDP in 1983, showed a surplus of 8.4 percent in 1990.
- The volatility in real output growth rate was reduced to a good extent. All the approaches employed demonstrated enhancement in the real GDP growth rate.
- Though the inflation rate was brought down during the implementation of programmes, it was still ranging between 15% - 20%.
- Foreign exchange reserves growth revealed better performance during programme years.
- On an average the established targets were met.
- The Fund supported programmes enhanced the dependency of the Chilean economy. The increase in dependency of the Chilean economy was more than that of the 'control group'. The results were statistically significant at 5 percent level of significance.
- The intermediate variables revealed good performance during the programme years. The overall budget deficit was wiped out and it showed a surplus in 1987 onward, excepting 1988.
- Domestic credit expansion was slowed down and was brought under control from 1986 onward.
- The money supply growth rate brought down to an extent, but there was the scope left for further reduction.

- The interest rates were quite high in the beginning, but during the programme implementation these were bought down to an extent.
- The domestic currency depreciated continuously over the programme years.
- The Chilean economy revealed better performance for six different programme years out of total nine years. When comparison was made with the control group, the Chilean economy revealed poor performance for two programme years out of total nine programme years.
- In sum, the Chilean economy revealed satisfactory performance under the Fund-supported programmes. Reasons for contradictory results shown by generalized evaluation approach have already been explained (Table 7.8).

Conclusions

The Chilean authorities implemented the IMF supported programmes for nine different years. A clear improvement was seen in the different sectors of the economy. Consumption as proposition of GDP declined to a considerable extent over the programme years, thus making domestic resources available for investment through increased domestic savings. Investment as percentage of GDP revealed a continuous increase over the programme years.

The external sector also revealed some improvement in the economy during the programme years. The important point is that improvement in overall balance of payments was not only due to increased inflow of foreign capital, but also to a large extent to improvement in current account.

The inflation rate was brought down during the programme years, but it could not be brought as per the expectations. The real output growth rate increase after the implementation of the Fund supported programmes and volatility in the growth rate was also reduced over the programme years. There was enhancement in the dependency of the Chilean economy during the programme years.

Table 7.8: Chile: Policy Variables, (1975-2002)

Year	Exchange rate (Ps per U.S. $)	Interest rate (%)	Money supply (% change)	Domestic credit (% change)	Budget deficit (as % of GDP)
1975	8.50	---	300.0	415.0	0.0
1976	17.4	---	413.5	172.3	1.4
1977	27.9	93.8	100.0	123.4	-1.1
1978	33.9	62.8	93.6	59.6	-0.1
1979	39.0	45.1	66.5	58.5	4.8
1980	39.0	37.5	61.8	51.4	5.4
1981	39.0	40.8	28.8	35.4	2.6
1982	73.4	47.9	34.9	67.6	-1.0
1983	87.5	28.0	21.5	25.0	-2.6
1984	128.2	27.6	22.4	51.1	-3.0
1985	183.8	32.0	47.2	48.9	-2.4
1986	204.7	19.0	25.3	21.2	-1.0
1987	238.1	25.2	35.0	20.0	0.5
1988	247.2	15.1	27.1	12.3	-0.2
1989	297.3	27.7	31.2	11.4	1.8
1990	337.0	40.3	23.6	20.3	0.8
1991	374.9	28.6	28.0	14.0	1.5
1992	382.3	23.9	23.3	19.8	2.2
1993	431.0	24.3	23.3	24.2	1.9
1994	404.1	20.3	11.3	8.8	1.6
1995	407.1	18.2	25.8	22.3	2.3
1996	425.0	17.4	19.5	16.4	2.3
1997	439.8	15.7	16.3	14.2	2.0
1998	473.8	20.2	9.5	11.7	0.3

Contd...

1999	530.1	12.6	14.7	8.8	-1.5
2000	572.7	14.8	6.2	13.9	0.1
2001	656.2	11.9	-5.4	15.0	---
2002	712.4	7.8	-0.3	6.4	---

Sources: Compiled and computed form *IMF-International Financial Statistics*, various issues, and *UN-National Accounts Statistics, Main Aggregates and detailed Tables*, various issues.

The results were statistically significant at 5 percent level of confidence.

Finally, the Chilean economy `showed a satisfactory macroeconomic performance under the Fund-supported programmes.

Appendix 7A: Chile: Statistics on Macroeconomic Variables (1975-2002)

Year	CN/ GDP	INV/ GDP	DS/ GDP	X/M	CA/ GDP	OB/ GDP	INFR (%)	RGDP Gr	FOREX Gr (%)	X/ GDP	M/ GDP
1975	88.7	14.1	11.3	116.0	-6.8	-8.4	374.7	-12.9	29.8	21.5	18.5
1976	82.9	12.4	17.1	126.8	1.5	4.2	211.8	3.5	1011.5	21.1	16.7
1977	87.4	14.6	12.6	96.9	-4.1	0.9	91.9	9.9	3.2	16.4	16.9
1978	85.5	17.8	14.5	82.5	-7.1	4.7	40.1	8.2	181.4	16.1	19.5
1979	85.0	17.7	15.0	92.3	-5.7	3.4	33.4	8.3	83.6	13.7	14.9
1980	83.2	21.0	16.8	91.1	-7.1	4.5	35.1	7.8	63.3	16.9	18.6
1981	87.6	22.7	12.4	61.4	-14.5	0.2	19.7	5.5	2.7	12.0	19.5
1982	90.6	11.3	9.4	105.1	-9.5	-5.6	9.9	-14.1	-44.9	15.2	14.5
1983	87.4	9.8	12.6	139.3	-5.7	-21.7	27.3	-0.7	18.2	19.4	13.9
1984	87.4	13.6	12.6	114.6	-11.0	-10.8	19.9	6.4	12.8	19.1	16.6
1985	83.5	13.7	16.5	139.4	-8.8	-16.3	30.7	2.5	6.8	23.9	17.1
1986	81.6	14.6	18.4	135.4	-7.1	-16.7	19.5	5.6	-4.0	24.9	18.4
1987	79.0	16.9	21.0	130.8	-4.3	-10.1	19.9	5.7	4.7	27.6	21.1
1988	75.8	17.0	24.2	145.9	-0.8	-3.8	14.7	7.4	26.5	31.9	21.9
1989	76.0	20.3	24.0	124.3	-3.0	1.7	17.0	10.0	15.7	31.8	25.6
1990	76.9	20.2	23.1	118.1	-3.0	8.4	26.0	2.1	68.3	29.9	25.3
1991	72.9	20.0	23.1	119.1	-0.3	3.8	21.8	8.1	16.0	27.1	22.6
1992	74.8	22.4	25.2	107.8	-2.2	5.8	15.4	12.2	30.2	23.0	21.3
1993	75.9	24.9	24.1	90.3	-5.4	0.9	12.7	7.0	5.1	19.4	21.5
1994	74.6	33.3	25.4	106.7	-2.8	5.5	11.4	5.7	35.7	20.5	19.2
1995	76.2	23.9	23.8	109.4	-1.9	1.6	8.2	10.6	8.0	22.6	20.6
1996	75.5	24.9	24.5	93.4	-4.1	2.9	7.4	7.4	4.5	18.0	19.3
1997	74.0	25.4	26.0	91.4	-4.4	3.7	6.1	6.6	14.9	19.7	21.5
1998	76.7	26.0	23.3	85.5	-4.9	-2.5	5.1	3.2	-11.5	17.6	20.5

Contd...

1999	76.1	21.9	23.9	111.9	-0.1	-0.9	3.3	-1.0	-7.2	19.5	17.4
2000	75.5	22.3	24.5	108.6	-1.2	0.3	3.8	4.4	2.8	22.0	20.3
2001	76.5	21.6	23.5	112.0	-1.6	-0.9	3.6	5.3	-2.4	26.6	23.8
2002	75.6	21.2	24.4	114.2	-1.3	-0.3	2.5	2.2	5.4	27.6	24.2

Sources: Compiled and computed form *IMF-International Financial Statistics*, various issues, and *UN-National Accounts Statistics, Main Aggregates and detailed Tables*, various issues.

8

Mexico: Lack of Sustainable Development

Mexico is a middle income country. It has an area of 1,958,000 square kilometres. About 70 percent of its population lives in urban areas. Mexico has a highly diversified economy. Although good farming conditions exist in a relatively small area, irrigation has increased the amount of arable land. Beans, corn, coffee, soya-beans, sorghum, and tomatoes are its most important agricultural commodities. Livestock and fishing are also important industries. Mexico is endowed with rich mineral deposits, particularly of silver, lead copper and iron. Mexico is also a leading producer of oil and natural gas.

Tourism accounts for an increasingly important part of its economy. The industrial sector includes metal, chemicals, and vehicle assembly plants, as well as free trade zones, including assembly plants along the border with the United States.

During 1950s and 1960s, Mexico experienced rapid industrialization, widely characterized as a period of 'stabilizing development', and enjoyed high growth, low inflation and moderate debt accumulation. This was achieved through the maintenance of a tight fiscal stance, accompanied by inward looking policies. The strategy was highly successful in the beginning but not sustainable as it was framed by high protective barriers, focusing on import substitution and rapid expansion of the domestic credit.

In early 1970s, the policy of private sector led growth was replaced by a policy of 'shared development' with the government adopting an active policy of public sector led growth, which further boosted output and employment. A new government responded with economic measures supported by an extended arrangement in the last quarter of 1976.

After 1975, Mexico has adopted a number of programmes supported by the Fund, as detailed in Table 8.1.

1977-1979 Adjustment Programme

The 1977-79 economic adjustment programme was supported by an extended arrangement, which was approved by the Fund in October 1976, authorizing to purchase up to the equivalent of SDR 518 million. The programme was designed to restore an adequate rate of real economic growth and reduction of inflationary pressures. The following measures were to be implemented to supplement the new exchange rate regime (the peso was severed from its fixed peg to US dollar and started floating independently); some export taxes were designed to mitigate the impact on domestic prices of the exchange rate adjustment and to increase government revenues, the suspension; with a few exceptions, of the tax rate regime; and the progressive dismantling of unnecessary import controls and tariff reduction for import products required for domestic production. Moreover, price control for essential consumer goods and raw materials were to be continued and widened to avoid undue domestic price increases. Price adjustments were to be permitted on the basis of cost increases, particularly in case of agriculture products so as not to discourage their production. In addition, the programme included other fiscal and monetary measures to provide an increase in the revenue of public sector, combined with tight control in current public expenditures, thus reducing the need of financing from abroad.

The following conclusions have been drawn regarding the macroeconomic performance of the 1977-79 programme:

- Mexican economy showed somewhat satisfactory performance during 1977-79.
- Mexican economy performed better than the 'control group' during 1977-79.

From 1977 to 1981, Mexico registered a high rate of economic growth- more than 8 percent a year and a rapid expansion of employment, but this was accompanied by an acceleration of

Table 8.1: Mexico: Lending Arrangements with IMF, 1975-2002

(Amount expressed in millions of SDRs)

Facility	Date of arrangement	Date of expiration	Amount approved	Balance not drawn	Programme years	remarks
EA	28.10.1976	27.10.1979	518.0	418.0	1977,1978,1979	Programme implemented
EA	23.12.1982	31.12.1985	3410.6	908.0	1983,1984,1985	Programme implemented
SBA	19.11.1986	01.04.1988	1400.0	0	1986,1987	
EA	26.05.1989	25.05.1992	3729.6	466.2	1989,1990,1991	
SBA	01.02.1995	15.02.1997	12070.2	3312.2	1995,1996	
SBA	07.07.1999	30.11.2000	3103.0	1163.5	1999,2000	

Source: IMF Survey, various issues.

inflation and weakening of the country's external situation. Consumer price inflation reached 28.7 percent by the end of 1981, while the current account deficit widened to US$ 12.9 billion in 1981, from US$ 7.5 billion in 1980. The most important factor behind these worsening trends was the expansionary stance of public sector which registered an overall deficit equivalent to 15 percent of GDP in 1981.

The marked deterioration of the public sector finances, together with a change in outlook in the international markets for petroleum and Mexico's other export commodities, led to growing doubt about the sustainability of the exchange rate policy then being pursued and gave rise to recurring episodes of capital flight. In early 1982, the Mexican authorities ceased supporting the exchange rate of peso, resulting in a substantial depreciation of currency. Large wage increases for the public sector in this period added the difficulties and had an adverse effect on confidence.

The expansionary fiscal policies culminated in the financial crisis of 1982, when inflation rate was nearly 100 percent, international reserves were virtually depleted, and the Mexican authorities imposed strict exchange and trade controls, nationalized the banking system, and announced a partial moratorium on external debt-debt service payments.

1983-1985 Adjustment Programme

On December23, 1982, the Fund approved an extended arrangement for Mexico authorizing purchases up to the equivalent of SDR 3410 million in support of the government's economic programme for 1983-85. The programme envisaged a reduction of the public sector deficit, from equivalent to 16.5 percent of GDP in 1982 to 8.5 percent in 1983, 5.5 percent in 1984 and 3.5 percent in 1985. Such a cutback in the overall deficit of the public sector was expected to lower the pressure on domestic prices, make provisions for reasonable volume of credit to the private sector and help rebuild net international reserves. To reduce public expenditure, the authorities decided to adopt measures of a structural nature as well as to implement general restraint by keeping all expenditure items under close scrutiny. The authorities were assigning high priorities to hold down current and operating expenditure, by increasing productivity, eliminating or reducing subsidies to both the private and public sectors and by cutting back the growth of wage bill through a freeze in hiring and a pursuit of a restraint wage policy in the public sector.

The inflation rate was expected to be reduced from the range of 90-100 percent in 1981 to about 55 percent during 1983 and to progressively lower levels in the succeeding years. The current account deficit was expected to decline to US $4.25 billion in 1983, with a further reduction taking place in 1984 and 1985. Together with the pursuit of tight monetary and flexible exchange rate policies, these developments were designed to permit a more efficient management of the country's resources and to reduce the scope and weight of restrictions that were being applied to external transactions. The strengthening of the fiscal and balance of payments situation under programme was intended to lower Mexico's reliance on external financing over the coming years and thereby contribute to an easing of debt service problems that Mexico had experienced in the past. Domestic credit policy was designed to insure that the private sector receives an appropriate of private domestic financial savings. Interest rates were to be managed flexibly, so they could play their role in allocating credit and in promoting savings.

The following conclusions have been drawn regarding the 1983-85 economic adjustment programme:

- Mexican economy showed better macroeconomic performance in 1983, while poor performance during 1984-85.
- Mexican economy showed better macroeconomic performance as compared to the 'control group' in 1983, but poor performance during 1984-85.
- Only current account target was met.

An IMF publication also supported the above mentioned conclusions. "Mexican economy performed well in 1983, the economic performance began to falter in the later part of 1984 and worsened in 1985; reflecting the weakness of petroleum market, the devastating earth quake which struck in Sept 1985, and slippage in domestic policy implementation. Economic growth slowed down, price pressures increased, and the balance of payments swung into deficit, despite the efforts of authorities to implement a more flexible exchange rate policy, a tight credit policy, cutbacks in public sector outlays and a liberalization of import restrictions" (Tables 8.2, 8.3, 8.4 and 8.5).

1986-1987 Adjustment programme

In November 1986, the Fund approved a stand-by arrangement for the government of Mexico, authorizing purchases up to the equivalent of SDR 1400 million to support the government's economic adjustment programme for 1986-87. The economic programme relied on demand management measures, and on structural adjustment measures to restore growth in the economy in the context of financial stability. The programme had been framed in a medium tern context to encompass both measures to deal with pressing domestic and external imbalances and supply policies to increase efficiency and thus reinforce the country's growth potential. The policies being implemented were expected to restore balance of payments viability over the medium term to help break the inflationary trend, to strengthen savings in the economy and improve efficiency in the use of resources as the basis for sustained growth.

The Mexican authorities believed that, economy already in recession, any attempt to compensate immediately and in the full for loss of export earnings through adjustment alone could not be sustained. The authorities planned to implement fiscal measures to cut financial deficit to equivalent 3 percent points of GDP by the end of 1987. These measures were expected to include increases in revenues and cutbacks in spending in relation to GDP. The authorities planned to conduct monetary and credit policies consistent with the objective of reducing rate of inflation and attaining their balance of payments targets. As a result of the

Table 8.2: Mexico: Programme Effects: Before-after Approach

The difference between means method

Variable		1977	1978	1979	1983	1984	1985	1986	1987	1989	1990	1991	1995	1996	1999	2000	Effect	t-value
CN/GDP	Pre	79.0	77.0	77.0	72.6	69.7	72.2	73.9	77.5	75.9	78.8	79.2	83.1	77.5	77.7	77.9	+	0.615
	Pro	77.0	77.0	75.3	69.7	72.2	73.9	77.5	74.1	78.8	79.2	79.5	77.5	74.7	77.9	78.5		
INV/GDP	Pre	21.6	22.8	23.6	21.2	20.3	19.9	21.2	18.2	21.0	23.8	21.8	19.3	16.1	20.8	21.2	-	0.277
	Pro	22.8	23.6	26.0	20.3	19.9	21.2	18.2	18.5	23.8	21.8	18.6	16.1	17.8	21.2	20.9		
DS/GDP	Pre	21.0	23.0	23.0	27.4	30.3	27.8	26.1	22.5	24.1	21.2	20.8	16.9	22.5	22.3	22.1	+	0.615
	Pro	23.0	23.0	24.7	30.3	27.8	26.1	22.5	25.9	21.2	20.8	20.5	22.5	25.3	22.1	21.5		
X/M	Pre	56.7	75.9	74.1	140	272	207	158	136	106	94.3	101	76.7	109	93.6	96.0	+	0.310
	Pro	75.9	74.1	74.3	272	207	158	136	164	94.3	101	85.4	109	107	96.0	95.3		
CA/GDP	Pre	-3.8	-2.3	-3.1	-3.8	3.8	2.4	0.6	-1.3	-1.4	-2.0	-3.0	-7.0	-0.6	-3.8	-2.9	+	0.866
	Pro	-2.3	-3.1	-4.1	3.8	2.4	0.6	-1.3	2.8	-2.0	-3.0	-4.7	-0.6	-0.8	-2.9	-3.1		
OB/GDP	Pre	-1.0	0.8	0.4	-7.0	-3.0	-0.4	-2.0	-0.3	-6.4	-0.1	0.9	-4.0	-6.2	0.7	0.8	+	2.471*
	Pro	0.8	0.4	0.2	-3.0	-0.4	-2.0	-0.3	2.9	-0.1	0.9	2.5	-6.2	1.3	0.8	1.2		
INFR	Pre	15.8	29.0	17.5	58.9	102	65.5	57.7	86.2	114	20.0	26.7	7.0	35.0	15.9	16.6	-	0.036
	Pro	29.0	17.5	18.2	102	65.5	57.7	86.2	132	20.0	26.7	22.7	35.0	34.4	16.6	9.5		
RGDP Gr	Pre	4.2	3.4	8.3	-0.6	-5.3	3.7	2.7	-3.7	1.2	3.3	4.4	4.4	-6.2	4.8	3.9	+	0.605
	Pro	3.4	8.3	9.2	-5.3	3.7	2.7	-3.7	1.7	3.3	4.4	4.2	-6.2	5.1	3.9	6.9		
FOREX Gr	Pre	1.6	34.1	12.2	-77.7	358	91.5	-32.5	15.4	-48.5	21.7	58.9	-75.5	14.9	11.8	-1.5	+	0.712
	Pro	34.1	12.2	4.8	358	91.5	-32.5	15.4	108	21.7	58.9	81.4	14.9	25.7	-1.5	13.3		
Memorandum Items																		
X/GDP	Pre	3.8	5.1	5.9	12.7	15.3	13.9	12.0	12.6	11.9	11.5	11.2	14.3	30.2	28.3	27.6	Pre<	1.602
	Pro	5.1	5.9	6.7	15.3	13.9	12.0	12.6	14.9	11.5	11.2	13.4	30.2	32.9	27.6	29.0	Pro	
M/GDP	Pre	6.8	6.7	7.9	9.1	5.6	6.7	7.6	9.3	11.2	12.2	11.2	18.7	27.5	30.2	28.7	Pre<	1.692
	Pro	6.7	7.9	9.0	5.6	6.7	7.6	9.3	9.1	12.2	11.2	15.7	27.5	30.7	28.7	30.4	Pro	

Notes: (1) + sign indicates better performance, - sign indicates poor performance and 0 indicates performance. (2) The * sign means significant at % level of significance.

Table 8.3: Mexico: Programme Effects: Before-after Approach

Total number program years method

Variable	1977	1978	1979	1983	1984	1985	1986	1987	1989
CN/GDP	+	0	+	+	-	-	-	+	-
INV/GDP	+	+	+	-	-	+	-	+	+
DS/GDP	+	0	+	+	-	-	-	+	-
X/M	+	-	+	+	-	-	-	+	-
CA/GDP	+	-	-	+	-	-	-	+	-
OB/GDP	+	-	-	+	+	-	+	+	+
RGDP Gr	-	+	+	-	+	-	-	+	+
INFR	-	+	-	-	+	+	-	-	+
FOREX Gr	+	-	-	+	-	-	+	+	+
No of variables with better performance	7	3	5	6	3	2	2	8	5
No of variables with poor performance	2	4	4	3	6	7	7	1	4
No of variables with same performance	0	2	0	0	0	0	0	0	0

Contd...

Variable	Performance (no. of years)								
	1990	1991	1995	1996	1999	2000	Better	Poor	Same
CN/GDP	-	-	+	+	-	-	6	8	1
INV/GDP	-	-	-	+	+	-	8	7	0
DS/GDP	-	-	+	+	-	-	6	8	1
X/M	+	-	+	-	+	-	7	8	0
CA/GDP	-	-	+	-	-	+	5	10	0
OB/GDP	+	+	-	+	+	+	11	4	0
RGDP Gr	+	-	-	+	-	+	8	7	0
INFR	-	+	-	+	-	+	7	8	0
FOREX Gr	+	+	+	+	-	+	10	5	0
No of variables with better performance	4	3	5	7	3	5	68 (50.4)		
No of variables with poor performance	5	6	4	2	6	4		65 (48.1)	
No of variables with same performance	0	0		0	0	0			2 (1.5)

Notes (1) + sign indicates better performance, - sign indicates poor performance and 0 indicates same performance. (2) Figures in parenthesis are percentages.

Table 8.4: Mexico: Programme Effects: With-without Approach

The difference between means method

Variable		1977	1978	1979	1983	1984	1985	1986	1987	1989
ΔCN/	MX	-2.0	0.0	-1.7	-2.9	2.5	1.7	3.6	-3.4	2.9
GDP	NPC	0.1	1.1	-0.6	-0.3	-0.4	0.3	0.5	-0.3	-0.6
ΔINV/	MX	1.2	0.8	2.4	-0.9	-0.4	1.3	-3.0	0.3	2.8
GDP	NPC	0.6	0.6	-0.1	-2.3	-1.3	-1.2	-0.2	1.0	0.6
ΔDS/	MX	2.0	0.0	1.7	2.9	-2.5	-1.7	-3.6	3.4	-2.9
GDP	NPC	-0.1	-1.1	0.6	0.3	0.4	-0.3	-0.5	0.3	0.6
ΔX/M	MX	19.2	-1.8	0.2	132	-64.9	-49.0	-21.7	27.8	-11.7
	NPC	-0.8	-5.5	10.8	4.3	4.9	-0.6	-6.2	-2.1	8.8
ΔCA/	MX	1.5	-0.8	-1.0	7.6	-1.4	-1.8	-1.9	4.1	-0.6
GDP	NPC	-0.5	-2.1	0.8	0.4	1.9	-0.8	0.0	-0.8	0.0
ΔOB/	MX	1.8	-0.4	-0.2	4.0	2.6	-1.6	1.7	3.2	6.3
GDP	NPC	0.6	-0.7	-1.0	-1.2	1.3	-0.5	0.3	0.0	0.5
ΔINFR	MX	13.2	-11.5	0.7	42.9	-36.3	-7.8	28.5	45.6	-94.2
	NPC	2.2	-3.7	4.8	3.8	11.1	5.6	-7.6	4.8	4.5
ΔRGDP	MX	-0.8	4.9	0.9	-4.7	9.0	-1.0	-6.4	5.4	2.1
Gr	NPC	-1.1	0.7	-0.1	-0.3	1.0	1.3	0.2	1.0	-0.8
ΔX/	MX	1.3	0.8	0.8	2.6	-1.4	-1.9	0.6	2.3	-0.4
GDP	NPC	0.3	-1.1	1.4	-1.8	0.6	-1.0	-1.0	0.6	1.1
ΔM/	MX	-0.1	1.2	1.1	-3.5	1.1	0.9	1.7	-0.2	1.0
GDP	NPC	0.8	0.1	0.4	-3.2	-1.4	-1.0	-1.3	1.6	0.9

Contd...

Variable		Effect 1990	t-value 1991	1995	1996	1999	2000		
ΔCN/ GDP	MX	0.4	0.3	-5.6	-2.8	0.2	0.6	+	0.698
	NPC	0.4	1.3	-0.2	0.2	0.1	-0.9		
ΔINV/ GDP	MX	-2.0	-3.2	-3.2	1.7	0.4	-0.3	+	0.160
	NPC	0.3	0.0	-0.1	-0.1	-1.3	0.1		
ΔDS/ GDP	MX	-0.4	-0.3	5.6	2.8	-0.2	-0.6	+	0.698
	NPC	-0.4	-1.3	0.2	-0.2	-0.1	0.9		
ΔX/M	MX	6.3	-15.6	33.1	-2.4	-2.4	-0.7	+	0.234
	NPC	-4.7	0.0	0.3	-1.3	6.1	1.4		
ΔCA/ GDP	MX	-1.0	-1.7	6.4	-0.2	0.9	-0.2	+	0.923
	NPC	-0.8	0.0	0.0	-0.3	0.1	-0.9		
ΔOB/ GDP	MX	1.0	1.6	-2.2	7.5	0.1	0.4	+	2.840*
	NPC	-0.4	0.2	-0.6	0.6	0.2	-0.5		
ΔINFR	MX	6.7	-4.0	28.0	-0.6	0.7	-7.1	+	0.095
	NPC	2.4	0.6	-3.6	-2.3	-3.2	-1.3		
ΔRGDP Gr	MX	1.1	-0.2	-10.6	11.3	-0.7	3.0	+	0.466
	NPC	1.4	0.0	-0.5	-0.3	-0.6	1.4		
ΔX/ GDP	MX	-0.3	2.2	15.9	2.7	-0.7	1.4	MX> NPC	1.738
	NPC	-0.6	-0.6	1.0	-0.8	-0.6	1.7		
ΔM/ GDP	MX	-1.0	4.5	8.8	3.2	-1.5	1.7	MX> NPC	1.769*
	NPC	1.9	-0.1	0.6	-0.9	-1.0	2.5		

Notes: (1) MX: Mexico and NPC: Non Programme Countries. (2) + sign indicates better performance, - sign indicates poor performance and 0 indicates same performance. (3) * sign indicates significant at 5% level of significance.

Table 8.5: Mexico: Programme Effects: With-without Approach

Total number program years method

Variable	1977	1978	1979	1983	1984	1985	1986	1987	1989
ΔCN/GDP	+	+	+	+	-	-	-	+	-
ΔINV/GDP	+	+	+	+	+	+	-	-	+
ΔDS/GDP	+	+	+	+	-	-	-	+	-
ΔX/M	+	+	-	+	-	-	-	+	-
ΔCA/GDP	+	+	-	+	-	-	-	+	-
ΔOB/GDP	+	+	+	+	+	-	+	+	-
ΔRGDP Gr	+	+	+	-	+	-	-	+	+
ΔINFR	-	+	+	-	+	+	-	-	+
No of variables with better performance	7	8	6	6	4	2	1	6	4
No of variables with poor performance	1	0	2	2	4	6	7	2	4
No of variables with same performance	0	0	0	0	0	0	0	0	0

Contd...

Variable	Performance (no. of years)								
	1990	1991	1995	1996	1999	2000	Better	Poor	Same
ΔCN/GDP	0	+	+	+	-	-	8	6	1
ΔINV/GDP	-	-	-	+	+	-	9	6	0
ΔDS/GDP	0	+	+	+	-	-	8	6	1
ΔX/M	+	-	+	-	-	-	6	9	0
ΔCA/GDP	-	-	+	+	+	+	8	7	0
ΔOB/GDP	+	+	-	+	-	+	12	3	0
ΔRGDP Gr	-	-	-	+	-	+	8	7	0
ΔINFR	-	+	-	-	-	+	7	8	0
No of variables with better performance	2	4	4	6	2	4	66 (55.0)		
No of variables with poor performance	4	4	4	2	6	4		52 (43.3)	
No of variables with same performance	2	0	0	0	0	0			2 (91.7)

Notes (1) + sign indicates better performance, (-) sign indicates poor performance and (0) indicates same performance. (2) Figures in parenthesis are percentages.

tightening of fiscal policies and the resumption of use of external credit by public sector, the authorities expected to limit the overall expansion of credit, while making room for private credit to support the recovery of economic activity. Interest rate policy was to be made flexible and responsive to market forces. The government policies were designed to facilitate in shift of economic resources to the export sector and to encourage efficient import substitution activities. The authorities stated their intention to encourage foreign investment, especially in ventures to expand exports capacity and activities that involve the transfer of technology.

The macroeconomic performance of the Mexican economy under the 1986-87 programme has been summarized below:

- Mexican economy showed better performance in 1987, but it had poor performance in 1986.
- Mexican economy had better performance as compared to the 'control group' in 1987, but relatively poor in 1986.

But, according to the IMF assessment, "The adjustment programme met with a considerable success. The balance of payments position improved significantly, and output began to recover in 1987. Furthermore, the authorities made significant strides in implementing trade liberalization and in privatizing public enterprises. Inflation remained high, however, and late in 1987, pressure on the balance of payments emerged, aggravated in part by the crash in the Mexican stock market."

Inflation decelerated throughout 1988, owing to policies put in place in December 1987. Though economic activity remained weak, real GDP grew by only 1.1 percent in 1988. Exports of goods and services grew by more than 3 percent in real terms, spurred in part by trade liberalization measures. Although the peso appreciated in real terms throughout 1988, its real effective value remained below the average in the preceding few years.

The external current account registered a deficit of $ 2.8 billion in 1988, following a $ 4.0 billion surplus in 1987. Although a sharp fall in international petroleum prices resulted in a decline of about one fourth in oil export receipts, continued growth of non petroleum exports resulted in a small increase in total exports. Imports rose by 55 percent, reflecting in part Mexico's substantial trade liberalization. The capital account also shifted into deficit, recording a deficit of $ 4.1billion in 1988, compared with a surplus of $ 2.5 billion in 1987. This shift reflected a decline in the level of official borrowing and a substantial early repayment of debt by private sector borrowers. As a result, the overall balance of payments recorded a deficit of almost $ 7 billion.

1989-1991 Adjustment Programme

On May 26, 1989, the Fund approved a three extended arrangement for the government of Mexico authorizing purchases up to the equivalent of SDR 3251 million to support the economic adjustment programme for 1989-91. The programme incorporated an important new feature- Fund support for debt reduction. This feature was to provide that 30 percent of each purchase under the extended arrangement may be set aside for debt reduction. For 1989-91, the government policies were aimed at consolidating gains with respect to inflation while the effects of structural reforms on economic performance were to be continued. Inflation was expected to decline to 18 percent in 1989 from 52 percent in 1988, and it was anticipated that gross domestic would increase by 1.5 percent on 1989, with a significant recovery to take place in 1990. Exchange rate policy was to be managed so as to be consistent with the balance of payments objectives, and monetary policy aimed at consolidating the recent gains in reducing inflation. Structural policies, many of which were already in place, covered a major overhaul of the tax system, the creation of conditions for increased direct foreign investment, continuing public enterprises reform, completion of trade liberalization efforts, the improvement of export competitiveness, and financial sector reforms to raise the efficiency of the banking system and to free interest rate.

The macroeconomic performance under the 1989-90 programme has been summarized below:

- Mexican economy had better performance in 1989, but it showed poor performance during 1990-91.
- Mexican economy did not perform better than the 'control group' during 1989-91.
- Though the overall external balance of payments and real GDP growth targets were met.

During 1994, investors' concern about the sustainability of the current account deficit began to increase, against the background of adverse political events in Mexico, intense competition for foreign savings in other emerging markets, and generally higher interest rates abroad. To contain capital outflows, the Mexican authorities raised interest rates, allowed the currency to move to the more depreciated limits of the exchange band, and substituted short-term indebtedness denominated in foreign currency for local currency- denominated debt. Nevertheless, there was a significant loss of external reserves.

Resurgence of investors' fear put further pressure on foreign exchange and financial markets and precipitated in the financial crisis and led to the floating of the peso in late December 1994.

1995-1996 Adjustment programme

The IMF approved an 18 month stand-by credit for Mexico of up to the equivalent of SDR 12070 million in support of the economic and financial programme for 1995-1996. This was the largest ever financial package approved by the IMF for a member country. The exceptional action was taken with a view to providing an adequate international response to Mexico's financial crisis and giving confidence to the international financial system.

The programme involved a two-pronged approach aimed at consolidating the progress made in the past several years and addressing the current liquidity problem of dealing with substantial short-term obligations falling due. The programme's specific objectives were: (1) the reduction in the current account deficit from 8 percent of GDP in 1994 to 4 percent of GDP in 1995, and to 3-3½ percent of GDP in 1996, and (2) a lowering of annualized rate of inflation to around 9 percent in the fourth quarter of 1995. Economic activity was expected to decline in the first half of 1995, as the effects of the change in relative prices and the financial adjustment. Real GDP was expected to grow by 1.5 percent in 1995. Gross domestic investment was expected to be equivalent to 21 percent of GDP in 1995.

To achieve these goals, the programme was cantered on a policy of wage, price, and credit restraint supported by an improvement in the fiscal position. The revised budget for 1995 provided for non financial public sector a surplus of 0.5 percent of GDP and a primary surplus of 3.4 percent. Credit policy was expected to play an important role in achieving the objectives of the programme. The programme provided for a reduction in the rate of credit expansion by the development banks of more than half. However, the development banks trust were allowed to provide net financing to priority sectors, including exports and agriculture.

The Bank of Mexico planned to support the floating exchange rate regime through limited intervention in the foreign exchange market. The authorities committed to review tax policies to at least maintain the surplus position of the public sector and improve the equity of the tax system.

The structural reform provided a reinforcement of the government's strategy for privatization and the granting of concessions to the private sector. Beginning in 1995 privatization was to involve basic infrastructure (rail, ports, airports, electricity generation, and radio and telecommunication). The privatization proceeds were to be used largely for the cancellation of the public external debt.

The following conclusions have been drawn regarding the macroeconomic performance of the Mexican economy under 1995-96 programme:

- Mexican economy showed better performance during 1995-96.
- Mexican economy showed somewhat better performance than the 'control group' during 1995-96.

- Only external current account deficit target could be achieved.

1999-2000 Adjustment Programme

On July 7, 1999, the IMF approved a stand-by arrangement for Mexico authorizing credit equivalent to SDR 3.1 billion to support the government's economic programme for 1999-2000. The IMF commended Mexico for the pursuit of sound economic policies and structural reforms, which had restored confidence and set the stage for sustainable growth. The Fund cautioned that the Mexican economy still remained vulnerable to shocks. The continued fragility of banking system was a major weakness and the Fund urged the authorities to accord this area top priority and to accelerate the pace of banking reforms. It emphasized the importance of enforcing the strict adherence to existing financial regulations upgrading the financial system's legal, regulatory, and supervisory framework consistent with the Basle core principles. The Fund supported the stance of monetary policy, within the context of existing floating exchange rate regime.

To reduce vulnerability to adverse shocks, the Mexican authorities were continuing their efforts to restructure the banking system, which was to play a key role in economic growth. The medium term strategy planned to consolidate the gains made in 1985-98 and set the economy on a sustainable growth path expanding employment and reducing poverty in the context of low inflation. The economic programme aimed to reduce inflation to 13 percent during 1999 and to 10 percent during 2000. Real GDP growth was expected to decline to 3 percent in 1999, reflecting in part, reduced access to international capital markets, but was set to recover to 5 percent in 2000. Accordingly, the external current account deficit was projected to decline to 2.2 percent of GDP in 1999 and then to increase to 3.1 percent of GDP in2000. The overall public sector deficit was projected, based on a conservative oil price assumption, at 1.25 percent of GDP in 1999.

The authorities also intended to continue carrying out structural reforms aimed at bolstering market confidence in the

Mexican economy and consolidating access to international capital markets on increasingly favourable terms.

The macroeconomic performance of the Mexican economy under the 1999- 2000 programme has been summarized below:

- Mexican economy showed poor performance during 1999-2000.
- Mexican economy showed poor performance as compared to the 'control group' during 1999-2000.
- Real GDP growth, and to some extent, inflation rate and current account deficit targets were met.

Macroeconomic Performance under Different Approaches

The macroeconomic performance of the Mexican economy-according to different approaches-has been summarized below:

Before-After Approach: The following important conclusions have been drawn in context of the macroeconomic performance of the Mexican economy during the Fund-supported programmes:

- When the total number of programme years method was employed, four variables viz., investment as percentage of GDP, overall balance of payments as percentage of GDP, real output growth rate and foreign exchange reserves growth revealed better performance of the economy. While, five variables, namely- consumption as percentage of GDP, domestic savings as percentage of GDP, trade account balance, current account balance and inflation rate revealed poor performance of the economy. (Table 8.3)
- According to the difference between means method, seven variables viz., consumption as percentage of GDP, domestic savings as percentage of GDP, exports as percentage of imports, current account as percentage of GDP, overall balance of payments as percentage of GDP, real GDP growth rate and foreign exchange reserves growth rate showed positive effects of the Fund supported programmes. While, two variables- investment as percentage of GDP and inflation rate revealed negative effects. (Table 8.2)

- During the implementation of Fund supported programmes, the dependency of the economy was enhanced, though the results were not statistically significant. (Table 8.2)

With-Without Approach: The following conclusions have been drawn regarding the macroeconomic performance of the Mexican economy under the Fund-supported programmes:

- According to the total number of programme years method, six variables viz., consumption as percentage of GDP, investment as percentage of GDP, domestic savings as percentage of GDP, current account as percent of GDP, overall balance as percentage of GDP and real GDP growth rate showed better performance of the Mexican economy as compared to that of the 'control group'. Two variables-exports as percentage of imports and inflation rate revealed poor performance of the Mexican economy. (Table 8.5)
- When the difference between means method was employed, all the variables viz., consumption as percentage of GDP, investment as percentage of GDP, domestic savings as percentage of GDP, exports as percentage of imports, current account as percentage of GDP, overall balance of payments as percentage of GDP, inflation rate and real GDP growth rate showed better performance of the Mexican economy in comparison of the performance of the 'control group'. (Table 8.4)
- Under the Fund supported programmes, the dependency of the Mexican economy increased more as compared to that of the 'control group'. The results were statistically significant at 5 percent level of significance. (Table 8.4)

Generalized Evaluation Approach: The generalized evaluation approach revealed positive effects of the Fund supported programmes on investment, domestic savings, and exports as percentage of imports, current account balance as percentage of GDP and overall balance as percentage of GDP. While, negative effect was seen on inflation rate, nominal GDP and real output growth rate. But, the positive effects shown on external sector an investment are doubtful. The deep analysis

(Table 8.2 and Appendix 8A) indicates that investment as percentage of GDP did not reveal an improvement during the programme years. Investment showed positive effect in regression analysis because it deteriorated more during non program years. This was also true to a large extent in the case of current account as percentage of GDP. The current account balance as percentage of GDP did not show much improvement during the programme years, but it not deteriorated like in non programme years. The overall balance of payments account showed the improvement- whatever it was- due to inflows of foreign capital through capital account Tables 8.6 and 8.7).

Overall Macroeconomic Performance

The following points are noteworthy in context of the overall macroeconomic performance of the Mexican economy under the Fund supported programmes:

- No improvement was clearly seen in consumption as percentage of GDP during programme years. Consumption, which was equivalent to 79 percent of GDP in 1976, became equivalent to 78.5 percent of GDP in 2000 and its value almost remained near these figures during programme years.
- Investment as percentage of GDP, which showed a little improvement during 1977-1979 economic adjustment programme, did not reveal any improvement after the implementation of the stated programme. The overall performance was disappointing.
- Domestic savings as percentage of GDP showed some improvement during 1977- 1979 and 1983 programmes. After 1983, it did not reveal improvement.
- The external sector's performance was also not satisfactory. Trade account showed deterioration during 8 programme years out of 15 programme years.
- The external current account balance as percentage of GDP did not reveal much improvement. The only achievement was that the widening deficit could be checked. Except 1983,

Table 8.6: Mexico: Programme effects: Generalized Evaluation (1975-2002)

Z	C	GDP	INV	Z_{-1}	FD/GDP	DCR	T	D	R^2	F
GDP	3804.1 (0.892)		4.947 (77.88)*					-25515.5 (0.488)	0.99	3124.2
INV	-6204.2 (0.717)	0.201 (77.89)*						4402.1 (0.434)	0.99	3118.0
DS	-8761.6 (0.480)	0.206 (37.86)*						27325.3 (1.278)	0.98	730.5
X/M	24.672 (1.232)			0.504 (3.063)*	-2.441 (1.338)	0.083 (0.316)	0.484 (0.540)	17.656 (1.302)	0.61	6.8
CA/ GDP	-5.012 (3.595)*			0.284 (1.912)*	-0.243 (2.456)*	-0.004 (0.027)	0.067 (1.837)*	2.362 (3.138)*	0.64	7.8
OB/ GDP	-1.135 (0.756)			0.150 (0.647)	0.307 (2.207)*	0.023 (1.153)	0.019 (0.290)	1.451 (1.225)	0.26	1.5
RGDP Gr	7.106 (2.639)*			0.054 (0.254)	0.434 (2.177)*	0.011 (0.392)	-0.177 (1.804)*	-0.461 (0.300)	0.30	1.9
INFR	-3.388 (0.286)			0.348 (2.346)*	-2.837 (2.451)*	0.204 (1.262)	0.219 (0.419)	9.215 (1.152)	0.72	11.1

Note: (1) Figures in parenthesis are t-values. (2) *sign indicates significant at 5% level of significance.

Table 8.7: Mexico: Programme Effects (summary)

Variable	Before-After Approach		With-Without Approach		Generalized Evaluation
	Difference between means method	Total number of programme years	Difference between means method	Total number of programme years	
CN/ GDP	+	-	+	+	N A
INV/GDP	-	+	+	+	N A
DS/GDP	+	-	+	+	N A
X/M	+	-	+	-	+
CA/GDP	+	-	+	+	+*
OB/GDP	+*	+	+*	+	+
RGDP Gr	+	+	+	+	-
INFR	-	-	+	-	-
FOREX Gr	+	+	N A	N A	N A
GDP	N A	N A	N A	N A	-
INV	N A	N A	N A	N A	+
DS	N A	N A	N A	N A	+
Total	7	4	8	6	5
Better	2	5	0	2	3
Poor	0	0	0	0	0
Same					

Note: (1) + sign indicates better performance,-sign indicates poor performance and 0 sign indicates same performance. (2) * sign indicates significance at 5% level of significance.

1984,1985 and 1987, all the programme years showed deficit in current account- usually being equivalent to 3%- 4% of GDP.

- The overall balance of payments showed improvement during the programme years. It showed improvement during 11 programme years out of total 15 years. But, the improvement in overall balance of payments was not through the current account. It was due to increased foreign capital in flows, perhaps because of IMF's 'seal of approval'.
- No satisfactory results were achieved in context of inflation rate during programme years. Improvement was seen 2000 onward.
- Not much success was achieved in the case of real output growth rate. Though there was on average no decline in real GDP growth rate, the volatility was still present during the programme years.
- Positive performance was shown by foreign exchange reserves growth rate.
- Few of the established targets were met.
- The dependency of the Mexican economy increased during the programme years. The results were statistically significant.
- The 1990 onward, the better management of instrumental variables was achieved. The overall budget balance, which showed large deficits till 1989, remained under control 1990 onward.
- There was huge domestic credit expansion before 1992, but it was largely under control since that.
- The money supply growth rate was quite high till 1991, but it was brought down to a good extent since then.
- Interest rates remained high during 1981-1990. These were largely under control after 1990, excepting 1995 and 1996.
- The foreign exchange management remained flexible. Despite this, no improvement was found in external sector accounts.
- The Mexican economy showed some improvement during seven programme years out of total fifteen programme years.

When comparison was made with the control group, the number of programme years showing better performance declined to six.

- Finally, the Mexican economy did not reveal satisfactory performance during programme years (Table 8.8).

Conclusions

The Mexican authorities implemented the Fund-supported programmes for fifteen different years, but the economy did not show a satisfactory performance during the programme years. Despite the implementation- particularly 1990 onward- of tight credit policy, flexible foreign exchange management and tight fiscal policy, and to some extent control led money supply growth, the economy did not reveal sustainable improvement. Consumption as percentage of GDP, investment as percentage of GDP and domestic savings as percentage of GDP did not show positive improvement during programme years.

The external sector did not show noteworthy progress during the programme years. The current account did not reveal improvement, still having deficit. The overall balance of payments showed an improvement- generally moderate deficit or surplus-during programme years, owing to inflow of foreign capital.

The real output growth rate did not show improvement except the 1977-79 economic programme. The volatility was still present in real GDP growth. Disappointing results were also found in the case of inflation rate. The dependency of the Mexican economy increased during programme years. The results were statistically significant.

Finally, Mexican economy revealed poor performance under the Fund-supported programmes. The economy could not achieve stable and viable economic position.

Table 8.8: Mexico: Policy Variables, (1975-2002)

Year	Exchange rate[1] (Ps per U.S. $)	Interest rate (%)	Money supply (% change)	Domestic credit (% change)	Budget deficit (as % of GDP)
1975	12.5	---	16.5	27.1	-4.9
1976	20.0	---	46.0	21.3	-4.7
1977	22.7	10.6	38.0	41.4	-3.3
1978	22.7	11.2	33.1	32.1	-2.7
1979	22.8	13.2	35.8	43.9	-3.3
1980	23.3	20.6	36.7	39.0	3.1
1981	26.2	29.5	49.0	48.8	-6.7
1982	96.5	43.6	58.0	96.6	-15.4
1983	143.9	54.7	61.9	56.2	-7.9
1984	192.6	48.3	68.5	51.3	-7.1
1985	371.7	59.5	43.3	69.7	-8.4
1986	923.5	84.9	78.4	101.7	-13.2
1987	2209.7	97.2	147.2	104.4	-13.6
1988	2281.0	63.6	-17.5	66.9	-10.2
1989	2641.0	36.3	115.4	45.6	-5.4
1990	2945.0	31.2	104.1	41.7	0.8
1991	3.07	19.3	48.7	36.6	2.9
1992	3.12	15.6	23.9	27.5	4.1
1993	3.11	15.0	15.2	11.9	0.5
1994	5.33	14.1	19.2	24.1	0.0
1995	7.64	48.4	31.7	5.4	-0.5
1996	7.85	31.4	25.3	-17.5	-0.2
1997	8.08	19.8	33.8	113.6	-1.0
1998	9.87	24.7	19.7	10.5	-1.4

Contd...

1999	9.51	21.4	11.7	1.0	-1.5
2000	9.57	15.2	24.8	0.2	-1.2
2001	9.14	11.3	12.4	0.5	-0.7
2002	10.31	7.1	8.9	15.3	-1.7

Note: (1) New Pesos per U S Dollar 1991 onwards. Sources: Compiled and computed form *IMF-International Financial Statistics*, various issues, and *UN-National Accounts Statistics, Main Aggregates and detailed Tables*, various issues.

Appendix 8A: Mexico: Statistics on Macroeconomic Variables (1975-2002)

Year	CN/ GDP	INV/ GDP	DS/ GDP	X/M	CA/ GDP	OB/ GDP	INFR (%)	RGDP Gr	FOREX Gr (%)	X/ GDP	M/ GDP
1975	78.9	23.7	21.1	44.1	-4.6	0.2	15.2	5.6	21.7	3.3	7.5
1976	79.0	21.6	21.0	56.7	-3.8	-1.0	15.8	4.2	1.6	3.8	6.8
1977	77.0	22.8	23.0	75.9	-2.3	0.8	29.0	3.4	34.1	5.1	6.7
1978	77.0	23.6	23.0	74.1	-3.1	0.4	17.5	8.3	12.2	5.9	7.9
1979	75.3	26.0	24.7	74.3	-4.1	0.2	18.2	9.2	4.8	6.7	9.0
1980	72.8	28.1	27.2	80.0	-5.8	0.4	26.4	8.3	43.7	8.4	10.5
1981	72.7	29.0	27.3	81.6	-6.7	0.5	27.9	7.9	38.0	8.2	10.0
1982	72.6	21.2	27.4	140.2	-3.8	-7.0	58.9	-0.6	-77.7	12.7	9.1
1983	69.7	20.3	30.3	271.9	3.8	-3.0	101.8	-5.3	358.3	15.3	5.6
1984	72.2	19.9	27.8	207.0	2.4	-0.4	65.5	3.7	91.5	13.9	6.7
1985	73.9	21.2	26.1	158.0	0.6	-2.0	57.7	2.7	-32.5	12.0	7.6
1986	77.5	18.2	22.5	136.3	-1.3	-0.3	86.2	-3.7	15.4	12.6	9.3
1987	74.1	18.5	25.9	164.1	2.8	2.9	131.8	1.7	107.7	14.9	9.1
1988	75.9	21.0	24.1	106.0	-1.4	-6.4	114.2	1.2	-48.5	11.9	11.2
1989	78.8	23.8	21.2	94.3	-2.0	-0.1	20.0	3.3	21.7	11.5	12.2
1990	79.2	21.8	20.8	100.6	-3.0	0.9	26.7	4.4	58.9	11.2	11.2
1991	79.5	18.6	20.5	85.4	-4.7	2.5	22.7	4.2	81.4	13.4	15.7
1992	81.7	19.5	18.3	74.3	-6.7	0.4	15.5	3.6	7.3	12.6	17.0
1993	82.9	18.5	17.1	79.3	-5.8	1.7	9.8	1.9	35.2	12.8	16.2
1994	83.1	19.3	16.9	76.7	-7.0	-4.0	7.0	4.4	-75.5	14.3	18.7
1995	77.5	16.1	22.5	109.6	-0.6	-6.2	35.0	-6.2	14.9	30.2	27.5
1996	74.7	17.8	25.3	107.2	-0.8	1.3	34.4	5.1	25.7	32.9	30.7
1997	74.1	19.5	25.9	100.5	-1.9	3.5	20.6	6.8	46.7	28.1	27.9
1998	77.7	20.8	22.3	93.6	-3.8	0.7	15.9	4.8	11.8	28.3	30.2

Contd...

1999	77.9	21.2	22.1	96.0	-2.9	0.8	16.6	3.9	-1.5	27.6	28.7
2000	78.5	20.9	21.5	95.3	-3.1	1.2	9.5	6.9	13.3	29.0	30.4
2001	81.3	19.9	18.7	94.0	-2.0	1.1	6.4	0.0	26.2	25.2	26.8
2002	81.1	19.3	18.9	95.3	-2.2	1.1	5.0	0.6	12.4	25.0	26.3

Sources: Compiled and computed form *IMF-International Financial Statistics*, various issues, and *UN-National Accounts Statistics, Main Aggregates and detailed Tables*, various issues.

9

India: Remarkable Macroeconomic Performance

India, the second most populous country in the world is characterized by considerable racial, religious, cultural and linguistic diversity. Although agriculture supports much of the population, manufacturing, and services play an important role. Agriculture, forestry, fishing, and related activities employ a major part of labour force and account for about fourth of gross domestic product. Food grains are the principal farm product. Among non-agricultural activities, manufacturing, construction, electricity, gas, and water supplies account for about one third of gross domestic product. India possesses major reserves of coal and iron ore, and has developed a broad diverse industrial base.

The Indian economy made considerable progress during the greater part of 1970s: real economic growth exceeded 6 percent a year, inflationary pressures were held in check, and agriculture production expanded considerably, so that food imports were virtually eliminated and sizable food stock were accumulated. A severe drought was experienced in 1979/80 and affected industrial and agricultural output. Although situation improved in 1980/81 within a year of normal monsoon, the intervening rise in oil prices weakened the balance of payments. The current account balance moved from a moderate surplus into deficit in 1979/80. This deficit widened to the equivalent of 2 percent of GDP in 1980/81 and was expected to remain under pressure over the coming years. To improve the situation, the Indian authorities implemented a comprehensive adjustment programme for fiscal years: 1981/82, 1982/83 and 1983/84.

The detail of the Fund supported programmes implemented by India is given in Table 9.1.

Table 9.1: India: Lending Arrangements with IMF, 1975-2002

(Amount expressed in millions of SDRs)

Facility	Date of arrangement	Date of expiration	Amount approved	Balance not drawn	Programme years[1]	remarks
EA	09.11.1981	08.11.1984	5000	1100	1982,1983,1984	
SBA	08.01.1991	07.04.1991	552	0	1992	
SBA	31.10.1991	30.06.1993	1656	0	1992,1993	

Note: 1. Fiscal years ending in the year stated.

Source: IMF Survey, various issues.

1981/82-1983/84 Adjustment Programme

This programme was supported by the Fund under a three year extended arrangement, for SDR 5000 million, approved on November 9, 1981. The programme aimed at achieving a high rate of economic growth, slowing inflation, and strengthening the balance of payments over the medium term. The programme contained:

- Demand management policies to promote domestic financial stability.
- Measures to mobilize increased domestic savings, in particular public savings, to support a set up in investment of structural adjustment.
- Further liberalization of trade restrictions to improve the efficiency of the economy.

The average growth of GDP was targeted at 5.2 percent during the plan period of 1980/81-1984/85. The investment was planned to increase from 21.8 percent of GDP in 1979/80 to 25.1 percent by 1984/85. Gross domestic savings were projected to rise from 21.2 percent of GDP in 1979/80 to 24.5 percent by 1984/85.

The programme strategy was incorporated into sixth five year plan (1980/81-1984/85). The sixth plan addressed a number of tax and non tax measures that were to be taken to meet ambitious investment goals. Given that the nominal tax rate and rate of private sector savings were already high, the plan emphasized the need to increase public sector savings by raising administrative prices, reducing subsidies (e.g. for fertilizer), and fostering greater efficiency in the utilization of existing capital.

For a time, negotiations between the Fund and India were at a stalemate. The Fund, therefore, advised India to come with commitments for a one year programme. The government took a powerful revenue raising measures. Most importantly, in July 1981, it raised the price of domestic crude oil from an average of \$46.92 to \$141.84 (an increase of 200 percent), and it further reduced its subsidy burden by over to \$ 900 million by increasing fertilizer prices for the second time in just over one year, The government also raised the prices of most petroleum products. In addition, the tariffs of electricity boards in a number of states were raised.

Reduction of external restrictions in the Indian economy was a second and even more sensitive issue that figured prominently in India- IMF negotiations.

Thus, the text of the extended arrangement and accompanying documentation committed the Indian government to set a performance criteria and economic policies that showed the policy approach and broad objectives of its sixth plan. The performance criteria were as given below:

- In the first year of the extended arrangement India had (1) to have ceiling on the domestic credit to the banking system and on net credit to government and (2) to limit contracting or guaranteeing of medium term loans of maturity of 1-12 years to no more than SDR 1.4 billion.
- Second and third instalments were dependent on subsequent consultations and additional performance clauses.
- During the extended arrangement, India had not to impose or to intensify import restrictions for balance of payments reasons, to impose or intensify restrictions on payments and transfers for current international transactions, to introduce multiple currency practices.

In addition to these, India further committed itself to a wide ranging adjustments including a massive investment programme with emphasis on energy production, alleviation of infrastructural constraints, efficiency in the private sector and continued flexibility in pricing policy. Monetary and financial policies were intended to contain inflationary pressures and to pursue a practical exchange rate policy. Other measures included the strengthening of the export efforts, consolidating the progress achieved in the previous years in context of trade liberalization.

In India, opposition came principally from the left, but also from others sceptical of the government's policy to manage the economy. According to these critics, the IMF loan was unnecessary; its policy conditions intrusive and their impact inequitable, and the outcome of the programme likely ineffective as a mean to solve the balance of payments problem. Jyoti Basu, then the chief minister of West Bengal quoted, "IMF loan would imply a total reversal of India's economic policy of self reliance and would compromise certain constitutional principles as well". Hannan Ezekiel, then the editor of Bombay Economic Times, agreed with the left that poor ought not to be made to bear much of the burden of adjustment.

In defending this programme before the Parliament, the government stated that: (1) they had not agreed anything other than what was in the official plan, (2) if pushed too hard by the IMF on any issue, they would not continue the programme, (3) if the rate of growth of output was not sufficiently high to enable them to afford the programme they would not continue to draw resources from the Fund, and (4) if the economic conditions improved sufficiently, they would not draw.

Outside of India, the main criticism of the extended programme came from the US government. Whereas the left viewed IMF conditionality as an affront and a distortion of Indian priorities, the United States claimed that the conditions were too easy.

All purchases, totalling to SDR 3900 million, were made through April, 1984. The authorities informed the IMF to cancel the arrangement, because India's external accounts had improved significantly. According to an IMF publication, "In assessing the performance of 1981/82-1983/84 programme, account must be taken of the external environment, which was less favourable, and severe drought of 1982/83. Despite these adverse developments, the programme achieved a success".

The targets established in the programme have been given in Table 9.2.

Though inflation rate could not be lowered, it was brought almost under control and average growth was 5.9 percent during 1981/82-1983/84. Balance of payments position improved significantly during the programme period. Production of food grains touched a record level in 1981/82 and improved again in 1983/84. After strong growth in 1981/82, the industrial production

Table 9.2: India: The 1981/82-1983/84 Economic Programme Targets

Variable	Target	Year/Period	Actual
Real GDP Growth	5.2 %	1981/82-1983/84	5.9 %
Inflation	Decline	1981/82-1983/84	No Decline
Current Account Deficit	2.2 % of GDP	1983/84	1 % of GDP
Bal. of Payments Deficit	SDR 2.0 billion	1983/84	SDR 1.0 billion
Investment	26.5 % of GDP	1983/84	20.7 % of GDP
Gross Domestic Savings	24.5 % of GDP	1983/84	19.0 % of GDP
Public Savings	5 % of GDP	1983/84	5.6 % of GDP
Budget Deficit	6-7 % of GDP	1981/82-1983/84	6 % of GDP
Domestic Credit Expansion	19.4 %	1981/82-1983/84	19.8 %
Bank Credit to Govt.	16 %	1981/82-1983/84	19.6 %
Narrow Money	11 %	1981/82-1983/84	14.6 %
Broad Money	15 %	1981/82-1983/84	17.1 %
Medium Term Loan	SDR 1.4 billion	1981/82	Below Target

had been subdued not only because of weak demand, both domestic and foreign, but also because of production difficulties in several important industries.

The monetary targets established in the programme had been observed and overall budget deficit remained within originally envisaged limit. Monetary and fiscal policies were adapted according to the changing circumstances, in particular following the drought related slowdown in growth, and policies to maintain the momentum of adjustment were strengthened.

Plan expenditure rose significantly during the programme period and the investment, in real term, was also higher as compared to earlier plans. Major success was in the area of public savings, which rose from 3.6 percent of GDP in 1980/81 to 5.6 percent in 1983/84. The saving performance of the states fell short of the programme targets because of the pressure on state budgets from increased wage and material costs and limited progress in raising additional resources in the area of electric power generation, irrigation and road transportation where abundant opportunities existed.

The complex network of industrial regulations was streamlined and liberalized. Free access to foreign technology was provided and foreign collaboration arrangements had expanded rapidly. Price reforms were also adopted. Controls on steel prices were lifted and prices for 30 percent of domestic production were determined on the free market.

The import regime was considerably liberalized during 1981/82-1983/84. The strategy aimed at modernization of industry, technology up gradation, efficiency improvement and expanding export base.

The following conclusions have been drawn regarding the 1981/82-1983/84 economic programme:

- Indian economy had poor macroeconomic performance in 1981/82, while a satisfactory performance during 1982/82-1983/84.

- Indian economy showed better macroeconomic performance as compared to the 'control group' during 1981/82-1982/83, while poor performance in 1983/84.
- Real GDP growth, current account deficit and overall balance of payments targets were met, while inflation rate, domestic savings and investment targets could not be achieved.
- In sum, the economy showed satisfactory performance during the programme period (Tables 9.3, 9.4, 9.5 and 9.6).

During the second half of the 1980s, a combination of strong domestic demand and steps to liberalize the economy contributed to an increase in economic growth to about 6 percent a year. At the same time, authorities started the process of shifting to a more outward orientation of the economy by directly encouraging exports and by increasing the flexibility of exchange rate, resulting in unprecedented growth in exports. At the same time, however, a large fiscal deficit contributed to increasing inflation and deterioration in India's external position.

In August 1990, the crisis in the Middle East had severe and wide spread effects on the economy. Revenue losses and expenditure related to the crisis had weakened India's budgetary position, international reserves had fallen, and higher energy prices led to a slow down of economic activity.

The government had responded to these events by passing through world oil price increases with a view to reducing the growth of oil consumption. To offset the effect of the Middle East situation on budget, the government increased direct and indirect taxes and cut expenditure. Monetary policy was kept tight and imports by government agencies were reduced.

The government committed to continue the adjustment process in fiscal years: 1991/92, 1992/93.

1991/92-1992/93 Adjustment Programme

The IMF approved the use of financial resources by the government of India for SDR 551.9 million, under first credit tranche stand-by arrangement for three months on January 8, 1991. The government announced to sharply reduce the fiscal

Table 9.3: India: Programme Effects: Before-after Approach

Variable		Programme years					The difference between means method	
		1982	1983	1984	1992	1993	Effect	t-value
CN/GDP	Pre	82.6	80.8	80.5	79.6	79.6	+	1.383
	Pro	80.8	80.5	81.0	79.6	78.2		
INV/GDP	Pre	20.9	25.1	22.9	21.8	20.8	-	0.134
	Pro	25.1	22.9	20.7	20.8	21.2		
DS/GDP	Pre	17.4	19.2	19.5	20.4	20.4	+	1.383
	Pro	19.2	19.5	19.0	20.4	21.8		
X/M	Pre	57.8	53.8	63.6	76.0	85.8	+	1.378
	Pro	53.8	63.6	65.1	85.8	87.3		
CA/GDP	Pre	-1.0	-1.5	-1.3	-3.3	-1.6	+	0.927
	Pro	-1.5	-1.3	-1.0	-1.6	-1.6		
OB/GDP	Pre	-1.0	-1.2	-0.9	-2.1	0.0	+	1.529
	Pro	-1.2	-0.9	-0.4	0.0	0.3		
INFR	Pre	11.4	13.1	7.9	9.0	13.9	-	0.095
	Pro	13.1	7.9	11.9	13.9	9.5		
RGDP Gr	Pre	6.5	6.5	3.8	5.5	1.1	+	0.012
	Pro	6.5	3.8	7.4	1.1	4.7		
FOREX Gr	Pre	-10.2	-37.7	-6.0	-61.2	197	+	0.446
	Pro	-37.7	-6.0	22.0	197	52.5		
Memorandum Items								
X/GDP	Pre	5.0	4.5	5.0	6.1	6.7	Pre<Pro	0.405
	Pro	4.5	5.0	4.5	6.7	7.1		
M/GDP	Pre	8.6	8.4	7.8	8.0	7.8	Pre>Pro	1.561
	Pro	8.4	7.8	6.8	7.8	8.1		

Notes: (1) + sign indicates better performance, - sign indicates poor performance and 0 indicates performance.

Table 9.4: India: Programme Effects: Before-after Approach

Total number program years method

Variable	Programme years					Performance (no. of years)		
	1982	1983	1984	1992	1993	Better	Poor	Same
CN/GDP	+	+	-	0	+	3	1	1
INV/GDP	+	-	-	-	+	2	3	0
DS/GDP	+	+	-	0	+	3	1	1
X/M	-	+	+	+	+	4	1	0
CA/GDP	-	+	+	+	0	3	1	1
OB/GDP	-	+	+	+	+	4	1	0
RGDP Gr	0	-	+	-	+	2	2	1
INFR	-	+	-	-	+	2	3	0
FOREX Gr	-	+	+	+	-	3	2	0
No of variables with better performance	3	7	5	4	7	26 (57.8)		
No of variables with poor performance	5	2	4	3	1		15 (33.3)	
No of variables with same performance	1	0	0	2	1			4 (8.9)

Notes (1) + sign indicates better performance, - sign indicates poor performance and 0 indicates same performance. (2) Figures in parenthesis are percentages.

Table 9.5: India: Programme Effects: With-without Approach

Variable		Programme years					The difference between means method	
		1982	1983	1984	1992	1993	Effect	t-value
Δ CN/GDP	IN	-1.8	-0.3	0.5	0.0	-1.4	+	2.503*
	NPC	1.0	2.7	-0.3	1.3	0.9		
ΔINV/GDP	IN	4.2	-2.2	-2.2	-1.0	0.4	+	0.324
	NPC	0.6	-0.4	-2.3	0.0	-0.2		
ΔDS/GDP	IN	1.8	0.3	-0.5	0.0	1.4	+	2.503*
	NPC	-1.0	-2.7	0.3	-1.3	-0.9		
ΔX/M	IN	-4.0	9.8	1.5	9.8	1.5	+	1.669
	NPC	-4.7	0.7	4.3	0.0	-1.9		
ΔCA/GDP	IN	-0.5	0.2	0.3	1.7	0.0	+	2.018
	NPC	-2.6	-0.4	0.4	0.0	-0.1		
ΔOB/GDP	IN	-0.2	0.3	0.5	2.1	0.3	+	3.294*
	NPC	-0.4	-2.1	-1.2	0.2	-0.3		
ΔINFR	IN	1.7	-5.2	4.0	4.9	-4.4	+	0.382
	NPC	1.8	0.1	3.8	0.6	-2.3		
ΔRGDP Gr	IN	0.0	-2.7	3.6	-4.4	3.6	+	0.672
	NPC	-1.0	-4.3	-0.3	0.0	0.9		
Memorandum Items								
ΔX/GDP	IN	-0.5	0.5	-0.5	0.6	0.4	IN>	4.936*
	NPC	-2.3	-2.4	-1.8	-0.6	-0.9	NPC	
ΔM/GDP	IN	-0.2	-0.6	-1.0	-0.2	0.3	IN>	2.746*
	NPC	-0.9	-2.5	-3.2	-0.1	-0.7	NPC	

Notes: (1) IN: INDIA and NPC: Non Programme Countries. (2) + sign indicates better performance, - sign indicates poor performance and 0 indicates same performance. (3) * sign indicates significant at 5% level of significance.

Table 9.6: India: Programme Effects: With-without Approach

Total number program years method

Variable	Programme years					Performance (no. of years)		
	1982	1983	1984	1992	1993	Better	Poor	Same
ΔCN/GDP	+	+	-	+	+	4	1	0
ΔINV/GDP	+	-	+	-	+	3	2	0
ΔDS/GDP	+	+	-	+	+	4	1	0
ΔX/M	+	+	-	+	+	4	1	0
ΔCA/GDP	+	+	-	+	+	4	1	0
ΔOB/GDP	+	+	+	+	+	5	0	0
ΔRGDP Gr	+	+	+	-	+	4	1	0
ΔINFR	+	+	-	-	+	3	2	0
No of variables with better performance	8	7	3	5	8	31 (77.5)		
No of variables with poor performance	0	1	5	3	0		9 (22.5)	
No of variables with same performance	0	0	0	0	0			0 (0.0)

Notes (1) + sign indicates better performance, (-) sign indicates poor performance and (0) indicates same performance. (2)Figures in parenthesis are percentages.

deficit through strict expenditure control and revenue raising measures. It also intended to implement a wide range of policies to increase the efficiency and competitiveness of Indian economy. It committed to pay special attention to improve the financial position and efficiency of public enterprises.

On October 31, 1991, the IMF approved a stand-by credit for government of India authorizing drawings up to the equivalent of SDR 1656 million in support of the economic and financial programme for 1991/92-1992/93.

The programme sought an easing of external payments position and rebuilding of international reserves, economic growth of 3-3.5 percent in 1991/92 followed by gradual recovery in 1992/93 and a reduction in inflation rate to no more than 6 percent by the end of 1992/93. A large, sustained reduction in the overall public sector deficit was central to the authorities' strategy, both to reduce pressure on the external account and to release resources to private sector. The 1991/92 budget included, on the revenue side, a number of tax measures, a first step in selling shares in public enterprises, an increase in price of petroleum products, and measures to improve tax compliance. On the expenditure side, the budget relied on sharp cut in export subsidies, higher fertilizer prices, and the elimination of sugar subsidy; a tight constraint on defence expenditure and other outlays and lower transfers to public sector enterprises. The programme committed to continue to reduce the deficit, while initiating a major tax reform. In monetary field, the programme provided for a continuation of monetary tightness adopted in the course of 1991/92 in response to external liquidity crisis and the build up in inflationary pressure. External sector policies were designed to exchange rate stability, a continuation of reforms to integrate Indian economy more closely into the world economy, and the temporary maintenance of measures to hold down imports. The detail of targets established in the programme has been given in Table 9.7.

Table 9.7: India: The 1991/92-1992/93 Economic Programme Targets

Variable	1991/92		1992/93	
	Target	Actual	Target	Actual
Real GDP Growth (%)	3.5	1.1	4.0	4.7
Inflation (%)	9.0	13.9	6.0	9.5
Current Account Deficit (% of GDP)	2.7	1.6	2.6	1.6
Budget Deficit (% of GDP)	6.5	5.4	5.0	5.3
Public Sector Deficit (% of GDP)	10.0	10.0	8.5	8.5
Foreign Exchange Reserves (US $ Bn)	2.2	3.6	3.2	5.5
Broad Money Growth (%)	13.0	18.3	12.0	16.4
Reserve Money Growth	15.6	13.3	12.0	8.3
External Borrowings (US $ Mn)	----	----	3500	1500

Indian economic programme, 1991/92-1992/93 included structural reforms aimed at reducing government intervention, enhancing domestic competition and accelerating the country's integration into world economy. The authorities announced three major initiatives in July 1991, namely, the virtual abolition of the complex system of industrial licensing, measures to enhance competition between public sector and private sector and a significant liberalization of foreign investment. In the financial sector, the three priority areas for action under the programme were to achieve a more market oriented allocation of credit, strengthening the capital base of a number of banks, and improve supervision procedures; and build up capital markets, including term lending institutions.

Balance of payments position improved during the programme period and particularly after the implementation of programme. The terms of trade improved during 1991/92-1992/93. Inflation rate was brought largely under control, though the established targets were not met. Exports as well as imports improved after 1991. The foreign exchange level exceeded the targets established in the programme. Domestic savings as percentage of GDP showed some improvement during the programme years, while a little disappointment was shown by investment as percentage of GDP. The dependency of the economy was enhanced during the programme years. The real GDP growth- though it could not achieve 1991/92 target of the programme- got momentum1992 onward.

The monetary targets established under the programme had been observed. The five targets, which the government fulfilled, pertained to net domestic assets of R.B.I., net R.B.I. credit to central government, the fiscal deficit, external debt levels and net official exchange reserves.

The key structural reforms were made during the program period. These included: deregulation of industry, promotion of increased competition by the opening of the areas previously reserved for public sector and policies to attract foreign investment, deregulation of foreign trade, tax system reform

(Chelliah Committee). The role of market forces increased in price determination.

The following conclusions have been drawn regarding the macroeconomic performance of the Indian economy during 1991/92-1992/93:

- Indian economy showed satisfactory performance during 1991/92-1992/93.
- Indian economy performed better than the 'control group'.
- Targets for real GDP growth and external current account deficit were achieved. Target established for inflation rate was not met.

Macroeconomic Performance under Different Approaches

The macroeconomic performance of the Indian economy – according to different approaches- during programme years has been described below:

Before-After Approach: The following conclusions have been drawn regarding the macroeconomic performance of the Indian economy during the programme years.

- According to the total number of programme years method, seven variables viz., consumption as percentage of GDP, domestic savings as percentage of GDP, exports as percentage of imports, current account balance as percentage of GDP, overall balance of payments as percentage of GDP, real output growth rate and foreign exchange reserves growth rate showed better performance of the Indian economy during the programme years. While, two variables- inflation rate and investment as percentage of GDP revealed poor performance during programme years. (Table 9.4)
- According to the difference between means method, seven variables, namely: consumption as percentage of GDP, domestic savings as percentage of GDP, exports as percentage of imports, current accounts as percentage of GDP, overall balance of payments as percentage of GDP, foreign exchange reserves growth rate and real output growth rate showed better performance of the Indian economy during the

programme years. Only two variables viz., investment as percentage of GDP and inflation rate revealed poor performance. (Table 9.3)

- The dependency of the Indian economy increased during the programme years, though the results were not statistically significant. (Table 9.3)

With-Without Approach: The following conclusions have been drawn in context of macroeconomic performance of the Indian economy during the programme years.

- When the total number of programme years method was employed, the Indian economy showed better performance during the programme years in comparison of the 'control group' in the case all the variables: consumption as percentage of GDP, investment as percentage of GDP, domestic savings as percentage of GDP, exports as percentage of imports, current account balance as percentage of GDP, overall balance of payments as percentage of GDP, inflation rate and real GDP growth rate. (Table 9.6)
- According to the difference between means method too, the Indian economy showed better performance as compared to the 'control group' in the case of all the variables i.e. consumption as percentage of GDP, investment as percentage of GDP, domestic savings as percentage of GDP, exports as percentage of GDP, current account balance as percentage of GDP, overall balance of payments as percentage of GDP, inflation rate and real output growth rate. The results were statistically significant at 5 percent level of significance in the case of consumption as percentage of GDP, domestic savings as percentage of GDP and overall balance of payments as percentage of GDP. (Table 9.5)
- The dependency of the Indian economy increased more than that of the 'control group' during the programme years. The results were statistically significant at 5 percent level of significance. (Table 9.5)

Generalized Evaluation Approach: The results obtained by the generalized evaluation approach contradicted the results of another two approaches, before- after and with- without approaches. The reason was obvious, the continuous improvement in the economic position of the economy even after the implementation of the Fund supported programmes. Though the Indian economy showed good performance during the programme years, the improvement was even more during non programme years- particularly 1993 onward (Table 9.3 and Appendix 9A). For example, when a regression equation was fitted for the period 1975- 2002 the programme dummy variable showed the negative effect of the Fund supported programmes on real GDP growth rate, but the programme dummy variable showed positive effect on real GDP growth rate when the period was 1975- 1993 (Tables 9.8 and 9.9). Because of the very good performance from 1993 onward, the generalized evaluation approach undermined the favourable effects of the Fund supported programmes on most of the macroeconomic variables. So, in inferring the conclusions regarding the effects of the Fund supported programmes, the results of the generalized evaluation approach have not been given much weight.

Overall Macroeconomic Performance

The following important points have been inferred regarding the overall macroeconomic performance of the Indian economy under the Fund supported programmes:

- Consumption as percentage of GDP revealed positive effects the Fund supported programmes on the Indian economy. When the performance was compared with that of the 'control group', it was better and statistically significant at 5 percent level of significance.
- Investment as percentage of GDP, though it did not reveal improvement as per before-after approach, showed better performance of the economy in comparison of the 'control group'.
- Domestic savings as percentage of GDP showed improvement during the programme years. When the performance was

Table 9.8: India: Programme Effects: Generalized Evaluation (1975-2002)

Z	C	GDP	INV	Z_{-1}	FD/GDP	DCR	T	D	R^2	F
GDP	-71.658 (0.577)		4.531 (94.30)*					165.631 (0.805)	0.99	4718.3
INV	21.093 (0.775)	0.220 (94.31)*						-39.424 (0.872)	0.99	4738.8
DS	-36.297 (1.254)	0.230 (81.88)*						-59.046 (1.228)	0.99	4597.5
X/M	79.722 (2.870)*			0.379 (1.851)*	1.839 (1.395)	-1.204 (1.928)*	-0.097 (0.432)	-1.689 (0.362)	0.58	6.1
CA/GDP	2.216 (1.6440			0.404 (1.842)*	0.390 (2.480)*	-0.011 (0.212)	-0.013 (0.516)	-0.329 (0.670)	0.70	10.2
OB/GDP	3.585 (2.016)*			0.061 (0.226)	0.401 (2.594)*	-0.047 (0.659)	0.027 (1.021)	-1.178 (1.658)	0.52	4.7
RGDP Gr	8.791 (2.073)*			-0.307 (1.611)	-0.111 (0.287)	-0.153 (0.766)	0.011 (0.138)	-0.768 (0.523)	0.29	2.6
INFR	2.530 (0.415)			0.081 (0.587)	-0.916 (1.674)	-0.183 (0.648)	0.079 (0.714)	4.804 (2.285)*	0.30	2.8
Memorandum item: Generalized evaluation (1975-1990)										
RGDP Gr	12.05 (1.962)*			-0.380 (1.681)*	-1.199 (1.354)	-0.556 (1.463)	-0.362 (1.275)	1.428 (0.663)	0.28	1..9

Note: (1) Figures in parenthesis are t-values. (2) *sign indicates significant at 5% level of significance.

Table 9.9: India: Programme Effects (summary)

Variable	Before-After Approach		With-Without Approach		Generalized Evaluation
	Difference between means method	Total number of programme years	Difference between means method	Total number of programme years	
CN/ GDP	+	+	+*	+	N A
INV/GDP	-	-	+	+	N A
DS/GDP	+	+	+*	+	N A
X/M	+	+	+	+	-
CA/GDP	+	+	+	+	-
OB/GDP	+	+	+*	+	-
RGDP Gr	+	0	+	+	-
INFR	-	-	+	+	-
FOREX Gr	+	+	N A	N A	N A
'GDP	N A	N A	N A	N A	+
INV	N A	N A	N A	N A	-
DS	N A	N A	N A	N A	-
Total	7	6	8	8	1
Better	2	2	0	0	7
Poor	0	1	0	0	0
Same					

Note: (1) + sign indicates better performance,-sign indicates poor performance and 0 sign indicates same performance. (2) * sign indicates significance at 5% level of significance.

compared with that of the 'control group', it was better and statistically significant at 5 percent level of significance.

- Trade account represented by exports as percentage of imports, showed clear and continuous improvement over the program years. When the performance of the economy was compared with that of the 'control group', it was better and statistically significant at 10 percent level of significance.
- The current account as percentage of GDP showed the improvement during the programme years, though it could not reveal the surplus. When the performance of the economy was compared with that of the 'control group', it was better and statistically significant at 10 percent level of significance.
- The overall balance of payments account showed substantial improvement during the programme years. The results were statistically significant at 5 percent level of significance.
- Foreign exchange reserves growth rate showed positive performance during the programme years.
- The real GDP growth rate showed improvement during the programme years. When the comparison was made with the 'control group', the improvement got strengthened.
- The performance of inflation rate was also satisfactory. Though it could not be lowered, it was under control.
- Except inflation rate, domestic savings and investment, all other targets were met.
- The dependency of the Indian economy increased under the Fund supported programmes. When the comparison was made with 'control group', the enhancement in dependency of the Indian economy got strengthened and was statistically significant at 5 percent level of significance.
- As far as the performance of policy instruments is concerned, the success was met. The overall budget deficit could brought down to meet the established targets.
- The domestic credit expansion growth was brought down to an extent during the programme years. The established targets were nearly met in 1981/82- 1983/84 economic programme.

- The money supply growth was also brought down, though it could not met the established targets.
- The interest rates were increased during the programme years as per the general recommendation of the IMF.
- Another intermediate instrument, which was implemented according the Fund formulae, was the depreciation of domestic currency. The rupee substantially depreciated during the programme years.
- All the five programme years showed good improvement in macroeconomic position of the Indian economy.
- In sum, the performance of the Indian economy can be categorized as a good one (Table 9.10).

Conclusions

Both the programmes implemented by the Indian authorities showed good macroeconomic performance. Domestic savings as percentage of GDP, investment as percentage of GDP and consumption as percentage of GDP showed positive performances during the programmes years.

The external sector also revealed good performance. Trade account improved during programme years. The current account deficits could be lowered during the programme years. In the case of overall balance of payments, good success was met.

The real output growth rate also revealed favourable effect during programme years. Inflation rate could not show the desired results, though it remained under control. The dependency of the Indian economy increased during the programme years. The results were statistically significant.

Finally, the macroeconomic performance of the Indian economy during the Fund supported programme was good.

Table 9.10: India: Policy Variables, (1975-2002)

Year	Exchange rate (Rs per U.S. $)	Interest rate (%)	Money supply (% change)	Domestic credit (% change)	Budget deficit [1] (as % of GDP)
1975	8.74	---	14.0	16.5	-3.2
1976	8.88	---	24.5	17.9	-4.1
1977	8.21	---	19.2	14.9	-4.3
1978	8.19	13.5	21.1	15.7	-3.9
1979	7.91	14.5	17.7	20.3	-4.9
1980	7.93	16.5	15.9	22.9	-5.5
1981	9.10	16.5	17.4	21.9	-6.5
1982	9.63	16.5	17.2	21.4	-5.5
1983	10.50	16.5	16.9	16.2	-6.0
1984	12.45	16.5	18.0	20.8	-6.4
1985	12.17	16.5	16.9	17.4	-7.6
1986	13.12	16.5	17.9	18.6	-8.5
1987	12.88	16.5	16.3	15.0	-9.3
1988	14.95	16.5	18.3	18.0	-8.4
1989	17.04	16.5	15.7	16.4	-8.1
1990	18.07	16.5	15.1	15.7	-8.2
1991	25.83	17.9	18.3	14.2	-7.6
1992	26.20	18.9	16.8	12.5	-5.4
1993	31.38	16.3	16.9	13.3	-5.3
1994	31.38	14.8	20.3	12.6	-7.0
1995	35.18	15.5	10.9	9.3	-5.6
1996	35.93	16.0	18.7	19.7	-5.0
1997	39.28	13.8	17.6	11.9	-4.9
1998	42.48	13.5	18.1	15.7	-4.8

Contd...

1999	43.49	12.5	17.2	17.8	-5.2
2000	46.75	12.3	15.2	15.9	-5.4
2001	48.18	12.1	14.2	11.7	-5.2
2002	48.03	11.9	16.7	15.9	---

Note: 1. Fiscal year ending in the year stated.

Sources: Compiled and computed form *IMF-International Financial Statistics*, various issues, and *UN-National Accounts Statistics, Main Aggregates and detailed Tables*, various issues.

Appendix 9A: India: Statistics on Macroeconomic Variables (1975-2002)

Year	CN/ GDP[1]	INV/ GDP[1]	DS/ GDP[1]	X/M	CA/ GDP	OB/ GDP	INFR (%)	RGDP Gr	FOREX Gr (%)	X/ GDP	M/ GDP
1975	85.7	19.8	14.3	68.2	-0.2	0.4	5.7	9.7	14.6	4.6	6.8
1976	82.7	20.8	17.3	98.0	1.7	2.3	-7.6	1.5	205.8	5.9	6.0
1977	80.5	20.9	19.5	96.0	1.9	1.9	8.3	8.2	82.4	5.8	6.0
1978	81.1	19.8	18.9	84.8	0.5	1.5	2.5	6.6	28.8	5.2	6.2
1979	81.5	22.1	18.5	79.4	0.0	0.6	6.3	-4.8	11.4	5.5	7.0
1980	81.2	22.9	18.8	57.8	-1.0	-1.0	11.4	6.5	-10.2	5.0	8.6
1981	82.6	20.9	17.4	53.8	-1.5	-1.2	13.1	6.5	-37.7	4.5	8.4
1982	80.8	25.1	19.2	63.6	-1.3	-0.9	7.9	3.8	-6.0	5.0	7.8
1983	80.5	22.9	19.5	65.1	-1.0	-0.4	11.9	7.4	22.0	4.5	6.8
1984	81.0	20.7	19.0	69.0	-1.2	0.5	8.3	3.7	16.6	4.9	7.1
1985	80.6	21.1	19.4	57.3	-2.0	-0.2	5.6	5.5	10.2	4.3	7.5
1986	78.6	24.0	21.4	60.9	-2.0	-0.2	8.7	4.5	-1.9	4.1	6.7
1987	79.6	23.0	20.4	67.8	-2.0	0.1	8.8	4.9	2.9	4.4	6.5
1988	79.5	22.7	20.5	69.6	-2.5	0.0	9.4	9.7	-26.0	4.7	6.7
1989	78.2	23.9	21.8	77.2	-2.5	0.1	6.2	6.2	-25.2	5.7	7.4
1990	76.7	23.5	23.3	76.0	-3.3	-2.1	9.0	5.5	-61.2	6.1	8.0
1991	79.6	21.8	20.4	85.8	-1.6	0.0	13.9	1.1	197.0	6.7	7.8
1992	79.6	20.8	20.4	87.3	-1.6	0.3	9.5	4.7	52.5	7.1	8.1
1993	78.2	21.2	21.8	91.3	-0.7	1.5	10.0	5.0	79.5	8.2	9.0
1994	78.2	21.4	21.8	86.0	-0.5	3.0	12.4	7.3	97.6	7.6	8.8
1995	76.2	21.9	23.8	82.3	-1.5	-0.2	12.3	7.7	-9.6	8.4	10.2
1996	75.0	24.6	25.0	77.0	-1.5	0.9	10.4	7.0	13.0	8.5	11.0
1997	76.7	23.0	23.3	78.0	-0.7	1.2	11.4	4.6	23.2	8.4	10.7

Contd...

1998	75.8	22.6	24.2	76.0	-1.6	0.7	6.2	6.4	10.8	7.8	10.3
1999	76.9	21.2	23.1	80.9	-0.7	1.4	4.1	7.2	18.6	8.0	9.8
2000	77.5	21.2	22.5	75.7	-0.6	1.3	4.4	3.9	16.4	10.4	13.6
2001	77.7	22.0	22.3	77.9	0.4	2.7	3.2	5.1	21.4	10.3	13.2
2002	77.9	21.9	22.1	80.9	0.9	3.2	3.3	4.6	48.0	10.2	12.5

Note: 1.Fiscal year ending in the stated year.

Sources: Compiled and computed form *IMF-International Financial Statistics*, various issues, and *UN-National Accounts Statistics, Main Aggregates and detailed Tables*, various issues.

10

Bangladesh: Satisfactory Turn Around

Formerly East Pakistan, Bangladesh became independent in 1971. It is a small country with few natural resources, but a large population. Poverty is wide spread, low per capita income, high infant mortality, short life expectancy, and basic health care rudimentary. The country is highly vulnerable to droughts, floods, and cyclones.

Agriculture is the mainstay of Bangladesh's economy, accounting for about one half of gross domestic product. Much of the small industrial sector is agro based and the exports base is narrow. Workers' remittances-mainly from Middle East- are an important component of foreign exchange earnings. The balance of payments was characterized by large scale current account deficit, which were financed mainly foreign aid on highly liberal terms. Domestic savings were low. Import taxes are main source of budgetary revenue.

During 1974-75, the dominant factors affecting the economy of Bangladesh were severe floods, which caused extensive damage to the rice and jute crops. Rice production fell by about 3 percent from 1973/74 level. The need to purchase additional food grains abroad and low level of reserves led to a severe curtailment of other imports. Sluggish growth in total output and shortage of rice and other commodities resulted in a sharp increase in prices, particularly during the second half of 1974.

In such conditions, the Bangladesh authorities planned to implement the Fund supported programmes. The detail of the Fund supported programmes implemented by Bangladesh has been given in table 1. The latest arrangement was approved by the Fund on June 20, 2003 for three years under Poverty Reduction and Growth Facility.

1975/76 Adjustment programme

Bangladesh authorities implemented an economic adjustment programme for 1975/76, supported by a stand-by arrangement with the Fund. The programme aimed to stabilize the economy and place it on the path of sound and steady development. The programme projected a substantial rise in imports other than food grains, and foresaw an increase in the growth rate of the economy and a reduction in the rate of inflation.

The macroeconomic performance of the economy under the 1975/76 programme has been summarized below:

- Bangladesh economy showed good performance in 1975/76.
- Bangladesh economy performed better than the 'control group' in 1975/76.

Progress in agriculture development had been slow, with food grain production lagged behind the population increase throughout the 1970s, resulting in continued large imports of food. Over the same period, the production of jute and jute products, which accounted for two third of the country's exports, had not shown an upward trend, and other exports had not developed rapidly. Inflation, which began to re-emerge in mid 1976, had offset much of the beneficial effect of exchange rate changes. The balance of payments position had been under strain, and import shortages had hampered industrial activity, contributing to sluggish private investment (Table 10.1).

1979/80 Adjustment Programme

On July 31, 1979, the Fund approved for Bangladesh a stand-by arrangement authorizing purchases of currencies up to the equivalent to SDR 850 million in support of a financial programme for 1979/80 to stabilize the economy and to place it on the path of sound and steady development. The programme aimed strengthening the financial position of public sector, encouraging the improved allocation of resources, ensuring an environment needed for strengthening the balance of payments, and to restore domestic financial and price stability.

Table 10.1: Bangladesh: Lending Arrangements with IMF, 1975-2002

(Amount expressed in millions of SDRs)

Facility	Date of arrangement	Date of expiration	Amount approved	Balance not drawn	Programme years[1]	Remarks
SBA	28.07.1975	27.07.1976	62.5	0	1976	
SBA	31.07.1979	30.07.1980	85.0	0	1980	
EA	11.12.1980	10.12.1983	800.0	580.0	1981,1982	Cancelled in June 1982
SBA	28.03.1983	31.08.1983	68.4	0	1983	
SBA	02.12.1985	30.06.1987	180.0	0	1986	
SAF	06.02.1987	05.02.1990	135.1	0	1987,1988,1989	
PRGF	10.08.1990	13.09.1993	345.0	15.0	1991,1992,1993	

Note: 1.Fiscal years ending in the year stated.

Source: IMF Survey, various issues.

The following conclusions have been drawn regarding the 1979/80 economic programme:

- Bangladesh economy showed poor macroeconomic performance in 1979/80.
- The 'control group' had better performance than the Bangladesh economy in 1979/80.
- A severe drought and deterioration of the international economic environment were responsible for weak economic performance during the programme year.

1980/81- 1981/82 Adjustment Programme

In December 1980, the Fund approved an extended arrangement for the government of Bangladesh, for SDR 800 million in support of the economic programme for 1980/81-1982/83. The government's economic programme was formulated in within a broader framework of a five year plan for 1980/81-1984/85. The programme was directed to increase the level of aggregate production as quickly as possible and creating employment. Particular emphasis was placed on mobilizing public sector resources, encouraging private sector savings and investment, and strengthening the underlying external position. The overall aim of financial policy was to achieve an increase in domestic savings to finance increased investment, while maintaining a stable financial environment. Initiatives were being taken to encourage the development of non traditional exports and to increase the repatriation of remittances from workers abroad. The programme could be implemented only for 1980/81- 1981/82, because it was cancelled in June 1982.

The following conclusions have been drawn in context of the economic programme:

- Bangladesh economy showed better macroeconomic performance during 1980/81- 1981/82.
- Bangladesh economy performed somewhat better than the 'control group' during 1980/81- 1981/82 (Tables 10.2, 10.3, 10.4 and 10.5).

Table 10.2: Bangladesh: Programme Effects: Before-after Approach

The difference between means method

Variable		Programme years												Effect	t-value
		1976	1980	1981	1982	1983	1986	1987	1988	1989	1991	1992	1993		
CN/	Pre	101	93.1	97.9	96.8	99.6	97.7	97.0	96.6	97.7	98.0	95.8	86.1	+	0.346
GDP	Pro	99.7	97.9	96.8	99.6	99.7	97.0	96.6	97.7	98.1	95.8	86.1	87.7		
INV/	Pre	5.5	15.2	15.1	16.0	15.0	12.8	12.3	12.6	11.9	11.0	11.5	17.2	+	1.081
GDP	Pro	8.8	15.1	16.0	15.0	13.6	12.3	12.6	11.9	11.7	11.5	17.2	17.9		
DS/	Pre	-0.6	6.9	2.1	3.2	0.4	2.3	3.0	3.4	2.3	2.0	4.2	13.9	+	0.346
GDP	Pro	0.3	2.1	3.2	0.4	0.3	3.0	3.4	2.3	1.9	4.2	13.9	12.3		
X/M	Pre	24.8	34.4	30.5	29.3	33.3	36.0	35.7	39.8	42.4	46.4	54.6	62.5	+	1.769
	Pro	42.1	30.5	29.3	33.3	33.4	35.7	39.8	42.4	35.8	54.6	62.5	69.5		
CA/	Pre	-5.8	-0.6	-5.5	-7.9	-4.2	-3.2	-4.1	-1.4	-1.5	-1.9	0.3	0.6	+	0.284
GDP	Pro	-4.0	-5.5	-7.9	-4.2	-0.4	-4.1	-1.4	-1.5	-5.4	0.3	0.6	1.1		
OB/	Pre	-0.3	0.3	-2.5	-1.7	-0.8	-0.6	0.8	1.1	0.7	0.9	2.0	2.1	+	0.681
GDP	Pro	0.7	-2.5	-1.7	-0.8	3.0	0.8	1.1	0.7	-1.5	2.0	2.1	2.1		
INFR	Pre	21.9	14.7	13.4	16.2	12.5	10.7	11.0	9.5	9.3	8.1	6.4	3.6	+	1.565
	Pro	2.3	13.4	16.2	12.5	9.4	11.0	9.5	9.3	10.0	6.4	3.6	3.0		
RGDP	Pre	3.4	4.6	1.3	6.8	0.8	3.7	4.7	4.0	2.9	6.6	3.2	4.2	+	0.336
Gr	Pro	12.3	1.3	6.8	0.8	3.6	4.7	4.0	2.9	2.5	3.2	4.2	4.6		
FOREX	Pre	-5.8	18.8	-20.0	-53.8	24.5	-18.7	24.3	104	26.9	28.6	100	47.8	+	0.904
Gr	Pro	108	-20.0	-53.8	24.5	181	24.3	104	26.9	-51.2	100	47.8	33.8		
Memorandum Items															
X/	Pre	3.1	7.0	6.2	6.1	6.4	6.9	5.8	6.1	7.0	7.3 7.8	7.8	7.0	Pre<Pro	0.418
GDP	Pro	5.7	6.2	6.1	6.4	6.2	5.8	6.1	7.0	6.1		7.0	7.8		
M/	Pre	12.6	20.5	20.3	20.8	19.2	19.1	16.2	15.4	16.4	15.8	14.3	11.1	Pre>Pro	1.517
GDP	Pro	13.6	20.3	20.8	19.2	18.5	16.2	15.4	16.4	17.1	14.3	11.1	11.2		

Notes: (1) + sign indicates better performance, - sign indicates poor performance and 0 indicates performance.

Table 10.3: Bangladesh: Programme Effects: Before-after Approach

Total number program years method

Variable	Programme years												Performance (no. of years)		
	1976	1980	1981	1982	1983	1986	1987	1988	1989	1991	1992	1993	Better	Poor	Same
CN/GDP	+	-	+	-	-	+	+	-	-	+	+	-	6	6	0
INV/GDP	+	-	+	-	-	-	+	-	-	+	+	+	6	6	0
DS/GDP	+	-	+	-	-	+	+	-	-	+	+	-	6	6	0
X/M	+	-	-	+	+	-	+	+	-	+	+	+	8	4	0
CA/GDP	+	-	-	+	+	-	+	-	-	+	+	+	7	5	0
OB/GDP	+	-	+	+	+	+	+	-	-	+	+	0	8	3	1
RGDPGr	+	-	+	-	+	+	-	-	-	-	+	+	6	6	0
INFR	+	+	-	+	+	-	+	+	-	+	+	+	9	3	0
FOREX Gr	+	-	-	+	+	+	+	-	-	+	-	-	6	6	0
No of variables with better performance	9	1	5	5	6	5	8	2	0	8	8	5	62 (57.4)		
No of variables with poor performance	0	8	4	4	3	4	1	7	9	1	1	3		45 (41.7)	
No of variables with same performance	0	0	0	0	0	0	0	0	0	0	0	1			1 (0.9)

Notes (1) + sign indicates better performance, (-) sign indicates poor performance and (0) indicates same performance. (2) Figures in parenthesis are percentages.

Table 10.4: Bangladesh: Programme Effects: With-without Approach

The difference between means method

Variable		Programme years												Effect	t-value
		1976	1980	1981	1982	1983	1986	1987	1988	1989	1991	1992	1993		
ΔCN/	BN	-0.9	4.8	-1.1	2.8	0.1	-0.7	-0.4	1.1	0.4	-2.2	-9.7	1.6	+	0.831
GDP	NPC	-1.0	0.8	1.0	2.7	-0.3	0.5	-0.3	0.0	-0.6	1.3	0.9	0.1		
ΔINV/	BN	3.3	-0.1	0.9	-1.0	-1.4	-0.5	0.3	-0.7	-0.2	0.5	5.7	0.7	+	1.012
GDP	NPC	-0.1	0.7	0.6	-0.4	-2.3	-0.2	1.0	0.2	0.6	0.0	-0.2	0.4		
ΔDS/	BN	0.9	-4.8	1.1	-2.8	-0.1	0.7	0.4	-1.1	-0.4	2.2	9.7	-1.6	+	0.831
GDP	NPC	1.0	-0.8	-1.0	-2.7	0.3	-0.5	0.3	0.0	0.6	-1.3	-0.9	-0.1		
ΔX/M	BN	17.3	-3.9	-1.2	4.0	0.1	-0.3	4.1	2.6	-6.6	8.2	7.9	7.0	+	1.882*
	NPC	8.6	-11.3	-4.7	0.7	4.3	-6.2	-2.1	0.2	8.8	0.0	-1.9	-6.8		
ΔCA/	BN	1.8	-4.9	-2.4	3.7	3.8	-0.9	2.7	-0.1	-3.9	2.2	0.3	0.5	+	0.922
GDP	NPC	0.9	-2.3	-2.6	-0.4	0.4	0.0	-0.8	0.8	0.0	0.0	-0.1	-1.0		
ΔOB/	BN	1.0	-2.8	0.8	0.9	3.8	1.4	0.3	-0.4	-2.2	1.1	0.1	0.0	+	1.229
GDP	NPC	0.2	-1.6	-0.4	-2.1	-1.2	0.3	0.0	-0.5	0.5	0.2	-0.3	0.6		
ΔINFR	BN	-19.6	-1.3	2.8	-3.7	-3.1	0.3	-1.5	-0.2	0.7	-1.7	-2.8	-0.6	+	1.926*
	NPC	-6.0	1.3	1.8	0.1	3.8	-7.6	4.8	2.4	4.5	0.6	-2.3	0.0		
ΔRGD	BN	8.9	-3.3	5.5	-6.0	2.8	1.0	-0.7	-1.1	-0.4	-3.4	1.0	0.4	+	0.731
P Gr	NPC	2.1	1.7	-1.0	-4.3	-0.3	0.2	1.0	-2.5	-0.8	0.0	0.9	-1.1		
Memorandum Items															
ΔX/	BN	2.6	-0.8	-0.1	0.3	-0.2	-1.1	0.3	0.9	-0.9	0.5	-0.8	0.8	Pre>NPC	1.144
GDP	NPC	0.8	0.6	-2.3	-2.4	-1.8	-1.0	0.6	1.6	1.1	-0.6	-0.9	0.0		
ΔM/	BN	1.0	-0.2	0.5	-1.6	-0.7	-2.9	-0.8	1.0	0.7	-1.5	-3.2	0.1	Pre<NPC	0.813
GDP	NPC	-0.9	2.7	-0.9	-2.5	-3.2	-1.3	1.6	1.5	0.9	-0.1	-0.7	0.7		

Notes: (1) BN: Bangladesh and NPC: Non Programme Countries. (2) + sign indicates better performance, - sign indicates poor performance and 0 indicates same performance. (3) * sign indicates significant at 5% level of significance.

Table 10.5: Bangladesh: Programme Effects: With-without Approach

Total number program years method

Variable	Programme years												Performance (no. of years)		
	1976	1980	1981	1982	1983	1986	1987	1988	1989	1991	1992	1993	Better	Poor	Same
ΔCN/GDP	-	-	+	-	-	+	+	-	-	+	+	-	5	7	0
ΔINV/GDP	+	-	+	-	+	-	-	-	-	+	+	+	6	6	0
ΔDS/GDP	-	-	+	-	-	+	+	-	-	+	+	-	5	7	0
ΔX/M	+	+	+	+	-	+	+	+	-	+	+	+	10	2	0
ΔCA/GDP	+	-	+	+	+	-	+	-	-	+	+	+	8	4	0
ΔOB/GDP	· +	-	+	+	+	+	+	+	-	+	+	-	9	3	0
ΔRGDP Gr	+	-	+	-	+	+	-	+	+	-	+	+	8	4	0
ΔINFR	+	+	-	+	+	-	+	+	+	+	+	+	10	2	0
No of variables with better performance	6	2	7	4	5	5	6	4	2	7	8	5	61 (63.5)		
No of variables with poor performance	2	6	1	4	3	3	2	4	6	1	0	3		35 (36.5)	
No of variables with same performance	0	0	0	0	0	0	0	0	0	0	0	0			0 (0.0)

Notes (1) + sign indicates better performance, (-) sign indicates poor performance and (0) indicates same performance. (2) Figures in parenthesis are percentages.

1982/83 Adjustment programme

The Bangladesh authorities implemented an economic and financial programme for 1982/83 with support of a stand-by arrangement of SDR 68 million with the Fund. The main objective of the economic programme was to make progress toward achieving a sustainable balance of payments with reasonable growth and stability. The principal macroeconomic targets of the programme were to secure a rate of growth of about 3 percent, to reduce the external current account deficit to about 2 percent of GDP, and reduce the average rate of inflation, from 16 percent in 1981/82 to 12 percent in 1982/83. The main policy instruments were monetary restraint, exchange rate flexibility, and measures to increase the mobilization of domestic resources through administered price adjustments, reduction in budgetary subsidies and tax increases.

The following conclusions have been drawn regarding 1982/83 economic programme:

- Bangladesh economy showed better macroeconomic performance in 1982/83.
- Bangladesh economy performed better than the 'control group' in 1982/83.
- All targets established were met.

Bangladesh's economic performance weakened during 1984-85 following heavy floods that caused large losses to agriculture production and adversely affected the rest of the economy. The growth of real output declined, inflation accelerated, and the external current deficit widened. The government began to implement corrective measures consisting of restrictive monetary policies and a more flexible management of exchange rate.

The five years to 1984/85- the year before the country embarked on a comprehensive programme- were particularly difficult for Bangladesh's economy. With recurrent bad weather, worsening of terms of trade, and a stagnation in absorption, real gross domestic product growth averaged less than 4 percent a year, inflation averaged 12 percent a year, the external current account deficit was 9 percent of GDP on average, and gross official reserves covered less than two months of imports. In addition, the economy was beset with severe structural weaknesses, including a narrow export base, a low domestic savings rate, and an underdeveloped financial sector.

1985/86 Adjustment Programme

The Bangladesh authorities got an approval of a stand by arrangement with the Fund for SDR 180 million on December 4, 1985, in support of the 1985/86 economic and financial adjustment programme. The economic programme aimed at a reduction of the external current account deficit, an increase in the growth of real output and control of inflation. To these ends, the programme focused on mobilization of additional domestic resources through the adoption of new revenue measures and more efficient allocation of resources through the pursuit of appropriate pricing policies. A restraint monetary and credit policy was being implemented to contain inflationary pressure and stimulate domestic savings. Export promotion and diversification was to be pursued through the provision of adequate incentives and continuance of the process of liberalization of trade and payments system. In fiscal area, measures to enhance revenues and to curtail expenditure were a crucial component of the adjustment effort and were designed to reduce the overall budget deficit as a proposition to gross domestic product.

The performance of the economy under the programme has been summarized below:

- Bangladesh economy had better macroeconomic performance in 1985/86.
- Bangladesh economy performed better than the 'control group' in 1985/86.

1986/87- 1988/89 Economic Adjustment Programme

The Bangladesh authorities implemented an economic programme for 1986/87- 1988/89 supported by an extended arrangement of SDR 135 million approved by the Fund. The programme objectives were to raise the growth rate of GDP to at least 5 percent on average, moderate the rate of inflation and contain external current account deficit. To achieve these aims, the programme incorporated measures aimed at generating substantial additional domestic savings readdressing the problem facing the financial institutions and enhancing the flexibility in exchange rate management, while further liberalizing the trade and payments system.

The following conclusions have been drawn regarding the macroeconomic performance under the 1986/87- 1988/89 economic programme:

- Bangladesh economy performed better in 1986/87, but it showed poor performance during 1987/88- 1988/89.
- Bangladesh economy performed better than the 'control group' in 1986/87, but not during 1987/88- 1988/89.
- The targets established were not met.

According to IMF survey, "the little success of programme was partly reflected by the impact of floods in August 1987, which damaged crops, and infrastructure and disrupted supplies, besides causing considerable loss of life. Labour unrest also contributed to the lower rate of growth. In early September 1988, Bangladesh experienced severe floods which covered over three fourth of its land area. Barely two months after the floods, Bangladesh was struck by a major cyclone, which caused much loss of life, crops and livestock and damaged infrastructure".

1990/91- 1992/93 Economic Adjustment Programme

The Fund approved a three year arrangement in an amount equivalent to SDR 259 million for the government of Bangladesh under the enhanced structural adjustment facility (ESAF) on August 10, 1990.

The 1990/91- 1992/93 economic programme aimed at an average annual growth rate of 4.7 percent, a reduction in the rate of inflation, a further progress toward external payments viability and poverty alleviation. To these ends, the budget deficit was to be reduced during ESAF period by extensive revenue mobilization and restraint on current expenditure, and to be financed primarily by external concessional aid. The annual development programme was being expanded and rationalized to ensure adequate funding for high priority projects. In addition, public enterprises were required to make a larger contribution to the resource mobilization effort through more appropriate pricing and improved operating efficiency. Financial reforms under the programme focused on the development of markets and the viability of financial institutions, while exchange and trade liberalization were to continue over the programme period.

The strategy for poverty alleviation under the ESAF programme depended upon higher economic growth to permit increases in per capita income, employment generation, a reorientation of public expenditure toward the social sectors and human resource development.

The following conclusions have been drawn in context of the 1990/91- 1992/93 economic adjustment programme:

- Bangladesh economy showed better macroeconomic performance during 1990/91- 1992/93.
- Bangladesh performed better than the 'control group' during 1990/91- 1992/93.
- The programme was quite successful.
- Almost all the targets were met.

Macroeconomic Performance under Different Approaches

The macroeconomic performance of the Bangladesh economy under different approaches has been described below.

Before-After Approach: The following conclusions have been drawn regarding the macroeconomic performance of the Bangladesh economy under the Fund supported programmes.

- The total number of programme years method revealed that four variables viz., exports as percentage of imports, current account balance as percentage of GDP, overall balance of payments as percentage of GDP and inflation rate had better performance in the case of the Bangladesh economy during the programme years. While, five variables namely;

consumption as percentage of GDP, investment as percentage of GDP, domestic savings as percentage of GDP, real GDP growth rate and foreign exchange reserves growth rate had same performance as in the previous year. (Table 10.3)

- According to the difference between means method, all the nine variables- consumption as percentage of GDP, investment as percentage of GDP, domestic savings as percentage of GDP, exports as percentage of imports, current account balance as percentage of GDP, overall balance of payments as percentage of GDP, inflation rate, real GDP growth rate and foreign exchange reserves growth rate showed the positive performance of the Bangladesh economy during the programme years. But, the results were not statistically significant. (Table 10.2)
- The dependency (exports only) of the Bangladesh economy increased during the programme years. But, the results were not statistically significant. (Table 10.2)

With-Without Approach: The following conclusions have been drawn in context of the macroeconomic performance of the Bangladesh economy under the Fund supported programmes.

- According to the total number of programme years method, five variables viz., exports as percentage of imports, current account balance as percentage of GDP, overall balance of payments as percentage of GDP, real GDP growth rate and inflation rate showed better performance of the Bangladesh economy as compared to the 'control group'. In the case of two variables namely; consumption as percentage of GDP and domestic savings as percentage of GDP the Bangladesh economy revealed inferior performance as compared to the 'control group'. (Table 10.5)
- In the case of the difference between means method, all the variables- consumption as percentage of GDP, investment as percentage of GDP, domestic savings as percentage of GDP, exports as percentage of imports, current account as percentage of GDP, overall balance of payments as percentage of GDP, real GDP growth rate and inflation rate

showed better performance of the Bangladesh economy as compared to the 'control group' during the programme years. The results were statistically significant at five percent level of significance in the case of inflation rate and trade account balance. (Table 10.4)

- The dependency (exports only) of the Bangladesh economy increased more in comparison of that of the 'control group. The results were not statistically significant. (Table 10.4)

Generalized Evaluation Approach: The generalized evaluation approach showed positive effects of the fund supported programmes on three variables- nominal output, trade account balance and overall balance of payments as percentage of GDP – out of eight variables. As explained earlier too, the negative performance shown by the generalized evaluation approach does not necessarily mean that there was no improvement during the programme years. Actually, the improvement during non program years might be quite stronger than the improvement during the programme years. The same thing happened in the case of India and Chile. The Bangladesh economy showed good improvement during the programme years, but the improvement 1994 onward (non programme period) was even more strong (Table 10.2 and Appendix 10A). Ultimately, the regression fit for the entire period (1975- 2002) revealed unfavourable effects of the programmes on a number of variables employed (Tables 10.6 and 10.7).

Overall Macroeconomic Performance

The following important points have been inferred regarding the overall macroeconomic performance of the Bangladesh during programme years.

- Consumption as percentage of GDP showed favourable effects of the programmes. The consumption, which was equal to about one hundred percent of GDP in 1975/76, was brought down to 87.7 percent of GDP in 1992/93.
- Another variable, which showed much improvement during the programme years, was investment. Investment which was merely equivalent to 5.5 percent of GDP in 1974/75 rose

Table 10.6: Bangladesh: Programme Effects: Generalized Evaluation (1975-2002)

Z	C	GDP	INV	Z_{-1}	DCR	T	D	R^2	F
GDP	158.251 (3.482)*		4.255 (32.50)*				57.375 (1.112)	0.98	645.6
INV	-30.357 (2.669)*	0.230 (32.43)*					-17.399 (1.475)	0.98	669.1
DS	-44.143 (3.196)*	0.187 (21.68)*					-24.037 (1.677)	0.96	308.2
X/M	11.619 (5.586)*			0.754 (5.029)*	-0.300 (2.129)*	0.470 (1.538)	0.422 (0.171)	0.93	74.0
CA/GDP	-0.047 (0.025)			0.342 (1.806)*	-0.133 (2.905)*	0.076 (1.272)	-0.494 (0.728)	0.61	8.9
OB/GDP	2.265 (2.709)*			0.327 (2.159)*	-0.110 (4.030)*	-0.019 (0.692)	0.111 (0.260)	0.49	5.5
RGDP Gr	9.091 (3.979)*			-0.468 (2.703)*	-0.047 (0.841)	-0.057 (0.993)	-1.649 (1.705)*	0.30	2.9
INFR	4.821 (1.321)			0.255 (3.038)*	0.142 (1.446)	-0.119 (1.035)	0.354 (1.496)	0.53	6.5

Notes: (1) Figures in parenthesis are t-values. (2) *sign indicates significant at 5% level of significance.

Table 10.7: Bangladesh: Programme Effects (summary)

Variable	Before-After Approach		With-Without Approach		Generalized Evaluation
	Difference between means method	Total number of programme years	Difference between means method	Total number of programme years	
CN/ GDP	, +	0	+	-	N A
INV/GDP	+	0	+	0	N A
DS/GDP	+	0	+*	-	N A
X/M	+	+	+	+	+
CA/GDP	+	+	+	+	-
OB/GDP	+	+	+	+	+
RGDP Gr	+	0	+	+	-*
INFR	+	+	+*	+	-
FOREX Gr	+	0	N A	N A	N A
GDP	N A	N A	N A	N A	+
INV	N A	N A	N A	N A	-
DS	N A	N A	N A	N A	-
Total	9	4	8	5	3
Better	0	0	0	2	5
Poor	0	5	0	1	0
Same					

Note: (1) + sign indicates better performance,-sign indicates poor performance and 0 sign indicates same performance. (2) * sign indicates significance at 5% level of significance.

steadily during the programme years and was equal to 19.9 percent of GDP in 1992/93.

- A good performance was shown by domestic savings during the programme years. Domestic savings rose from equal to about 1 percent of GDP in 1975/76 to 12.3 percent of GDP in 1992/93.
- The external sector also shown good performance during the programme years. The trade account revealed substantial improvement under the Fund supported programmes. Exports, which were equivalent to 24.8 percent of imports in 1974/75 rose to 69.5 percent of imports in 1992/93.
- The current account had very good performance during the programme years. The current account deficit was equal to 5.8 of GDP in 1974/75, but it was wiped out during the programme years and there was a surplus in current account equal to 1.1 percent of GDP in 1992/93.
- The overall balance of payments as percentage of GDP improved substantially during the programme years. After the implementation of programmes for few years only, overall balance of payments started showing surplus.
- The real output showed good performance on two counts during the programme years. One, the volatility in growth rate was reduced to a good extent and two, there was on average an increase in the real output growth rate.
- The Bangladesh economy showed positive performance in context of inflation rate during the programme years. The results were statistically significant at five percent level of significance.
- Most of targets were met.
- The dependency (exports only) of the Bangladesh economy increased during the programme years. Though the results were not statistically significant.
- Intermediate policy variables also revealed good results. The overall budget deficit was largely under control during the program years.

- Domestic credit expansion rate had generally remained under controlled during the programme years.
- Money supply growth rate was also under control except a year or two.
- Interest rates were increased during the programme years. An increase is interest rate is generally recommended in the Fund supported programmes.
- As usually recommended by the IMF, the domestic currency was devalued against US dollar from year to year.
- The Bangladesh economy showed better performance during nine programme years out of total twelve programme years.
- In sum, the Bangladesh economy showed good macroeconomic performance under the Fund supported programmes (Table 10.8).

Conclusions

The Bangladesh economy showed good performance in every aspect. A good improvement was achieved in investment as percentage of GDP during the programme years. Consumption was reduced to a large extent as proportion of GDP. An appreciable success was met in context of domestic savings. Domestic savings, which were negligible in 1975 rose to the equivalent of 12.3 percent of GDP in 1992/93.

Considerable success was also met in the external sector. Trade account deficit was reduced to a large extent. The current account deficit was totally wiped out and it showed surplus 1991 onward. The overall balance of payments, which had deficits prior to the implementation of programmes, started showing surplus after a few years of programme implementation.

The inflation rate declined to a large extent and its volatility was also reduced. The real GDP growth became stable during the programme years. On an average, there was also an increase in real output growth rate. The dependency (exports only) of the Bangladesh economy had increased during the programme years, though the results were not statistical significant.

Table 10.8: Bangladesh: Policy Variables, (1975-2002)

Year	Exchange rate (Tk per U.S. $)	Interest rate (%)	Money supply (% change)	Domestic credit (% change)	Budget deficit[1] (as % of GDP)
1975	14.83	---	5.4	12.3	1.1
1976	14.95	6.8	18.5	21.5	-3.5
1977	14.40	7.0	23.7	23.9	0.2
1978	14.93	7.0	26.3	17.8	3.3
1979	15.64	7.0	22.0	23.9	0.5
1980	16.25	8.5	20.9	30.8	2.5
1981	19.84	8.5	16.8	26.7	-3.2
1982	24.07	8.5	11.9	11.8	1.2
1983	25.00	8.5	40.0	23.1	3.1
1984	26.00	8.5	36.1	29.2	0.8
1985	31.00	11.5	13.6	18.3	-1.5
1986	30.80	11.5	16.2	11.5	---
1987	31.20	11.5	18.8	7.6	---
1988	32.27	11.5	13.6	11.8	---
1989	32.27	11.5	18.7	22.9	-0.4
1990	35.79	11.5	10.2	8.7	---
1991	38.58	---	7.7	4.9	---
1992	39.00	15.0	13.6	6.5	---
1993	39.85	15.0	10.4	6.1	-5.4
1994	40.25	14.5	19.3	11.0	-4.6
1995	40.75	14.0	12.1	35.7	-5.3
1996	42.45	14.0	10.7	17.0	-4.5
1997	45.45	14.0	9.7	12.3	-4.4
1998	48.50	14.0	11.3	13.0	-4.1

Contd...

1999	51.00	14.1	15.4	15.3	-4.3
2000	54.00	15.5	19.2	13.7	-5.1
2001	57.00	15.8	14.6	17.1	-5.1
2002	57.90	16.0	13.2	12.1	-4.7

Note: 1.Fiscal year ending in the year stated.

Sources: Compiled and computed form *IMF-International Financial Statistics*, various issues, and *UN-National Accounts Statistics, Main Aggregates and detailed Tables*, various issues.

Finally, the success achieved by the Bangladesh economy under the Fund-supported programmes can be categorized as a good one. Increase in domestic savings, investment and stability in the economy were commendable.

Appendix 10A: Bangladesh: Statistics on Macroeconomic Variables (1975-2002)

Year	CN/ GDP[1]	INV/ GDP[1]	DS/ GDP[1]	X/M	CA/ GDP	OB/ GDP	INFR (%)	RGDP Gr	FOERX Gr (%)	X/GDP	M/GDP
1975	100.6	5.5	-0.6	24.8	-5.8	-0.3	21.9	3.4	-5.8	3.1	12.6
1976	99.7	8.8	0.3	42.1	-4.0	0.7	2.3	12.3	107.5	5.7	13.6
1977	95.2	11.7	4.8	40.9	-4.1	-0.6	4.8	1.7	-15.7	6.9	17.0
1978	96.2	12.2	3.8	36.2	-4.0	0.5	5.3	6.5	38.3	6.3	17.4
1979	93.1	15.2	6.9	34.4	-0.6	0.3	14.7	4.6	18.8	7.0	20.5
1980	97.9	15.1	2.1	30.5	-5.5	-2.5	13.4	1.3	-20.0	6.2	20.3
1981	96.8	16.0	3.2	29.3	-7.9	-1.7	16.2	6.8	-53.8	6.1	20.8
1982	99.6	15.0	0.4	33.3	-4.2	-0.8	12.5	0.8	24.5	6.4	19.2
1983	99.7	13.6	0.3	33.4	-0.4	3.0	9.4	3.6	180.7	6.2	18.5
1984	98.9	12.2	1.1	33.0	-3.5	0.0	10.5	4.2	-24.5	6.7	20.5
1985	97.7	12.8	2.3	36.0	-3.2	-0.6	10.7	3.7	-18.7	6.9	19.1
1986	97.0	12.3	3.0	35.7	-4.1	0.8	11.0	4.7	24.3	5.8	16.2
1987	96.6	12.6	3.4	39.8	-1.4	1.1	9.5	4.0	104.1	6.1	15.4
1988	97.7	11.9	2.3	42.4	-1.5	0.7	9.3	2.9	26.9	7.0	16.4
1989	98.1	11.7	1.9	35.8	-5.4	-1.5	10.0	2.5	-51.2	6.1	17.1
1990	98.0	11.0	2.0	46.4	-1.9	0.9	8.1	6.6	28.6	7.3	15.8
1991	95.8	11.5	4.2	54.6	0.3	2.0	6.4	3.2	100.3	7.8	14.3
1992	86.1	17.2	13.9	62.5	0.6	2.1	3.6	4.2	47.8	7.0	11.1
1993	87.7	17.9	12.3	69.5	1.1	2.1	3.0	4.6	33.8	7.8	11.2
1994	86.9	18.4	13.1	67.3	0.6	2.1	5.3	4.1	29.9	8.8	13.1
1995	86.9	19.1	13.1	61.6	-2.2	-1.4	10.2	4.9	-29.8	10.0	16.1
1996	85.1	20.0	14.9	63.8	-2.5	-1.0	2.4	4.6	-21.0	10.1	15.8
1997	89.1	20.6	10.9	73.8	-0.7	-0.3	5.4	5.4	-10.0	11.8	16.0
1998	82.6	21.6	17.4	76.6	-0.1	0.8	8.4	5.2	21.9	14.6	19.0

Contd...

1999	82.3	22.2	17.7	72.4	-0.8	-0.4	6.1	4.9	-15.4	12.0	16.5
2000	82.1	23.0	17.9	79.5	-0.7	0.0	2.3	5.9	-7.4	14.6	18.4
2001	82.0	23.1	18.0	74.8	-1.2	-0.3	2.0	5.3	-14.3	13.6	18.2
2002	81.8	23.1	18.2	78.4	1.6	1.1	3.3	4.8	31.9	13.2	16.8

Note: 1. Fiscal year ending in the year stated.

Sources: Compiled and computed form *IMF-International Financial Statistics*, various issues, and *UN-National Accounts Statistics, Main Aggregates and detailed Tables*, various issues.

11

Conclusions

The conclusions drawn in the context of macroeconomic performance of the countries i.e. Morocco, Ghana, Chile, Mexico, India and Bangladesh, under the Fund-supported programmes have been presented below.

Morocco

Moroccan economy implemented the Fund-supported programmes for twelve different years spanning from 1980 to 1992. The economy showed improvement in investment as proportion of GDP during these years. The Fund supported programmes' effect on consumption and domestic savings, both as percentage of GDP, was ambiguous.

External sector showed clear cut improvement during programme years. Trade account improved during programme years. Noteworthy performance was revealed by both the current account balance and overall balance of payments. The both accounts had steady improvement under the Fund supported programmes.

A remarkable success was achieved in the case of inflation rate. There was almost continuous decline in inflation during program years. The effect on foreign exchange reserves growth rate was not clear. The only disappointing effect was found on real GDP growth. All the three approaches revealed poor performance of real output. In addition to decline in real GDP growth rate, there was much variation in the growth rate. It also seems that the Fund supported programmes enhanced the dependency of the Moroccan economy, albeit the results were not statistically significant.

In brief, the Moroccan economy revealed satisfactory macroeconomic performance under the Fund-supported programmes.

Ghana

Ghana implemented the Fund-supported programmes for fifteen different years spanning from 1979 to 2001. Only one variable – investment as percentage of GDP- showed a statistically significant improvement during the programme years. Very disappointing results were shown by both the consumption and domestic savings. Consumption accounted generally for more than 90 percent of output, leaving a little portion for domestic savings. Increase in investment was largely due to inflow of foreign resources, especially after 1990, resulting in worsening external account position.

The external sector had very poor performance during the programme years. The situation became worse from bad in the case of all the three accounts i.e. trade account, current account and overall balance of payments. Overall balance of payments showed a surplus for few years i.e. 1987- 1995, but there was no improvement in current account during this period. This indicates that the temporary improvement in overall balance of payments was due to increased capital inflows induced by the IMF's 'seal of approval' and not due to current account or trade account.

Another disappointment was due to no improvement seen in inflation rate. The inflation rate remained high – though there was no further substantial increase- during programme years. An achievement was in context of volatility in real output growth. Real GDP growth rate became less volatile during programme years, but there was a little decline in real GDP growth rate on average basis. The Fund supported programmes led to enhance the dependency of the Ghanaian economy. The results were statistically significant at 5 percent level of significance.

Finally, the Fund supported programmes failed in improving the macroeconomic economic situation in Ghana. Even, there was deterioration in the economic position of the Ghanaian economy under the last two 1995-1997 and 1999-2001 programmes.

Chile

The Chilean authorities implemented the IMF supported programmes for nine different years. A clear improvement was seen in the different sectors of the economy. Consumption as proposition of GDP declined to a considerable extent over the programme years, thus making domestic resources available for investment through increased domestic savings. Investment as percentage of GDP revealed a continuous increase over the programme years.

The external sector also revealed some improvement in the economy during the programme years. The important point is that improvement in overall balance of payments was not only due to increased inflow of foreign capital, but also to a large extent to improvement in current account.

The inflation rate was brought down during the programme years, but it could not be brought down as per the expectations. The real output growth rate increased after the implementation of the Fund supported programmes and volatility in the growth rate was also reduced over the programme years. There was enhancement in the dependency of the Chilean economy during the programme years. The results were statistically significant at 5 percent level of confidence.

In brief, the Chilean economy showed a satisfactory macroeconomic performance under the Fund-supported programmes.

Table 11.1: Programme Effects: Summarized Performance

Country	Performance	Dependency
Morocco	Satisfactory	Enhanced
Ghana	Very Poor	Enhanced*
Chile	Satisfactory	Enhanced*
Mexico	Poor	Enhanced*
India	Good	Enhanced*
Bangladesh	Good	Enhanced

Note: (*) sign means significant at 5 % level of significance.

Mexico

The Mexican authorities implemented the Fund-supported programmes for fifteen different years, but the economy did not show a satisfactory performance during the programme years. Despite the implementation- particularly 1990 onward- of tight credit policy, flexible foreign exchange management and tight fiscal policy, and to some extent control money supply growth, the economy did not reveal sustainable improvement. Consumption as percentage of GDP, investment as percentage of GDP and domestic savings as percentage of GDP did not show positive improvement during programme years.

The external sector did not show noteworthy progress during the programme years. The current account did not reveal improvement, still having deficit. The overall balance of payments showed an improvement- generally moderate deficit or surplus-during programme years, owing to inflow of foreign capital.

The real output growth rate did not show improvement except the 1977-79 economic programme. The volatility was still present in real GDP growth. Disappointing results were also found in the case of inflation rate. The dependency of the Mexican economy increased during programme years. The results were statistically significant at 5 percent level of significance.

Finally, Mexican economy revealed poor performance under the Fund-supported programmes. The economy could not achieve stable and viable economic position.

India

Both the programmes implemented by the Indian authorities showed good macroeconomic performance. Domestic savings as percentage of GDP, investment as percentage of GDP and consumption as percentage of GDP showed positive performances during the programmes years.

The external sector also revealed good performance. Trade account improved during programme years. The current account deficits could be lowered during the programme years. In the case of overall balance of payments, good success was met.

The real output growth rate also revealed favourable effect during programme years. Though inflation rate could not show the desired results, it remained under control. The dependency of the Indian economy increased during the programme years. The results were statistically significant.

Finally, the macroeconomic performance of the Indian economy during the Fund supported programme was good.

Bangladesh

The Bangladesh economy showed good performance in every aspect. A good improvement was achieved in investment as percentage of GDP during the programme years. Consumption was reduced to a large extent as proposition of GDP. An appreciable success was met in context of domestic savings. Domestic savings, which were negligible in 1975 rose to the equivalent of 12.3 percent of GDP in 1992/93.

Considerable success was also met in the external sector. Trade account deficit was reduced to a large extent. The current account deficit was totally wiped out and it showed surplus1991 onward. The overall balance of payments, which had deficits prior to the implementation of programmes, started showing surplus after a few years of programme implementation.

The inflation rate declined to a large extent and volatility was also reduced. The real GDP growth became stable during the programme years. On an average, there was also an increase in real output growth rate. The dependency (exports only) of the Bangladesh economy had increased during the programme years, though the results were not statistical significant.

In brief, the success achieved by the Bangladesh economy under the Fund-supported programmes can be categorized as a good one. Increase in domestic savings, investment and stability in the economy were commendable.

The summarized main findings have been mentioned below:

- The Fund supported programmes are in fact a complex packages of measures geared to the particular circumstances of the country. They include both the demand and supply side policies. Aside from monetary and exchange policies a typical Fund supported programme calls for fiscal measures, such as reduction in government expenditure and increase in taxation, increase in domestic interest rates and producer prices to the realistic levels, policies to raise investment and its efficiency, trade liberalization, and wage restraint; in addition to some other policy measures.

- The openness of the economies was enhanced under the implementation of the Fund supported programmes. The results were statistically significant in the case of Ghana, India, Chile and Mexico.
- The programmes revealed good performance in the case of India and Bangladesh. The performance was satisfactory in the case of Chile and Morocco. The programmes failed in Ghana and Mexico. (Table 1)
- The success of the fund-supported programmes was not limited to any region/country. Although, this generalization is debatable because of small sample of countries included in the study.
- Generally, performance of overall balance of payments was stronger than that of current account during the programme years. It implies that inflow of foreign capital played a role, in general, in the improvement of overall balance of payments.

Suggestions

No general recommendations can be made as far as IMF's policy suggestions and the economic development are concerned. Case by case- not capsule approach- seems to be the most appropriate. The International monetary Fund has already moved toward this direction. Though, the policy might be economically sound, the democratic countries have faced political oppositions while implementing the policy resolutions. Despite the sincerity of the governments to implement the policies there have always been objections from the opposition parties, both on political and economic grounds. India and Morocco are examples. The policy instruments need to vary depending upon economic and political situation in the country concerned.

Blind following of the IMF directives may not be helpful, neither politically or economically, and the advice must be taken with caution and suitable adjustment must be made in the policy instruments. India, Bangladesh and Chile seem to have kept this point in view while implementing the programmes. Ghana and Mexico could not achieve stabilized economic position even after the implementation of the Fund supported programme for fifteen years. The smaller developing countries should also use the expertise in developing suitable policy instruments in their own countries. They can approach better placed developing countries in finding the suitable solution of the problem.

Some of the policy advices seem contradictory to the development requirements of the countries concerned. For example, whether the restriction on money supply can help the economic growth? Though it is very difficult to determine the optimal growth of money supply for the countries, the restriction on money supply may restrict the investment possibilities and retard the economic growth. Another area, in which the advice of IMF need not always lead to favourable situation are the suggestions about exchange rate adjustments. All the programme countries had made a number of adjustments in exchange rates, but the problem remains the same for them.

Appendices

Appendix 1

IMF Lendings and Sources of Funds

Lendings

A core responsibility of the IMF is to provide loans to countries experiencing balance-of-payments problems. This financial assistance enables countries to rebuild their international reserves, stabilize their currencies, continue paying for imports, and restore conditions for strong economic growth. Unlike development banks, the IMF does not lend for specific projects.

A member country may request IMF financial assistance if it has a balance of payments need—that is, if it cannot find sufficient financing on affordable terms to meet its net international payments. An IMF loan eases the adjustment policies and reforms that a country must make to correct its balance of payments problem and restore conditions for strong economic growth.

The volume of loans provided by the IMF has fluctuated significantly over time. The oil shock of the 1970s and the debt crisis of the 1980s were both followed by sharp increases in IMF lending. In the 1990s, the transition process in Central and Eastern Europe and the crises in emerging market economies led to further surges in the demand for IMF resources.

An IMF loan is usually provided under an "arrangement," which stipulates the specific policies and measures a country has agreed to implement in order to resolve its balance of payments problem. The economic program underlying an arrangement is formulated by the country in consultation with the IMF, and is presented to the Fund's Executive Board in a "Letter of Intent." Once an arrangement is approved by the Board, the loan is released in phased instalments as the program is carried out.

Over the years, the IMF has developed a number of loan instruments, or "facilities," that are tailored to address the specific circumstances of its diverse membership. Low-income countries may borrow at a concessional interest rate through the Poverty

Reduction and Growth Facility (PRGF). Non-concessional loans are provided through four main facilities: Stand-By Arrangements (SBA), the Extended Fund Facility (EFF), the Supplemental Reserve Facility (SRF), and the Compensatory Financing Facility (CFF). The IMF also provides emergency assistance to support recovery from natural disasters and conflicts, in some cases at concessional interest rates.

Except for the PRGF, all facilities are subject to the IMF's market-related interest rate, known as the "rate of charge," and some carry an interest rate premium or "surcharge." The rate of charge is based on the SDR interest rate, which is revised weekly to take account of changes in short-term interest rates in the major international money markets. The rate of charge was 3.39 percent as of February 28, 2005. Large loans carry a surcharge and must be repaid early if a country's external position permits.

The amount that a country can borrow from the Fund—its "access limit"—varies depending on the type of loan, but is typically a multiple of the country's IMF quota.

Poverty Reduction and Growth Facility (PRGF): Concessional lending arrangements to low-income countries are underpinned by comprehensive country-owned strategies, as specified in their Poverty Reduction Strategy Papers (PRSPs). In recent years, the largest number of IMF loans have been made through the PRGF. The interest rate levied on PRGF loans is only 0.5 percent, and loans are to be repaid over a period of 5½–10 years.

Stand-By Arrangements (SBA): The SBA is designed to help countries address short-term balance-of-payments problems and is the facility that provides the greatest amount of IMF resources. The length of a SBA is typically 12–18 months, and repayment is normally expected within 2¼–4 years. Surcharges apply to high access levels.

Extended Fund Facility (EFF): This facility was established in 1974 to help countries address more protracted balance-of-payments problems requiring fundamental reforms to the structure of the economy. Arrangements under the EFF are thus longer—

usually 3 years. Repayment is normally expected within 4½–7 years. Surcharges apply to high levels of access.

Supplemental Reserve Facility (SRF): This facility was introduced in 1997 to meet a need for very short-term financing on a large scale. The motivation for the SRF was the sudden loss of market confidence experienced by emerging market economies in the 1990s, which led to massive outflows of capital and required financing on a much larger scale than anything the IMF had previously been asked to provide. Countries are expected to repay loans within 2–2½ years, but may request an extension of up to six months. All SRF loans carry a substantial surcharge of 3–5 percentage points.

Compensatory Financing Facility (CFF): The CFF was established in 1963 to assist countries experiencing either a sudden shortfall in export earnings or an increase in the cost of cereal imports caused by fluctuating world commodity prices. The financial terms are the same as those applying to the SBA, except that CFF loans carry no surcharge.

Emergency Assistance: The IMF provides emergency assistance to countries that have experienced a natural disaster or are emerging from conflict. Emergency loans are subject to the basic rate of charge, although interest subsidies are available for PRGF-eligible countries, subject to availability. Loans must be repaid within 3¼–5 years.

IMF Concessional Lending and Debt Relief: The IMF provides two primary types of financial assistance to low-income countries: low-interest loans under the Poverty Reduction and Growth Facility (PRGF), and debt relief under the Heavily Indebted Poor Countries (HIPC) Initiative. These resources come from member contributions and the IMF itself, rather than from the quota subscriptions. They are administered under the PRGF and PRGF-HIPC Trusts, for which the IMF acts as Trustee.

The PRGF Trust was established to provide lending in support of PRGF arrangements and to subsidize the market rate of interest down to the concessional interest rate of 0.5 percent per annum. Loan resources in excess of $23 billion have been committed by 17 contributors to the Trust, while a larger number of IMF member countries have made subsidy contributions.

The PRGF-HIPC Trust was established to provide debt relief under the HIPC Initiative and to subsidize PRGF lending during the period 2002-05. The resources available to the Trust consists of grants and deposits from 93 member countries and contributions from the IMF itself. The bulk of the IMF's contribution comes from the investment income on the net proceeds from off-market gold transactions made during 1999-2000.

In addition to the above, there is a separate administered account financed by a group of member countries for interest subsidies on IMF emergency assistance to PRGF-eligible countries in post-conflict or natural disaster situations.

IMF's Lending Capacity: The IMF can only use the currencies of financially strong economies to finance lending. The IMF's Executive Board selects these currencies every three months. Most are issued by industrial countries, but the list also has included currencies of developing countries such as Botswana, China, and India. The IMF's holdings of these currencies, together with its own SDR holdings, make up its usable resources.

The amount the IMF has readily available for new (non-concessional) lending is indicated by its one-year forward commitment capacity. This is determined by its usable resources, plus projected loan repayments over the subsequent twelve months, less the resources that have already been committed under existing arrangements, less a precautionary balance. As of February 28, 2005, the Fund's one-year forward commitment capacity was $117 billion.

Sources of Funds

Most resources for IMF loans are provided by member countries, primarily through their payment of quotas. Concessional lending and debt relief for low-income countries are financed through separate contribution-based trust funds. The

IMF's annual operating expenses are largely paid for by the difference between its interest receipts and its interest payments.

The Quota System: Each member of the IMF is assigned a quota, based broadly on its relative size in the world economy, which determines its contribution to the IMF's financial resources. Upon joining the IMF, a country normally pays up to one-quarter of its quota in the form of widely accepted foreign currencies (such as the U.S. dollar, the euro, the yen, or the pound sterling) or Special Drawing Rights (SDRs). The remaining three-quarters is paid in the country's own currency.

Quotas are reviewed at least every five years. The quota review that was concluded in 1998 led to a 45 percent increase in IMF quotas to SDR 213 billion (about $327 billion as of end-February 2005). The review concluded in January 2003 resulted in no change in quotas.

Gold Holdings: Valued at current market prices, the IMF's gold holdings are worth about $45 billion as of end-February 2005, making the Fund one of the largest official holders of gold in the world. However, the IMF's Articles of Agreement strictly limit its use. Under some circumstances, the IMF may sell gold or may accept gold as payment by member countries; but the IMF is prohibited from buying gold or engaging in other gold transactions.

Borrowing Arrangements: If the IMF believes that its forward commitment capacity might fall short of its members' needs—for example, in the event of a major financial crisis—it can activate supplementary borrowing arrangements. The first and principal resort is the New Arrangements to Borrow (NAB), which was established in 1998. Under the NAB, 26 countries have agreed to lend SDR 34 billion (about $52 billion).

Appendix 2

IMF Efforts to Reduce Poverty in Poor Countries

The IMF provides low-income countries with policy advice, technical assistance, and financial support. Low-income countries receive more than half of the technical assistance provided by the Fund, and financial support is extended at low interest rates and over relatively long time horizons. Low-income countries with high external debt burdens are also eligible for debt relief.

Despite progress in recent decades, the extreme poverty prevalent in low-income countries is a critical problem facing the global community. At present, more than a billion people are living on less than $1 a day. More than three-quarters of a billion people are malnourished—about a fifth of them children. One-hundred and twenty-one of every 1000 children born in low-income countries die before reaching the age of five, the majority from malnutrition or disease that is readily preventable in high-income countries.

The Millennium Development Goals (MDGs) set by the United Nations are cantered on halving poverty between 1990 and 2015. How can they be achieved, when the causes of poverty and the reasons it persists are complex, varied, and not fully understood? There is little dispute that a sustained, rapid rate of growth in average per capita incomes is essential for meaningful poverty reduction. In turn, the factors that have been shown to promote such growth include openness to international trade, sound economic policies, strong institutions and legal frameworks, and good governance.

Accordingly, in the March 2002 Monterrey Consensus, the international community adopted a two-pillar strategy for achieving the MDGs. The first is the pursuit of sound policies and good governance by the low-income countries themselves. The second is larger and more effective international support, including official development assistance and trade liberalization to open markets to developing country exports.

The IMF is helping low-income countries make progress toward the MDGs and contributing to the approach embodied in the Monterrey Consensus through each of the Fund's three key functions—lending, technical assistance, and surveillance.

Poverty Reduction and Growth Facility (PRGF)

The IMF provides financial assistance to low-income countries experiencing balance of payments problems through its Poverty Reduction and Growth Facility (PRGF). The interest rate on PRGF loans is concessional (only 0.5 percent), and loans are repaid over a period of 10 years (with 5½ years' grace).

PRGF lending programs are based on Poverty Reduction Strategy Papers (PRSP). A PRSP is prepared by the government of a low-income country, in concert with civil society and development partners such as the IMF and World Bank, to describe the policies that will be employed to promote growth and reduce poverty in the country. In addition to economic policies, PRSPs typically cover structural and social policies that are needed to improve health and education, safeguard the environment, and combat HIV/AIDS, malaria, and other diseases. The IMF sees the PRSP approach as a key framework for implementing the Monterrey Consensus, and is working to ensure better alignment of PRGF lending programs with PRSPs.

Terms of the PRGF

- As of March 2005, 78 low-income countries are eligible for PRGF assistance.
- Eligibility is based principally on the IMF's assessment of a country's per capita income, drawing on the cut-off point for eligibility to World Bank concessional lending (currently 2003 per capita gross national income of $895).
- Loans under the PRGF carry an annual interest rate of 0.5 percent, with repayments made semi-annually, beginning 5½ years and ending 10 years after the disbursement.

An eligible country may normally borrow up to a maximum of 140 percent of its IMF quota under a three-year arrangement, although this may be increased to 185 percent of quota in exceptional circumstances. In each case, the amount will depend on the country's balance of payments need, the strength of its adjustment program, and its previous and outstanding use of IMF credit. The expected average access under the initial three-year arrangement is 90 percent of quota, and 65, 55, 45, 35, and 25 percent of quota for second through sixth-time users of the facility, respectively. "Low-access" PRGF arrangements with a standard level of 10 percent of quota may be used for members with little or no immediate balance of payments need. PRGF-eligible members with per-capita income above 75 percent of the cut-off for World Bank concessional lending, or members borrowing on commercial terms, may combine PRGF arrangements with lending from the IMF's non-concessional Extended Fund Facility.

Experience with the PRGF highlights a number of distinctive features:

First, the principle of **broad public participation and greater country ownership** is central to the PRGF. In this regard, discussions on the policies underlying PRGF-supported programs are more open, since they are based on the nationally-owned PRSP. With increased national ownership, PRGF conditionality has become more parsimonious, focused on the Fund's core areas of expertise, and limited to measures that have a direct and critical impact on the program's macroeconomic objectives.

Second, PRGF-supported programs reflect more closely **each country's poverty reduction and growth priorities**. Key policy measures and structural reforms aimed at poverty reduction and growth are identified and prioritized during the PRSP process, and if feasible, their budgetary costs are assessed. Countries' budgets under PRGF-supported programs reflect this analysis. Moreover, fiscal targets in PRGF-supported programs respond flexibly to changes in country circumstances and pro-poor policy priorities, while ensuring that the strategy can be financed in a sustainable, non-inflationary manner.

Third, PRGF-supported programs focus on strengthening **governance**, in order to assist countries' efforts to design targeted and well-prioritized spending. Of particular importance are measures to improve public resource management, transparency, and accountability. PRGF-supported programs also give more attention to the **poverty and social impacts** of key macroeconomic policy measures.

PRGF-supported programs are designed to cover only areas within the primary responsibility of the IMF, unless a particular measure is judged to have a direct, critical macroeconomic impact. Areas typically covered by the IMF include advising on prudent macroeconomic policies and related structural reforms such as exchange rate and tax policy, fiscal management, budget execution, fiscal transparency, and tax and customs administration.

When appropriate, the IMF draws on World Bank expertise in designing PRGF-supported programs, and the staffs of the Fund and Bank cooperate closely on conditionality. The Bank staff takes the lead in advising the authorities in the design of poverty reduction strategies in areas such as poverty assessments, monitoring, structural and sectoral issues, social issues, and costing priority poverty-reducing spending.

Concessional lending under the PRGF is administered by the IMF through the PRGF and PRGF-HIPC Trusts. The PRGF Trust borrows resources from central banks, governments, and official institutions generally at market-related interest rates, and lends them on a pass-through basis to PRGF-eligible countries. The difference between the market-related interest rate paid to PRGF Trust lenders and the rate of interest of 0.5 percent per year paid by the borrowing members is financed by contributions from bilateral donors and the IMF's own resources.

Heavily Indebted Poor Countries (HIPC) Initiative

Some low-income countries are eligible for the Heavily Indebted Poor Countries (HIPC) Initiative. The joint IMF-World

Bank HIPC Initiative aims to reduce the external debt burdens of heavily indebted poor countries. Fully implemented, the initiative would reduce the debts of 37 countries by about $55 billion (in net present value terms). The 27 HIPCs that have already obtained debt service relief are spending much more on social services than on debt service—on average four times as much—and have shown a marked increase in the share of health and education in the budgets under their PRGF programs.

The HIPC Initiative is a comprehensive approach to debt reduction for heavily indebted poor countries pursuing IMF- and World Bank-supported adjustment and reform programs. To date, debt reduction packages have been approved for 27 countries, 23 of them in Africa, providing $32 billion (net present value terms) in debt service relief over time.

The HIPC Initiative was first launched in 1996 by the IMF and World Bank, with the aim of ensuring that no poor country faces a debt burden it cannot manage. The Initiative entails coordinated action by the international financial community, including multilateral organizations and governments, to reduce to sustainable levels the external debt burdens of the most heavily indebted poor countries. Following a comprehensive review in September 1999, a number of modifications were approved to provide faster, deeper and broader debt relief and to strengthen the links between debt relief, poverty reduction and social policies. Countries' continued efforts toward macroeconomic adjustment and structural and social policy reforms—including higher spending on social sector programs like basic health and education—are now central to the enhanced HIPC Initiative.

Yet the HIPC Initiative is not a panacea. Even if all of the external debts of these countries were forgiven, most would still depend on significant levels of concessional external assistance, since their receipts of such assistance have been much larger than their debt-service payments for many years.

To be considered for HIPC Initiative assistance, a country must:

- face an unsustainable debt burden, beyond traditionally available debt-relief mechanisms;
- establish a track record of reform and sound policies through IMF- and World Bank-supported programs; and
- have developed a Poverty Reduction Strategy Paper (PRSP) through a broad-based participatory process (an interim strategy is sufficient to begin the process).

The first step is to carry out a debt sustainability analysis to determine the debt relief needs of the country. If a country's external debt ratio after traditional debt relief mechanisms is above a threshold for the value of debt to exports (or, in special cases, the value of debt to fiscal revenues), it qualifies for assistance under the Initiative. Once a country has made sufficient progress in meeting the criteria for debt relief, the Executive Boards of the IMF and World Bank formally decide on a country's eligibility, and the international community commits to reducing debt to the sustainability threshold. This is called the **decision point**.

Once a country reaches its decision point, it may immediately begin receiving **interim relief** on its debt service falling due. In order to receive the full and irrevocable reduction in debt available under the HIPC Initiative, however, the country must establish a further track record of good performance under IMF- and World Bank-supported programs. The length of this second period depends on (i) the satisfactory implementation of key policy reforms agreed at the decision point, (ii) the maintenance of macroeconomic stability, and (iii) the adoption and implementation for at least one year of the PRSP.

Once a country has met these criteria, it can reach its **completion point**, at which time lenders are expected to provide the full relief committed at the decision point.

The total cost of providing assistance to the 38 countries potentially qualified under the enhanced HIPC Initiative is estimated to be about $58 billion in 2004 net present value terms. A little over half of this will be provided by bilateral creditors, and the rest will come from multilateral lenders. The IMF's share of the cost is financed primarily by the investment income on the net proceeds from off-market gold sales in 1999 that were deposited to the IMF's PRGF-HIPC Trust. Additional contributions to this trust have been provided by member countries.

For the 27 countries for whom packages have already been approved, debt service falling due between 1998 and 2004 on average has dropped by more than half in relation to both exports and government revenue. Yet for debt reduction to have a tangible impact on poverty, the additional resources need to be targeted at the poor. Before the HIPC Initiative, eligible countries were, on average, spending slightly more on debt service than on health and education combined. This is no longer the case in the 27 countries receiving HIPC relief. Under their recent IMF- and World Bank-supported programs, these countries have increased markedly their expenditures on health, education and other social services and, on average, such spending is now almost four times the amount of debt service payments.

While country-by-country data demonstrate that these countries are seeing clear gains, it has taken time and effort to ensure that money is redirected to aid the poor in ways that most reduce poverty. And difficult problems remain. For example, in war-ravaged Rwanda and Ethiopia, pressing reconstruction needs may mean large new loans at the same time that old debt is being reduced.

Difficult problems also remain in HIPCs that have not yet been able to reach their decision points. Some of these countries are plagued by uneven policy records or poor governance, which in turn may be caused by the serious problems that their governments confront, including civil conflict. Some HIPCs have debts too large to write off given current funding for the Initiative. This is true, for example, in Liberia and Sudan, which are both afflicted by civil conflict. The IMF and the World Bank recently agreed to extend for an additional two years, to end-2006, the deadline—known as the "sunset clause"—for remaining HIPCs to begin to establish a policy track record that would allow their consideration for HIPC relief.

Maintaining a sustainable debt position while seeking the additional financing needed to make progress towards the MDGs remains a serious challenge for countries, even after debt relief under the HIPC Initiative. None of these are easy problems. But the IMF and World Bank are looking for solutions, with poverty reduction as the central focus.

Technical Assistance

Adequate policy-making capacity is critical for sustainable development and growth. The IMF provides assistance and training—generally free of charge—to help member countries strengthen the capacity of their institutions and officials to manage economic and financial policies. In recent years, the Fund has reinforced its efforts in low-income countries by establishing regional technical assistance centres in the Pacific, the Caribbean, East and West Africa, and in the near future in the Middle East.

IMF Emergency Assistance

The IMF provides emergency assistance to help member countries with urgent balance of payments financing needs in the wake of natural disasters or armed conflicts. Emergency financial assistance is designed to be disbursed rapidly and is supported by policy advice and, in many cases, technical assistance. Since 1962, 38 countries have received more than US$ 2.9 billion in emergency assistance from the IMF.

Since 1962, the IMF has provided emergency assistance to member countries afflicted by natural disasters—such as floods, earthquakes, hurricanes, or droughts. This assistance is aimed at meeting immediate foreign exchange financing needs arising from e.g., shortfalls in export earnings and/or increased imports, and avoid a serious depletion of external reserves.

In 1995, the IMF's policy on emergency assistance was expanded to cover countries in post-conflict situations. This assistance is limited to circumstances where a member with an urgent balance of payments need is unable to develop and implement a comprehensive economic program because its capacity has been damaged by a conflict, but where sufficient capacity for planning and policy implementation nevertheless exists. IMF financing can help a country directly and by catalyzing support from other sources, since Fund support must be part of a comprehensive international effort to address the aftermath of the conflict.

Emergency assistance loans are usually quick-disbursing and do not involve adherence to performance criteria. An IMF member requesting emergency assistance is required to describe the general economic policies that it proposes to follow. In addition, a member requesting post-conflict assistance is expected to indicate its intent to develop a more detailed policy program under one of the Fund's regular lending facilities. A request is granted when the IMF is satisfied that the member will cooperate with the Fund in finding solutions to its balance of payments difficulties.

Assistance has been typically limited to 25 percent of the member's quota in the IMF, although amounts up to 50 percent of quota can be and have been provided in certain circumstances. In March 2004, the Executive Board supported a proposal to extend emergency post-conflict assistance for up to three years, with access as much as 50 percent of quota, although no more than 25 percent of quota per year.

Emergency assistance loans are subject to the basic rate of charge, and should be repaid within 3¼ to 5 years. Since May 2001, for post-conflict cases which are eligible for the IMF's Poverty Reduction and Growth Facility (PRGF), the interest rate on loans has been subsidized down to 0.5 percent per year, with the interest subsidies financed by grant contributions from bilateral donors. In January 2005, the Executive Board agreed to provide a similar subsidization of emergency assistance for natural disasters upon request of the member country. Countries affected by the December 2004 tsunami in South Asia will be able to benefit from this initiative, as will members that have previously received emergency assistance for natural disasters but have not yet fully repaid such assistance.

Policy advice, covering the full range of macroeconomic policies and supporting structural measures, is an essential component of IMF emergency assistance. In post-conflict cases, technical assistance is also very important for rebuilding the capacity to implement macroeconomic policy. Areas of focus include rebuilding statistical capacity and establishing and reorganizing fiscal, monetary and exchange institutions to help restore tax and government expenditure capacity, payment, credit, and foreign exchange operations.

IMF and the Millennium Development Goals

The Millennium Development Goals (MDGs) are a set of development targets agreed by the international community, which centre on halving poverty and improving the welfare of the world's poorest by 2015. The IMF contributes to this effort through its advice, technical assistance, and lending to countries, as well as its role in mobilizing donor support. Together with the World Bank, it assesses progress toward the MDGs through an annual Global Monitoring Report.

In September 2000, at the United Nations Millennium Summit, world leaders agreed to eight specific and measurable development goals—now called the Millennium Development Goals (MDGs)—to be achieved by 2015. The first seven goals focus on eradicating extreme poverty and hunger; achieving universal primary education; promoting gender equality and empowering women; reducing child mortality; improving maternal health; combating HIV/AIDS, malaria and other diseases; and ensuring environmental sustainability. The eighth goal calls for the creation of a global partnership for development, with targets for aid, trade, and debt relief. A significant step toward meeting the MDGs was taken in Monterrey, Mexico, in March 2002, when the international community adopted a two pillar strategy, whereby sustained pursuit of sound policies and good governance by the low-income countries is to be matched by larger and more effective international support.

There are many ways in which the IMF helps poor countries achieve the sustained high levels of growth that establish the basis for poverty reduction—including through policy advice, technical assistance, financial support and debt relief. It also tries to ensure that developed countries' policies are supportive of low-income countries' development efforts, by advocating for increased foreign aid, the opening of markets to developing countries' exports, and the maintenance of a healthy enabling international economic climate.

The pressures to meet the MDGs by 2015 have further focused the IMF's efforts on helping countries assess the macroeconomic consequences of scaling up both their own policy efforts and external financial support. In this context, the IMF encourages countries to develop and analyze alternative frameworks for achieving the MDGs, and to make these underpin their poverty reduction strategies. Typically, one scenario might include a realistic projection that assumes good policy implementation and continued donor support at a level based on current trends and expectations. Another more ambitious projection would take account of absorptive and administrative constraints and try to identify policies to alleviate them so as to put the country on a higher growth path. This can help countries use the MDGs to design their policies, and guide donors in assessing the capacity of a country to absorb increased levels of aid and put it to effective use.

Increasingly, it is recognized that macroeconomic stability and growth depend heavily on structural and institutional factors. Therefore, in contributing to the achievement of the MDGs, the Fund works closely with partner agencies, especially the World Bank, but also other multilateral and bilateral providers of aid and financing.

The *Global Monitoring Report (*GMR) is an annual report that aims to assess how the world is doing in implementing the policies and actions needed to achieve the MDGs and related outcomes. It is produced jointly by the World Bank and the IMF, in collaboration with other international partners.

The first issue of the GMR, published in June 2004, showed that, on current trends, most MDGs would not be met by most countries. Some progress was being made, but it was uneven and too slow. The first goal of halving income poverty between 1990 and 2015 was likely to be achieved at the global level, but sub-Saharan Africa would fall well short. For the human development goals, the risks were much more pervasive across the regions. Likely shortfalls were especially serious with respect to the health and related environmental goals—child and maternal mortality, access to safe drinking water and basic sanitation. Few, if any, regions would achieve the mortality goals.

The GMR 2004 concluded that achievement of the MDGs required rising above current trends--and that, to that end, there was an urgent need for all parties to scale up action. In a comprehensive and integrated review of the global development policy agenda, the GMR 2004 identified priorities for action by developing countries, developed countries, and international agencies revolved around three elements: (1) accelerating reforms to achieve stronger economic growth; (2) empowering and investing in poor people by scaling up and improving the delivery of human development and related key services; and (3) speeding up the implementation of the Monterrey partnership, matching stronger reform efforts by developing countries with stronger support from developed countries and international agencies.

Building upon the previous year's conclusions and recommendations, which garnered wide consensus, the 2005 issue of the GMR tackles the question of how to generate momentum to accelerate progress and achieve the MDGs on schedule. With five years elapsed since the Millennium Declaration, and only ten to go until 2015, the year 2005 marks an important juncture. The report has a special focus on Sub-Saharan Africa, because this region is farthest from the MDGs and faces the toughest challenges in accelerating progress.

The report proposes a five-point agenda of accelerated and concerted actions by developing and developed countries: (1) anchor actions to achieve the MDGs in country-led development strategies; (2) improve the environment for stronger, private-led economic growth, as well as policies and governance; (3) scale up human development and relevant key services; (4) dismantle barriers to trade; and (5) substantially increase the level and effectiveness of aid.

Appendix 3

IMF Surveillance

A core responsibility of the IMF is to promote a dialogue among its member countries on the national and international consequences of their economic and financial policies. This process of monitoring and consultation, normally referred to as "surveillance", has evolved rapidly as the world economy has changed. IMF surveillance has also become increasingly open and transparent in recent years.

In today's globalized economy, where the economic and financial policies of one country may affect many other countries, international cooperation to monitor economic developments on a global scale is essential. With its nearly universal membership of 184 countries, the IMF provides the mechanism for this cooperation.

The importance of effective surveillance has been underscored by recent financial crises. In response, the IMF has undertaken many initiatives to strengthen its capacity to detect vulnerabilities and risks at an early stage, to help member countries strengthen their policy frameworks and institutions, and to improve transparency and accountability.

The IMF has a mandate under Article IV of its Articles of Agreement to exercise surveillance over the exchange rate policies of its members in order to ensure the effective operation of the international monetary system. In 1977, an Executive Board decision recognized that the IMF's appraisal of exchange rate policy requires a comprehensive analysis of the general economic situation and policy strategy of each member country. The decision also emphasized that the ultimate objective of surveillance is to help member countries achieve financial stability and sustainable economic growth.

The objectives of surveillance remain the same today as in 1977. However, the framework for surveillance has evolved significantly in order to promote the benefits and respond to the challenges of an increasingly open world economy, including the dramatic expansion of international capital flows. Surveillance today covers a wide range of economic policies, with the emphasis given to each varying in accordance with a country's individual circumstances.

Exchange rate, monetary and fiscal policies remain at the centre of IMF surveillance. The IMF provides advice on issues ranging from the choice of exchange rate regime, to ensuring consistency between the exchange rate regime and the stance of fiscal and monetary policies.

Structural policies—such as those governing a country's international trade, labour markets, and power sectors—became more important to IMF surveillance in the 1980s as economic growth slowed in many industrial countries in the wake of a major oil price shock. Debt crises in the developing world and the break-up of the Soviet Union further underlined the need for structural change in many countries. Today, structural issues are included in the IMF's policy dialogue with its member countries whenever they have an important impact on macroeconomic performance.

Financial sector issues have received increasing emphasis in IMF surveillance following a series of banking crises in both industrial and developing countries in the 1990s. In 1999, the IMF and the World Bank created a joint Financial Sector Assessment Program (FSAP) to assess the strengths and weaknesses of countries' financial sectors. In those countries that have participated, FSAP findings provide important inputs into IMF surveillance.

Institutional issues—such as central bank independence, financial sector regulation, corporate governance, and policy transparency and accountability—have also become increasingly important to IMF surveillance in the wake of financial crises and in the context of some member countries' transition from planned to market economies. In recent years, the IMF and the World Bank have taken a central role in developing, implementing, and assessing internationally recognized standards and codes in areas that are crucial for the efficient functioning of a modern economy.

Assessment of risks and vulnerabilities stemming from large and sometimes volatile capital flows have become more central to IMF surveillance in recent years. While crisis prevention has always been central to IMF surveillance, the growth and development of global capital markets has necessitated that the scope of surveillance be expanded beyond the traditional focus on the current account position and external debt sustainability.

"Article IV consultations", as IMF surveillance discussions are known, usually take place once a year. IMF economists visit the member country to gather information and hold discussions with government and central bank officials, and often private investors and labour representatives, members of parliament, and civil society organizations. Upon its return, the mission submits a report to the IMF's Executive Board for discussion. The Board's views are subsequently summarized and transmitted to the country's authorities.

In recent years, surveillance has become increasingly transparent. Before 1997, the IMF's assessments of member countries' policies were treated as confidential documents. Now, nine out of ten member countries agree to publication of a Public Information Notice (PIN), which summarizes the staff's and the Board's views, and four out of five countries agree to publication of the staff report itself (FY2004 data).

The IMF continuously reviews global economic trends and developments in what is known as multilateral surveillance. The IMF also regularly examines economic developments and policies pursued under regional arrangements such as the euro area and the West African Economic and Monetary Union. IMF surveillance of its member countries provides important input to the multilateral and regional surveillance processes, and vice verse.

Many of the Fund staff's views are published in its bi-annual World Economic Outlook (WEO), which discusses prospects for the world economy and provides in-depth analysis of specific issues and challenges. In addition, the bi-annual Global Financial Stability Report (GFSR) provides assessments of the stability of global financial markets and identifies potential systemic weaknesses that could lead to crisis.

Appendix 4

IMF Technical Assistance

The objective of IMF technical assistance, as described in its Articles of Agreement, "is to contribute to the development of the productive resources of member countries by enhancing the effectiveness of economic policy and financial management." In practice, the IMF fulfils this objective by helping countries build up their human and institutional capacity to design and implement effective macroeconomic and structural policies, put in place reforms that strengthen their financial sectors, and reduce vulnerability to crises.

Technical assistance is one of the benefits of IMF membership. It is normally provided free of charge to any requesting member country, within IMF resource constraints. About three-quarters of IMF technical assistance goes to low and lower-middle income countries, particularly in sub-Saharan Africa and Asia. Post-conflict countries are also major beneficiaries, with Timor-Leste, the Democratic Republic of Congo, and Afghanistan among the top ten recipients in recent years. A wide range of other countries seek technical assistance to strengthen their capacities. In helping individual countries reduce weaknesses and vulnerabilities, technical assistance also contributes to a more robust and stable global economy.

The IMF provides technical assistance in its areas of expertise, namely: macroeconomic policy, tax policy and revenue administration, expenditure management, monetary policy, the exchange rate system, financial sector sustainability, and macroeconomic and financial statistics. Since demand for technical assistance far exceeds supply, the IMF gives priority to providing assistance where it complements and enhances the IMF's other key forms of assistance, surveillance and lending.

The IMF's efforts to strengthen the international financial system have precipitated demands for technical assistance. For example, countries have asked for help to address financial sector weaknesses identified within the framework of the joint IMF-World Bank Financial Sector Assessment Program; adopt and adhere to international standards and codes for financial, fiscal, and statistical management; implement recommendations from off-shore financial centres assessments; and strengthen measures to combat money laundering and the financing of terrorism.

At the same time, there is a continuing demand for technical assistance to help low-income countries build capacity to design and implement poverty-reducing and growth programs, and to help heavily indebted poor countries undertake debt sustainability analyses and manage debt-reduction programs. The IMF also contributes actively to the Integrated Framework for trade-related technical assistance, which aims to assist the low-income countries expand their participation in the global economy.

The IMF attaches great importance to country ownership. The recipient country is fully involved in the entire process of technical assistance, from identification of need, to implementation, monitoring, and evaluation.

The IMF delivers technical assistance in various ways. Support is often provided through short staff missions of limited duration sent from headquarters, the placement of experts and/or resident advisors for periods ranging from a few weeks to a few years (if the intention is to field a long-term advisor, countries may be asked to make a financial or in-kind contribution). Assistance might also be provided in the form of technical and diagnostic reports, training courses, seminars, workshops, and "on-line" advice and support.

The IMF has increasingly adopted a regional approach to the delivery of technical assistance and training. It operates five regional technical assistance centres, in the Pacific, the Caribbean, East and West Africa, and in the Middle East. In addition to training offered at the IMF Institute in Washington D.C., the IMF also offers courses, workshops, and seminars for country officials through a network of six regional training institutes and programs.

IMF technical assistance is financed from both internal and external sources. The IMF finances directly technical assistance delivery, supervision, administrative, and other overhead costs; and this accounts for about one-fifth of its total net administrative budget. The IMF also administers funding provided by bilateral and multilateral donors. Such cooperation and resource sharing has two benefits: it leverages the resources available for technical assistance, and it helps avoid duplication of advice.

Bilateral donors include Australia, Austria, Brazil, Canada, China, Denmark, Finland, France, Germany, India, Ireland, Italy, Japan, Luxembourg, the Netherlands, New Zealand, Norway, Portugal, Russia, Singapore, Sweden, Switzerland, the United Kingdom, and the United States. Multilateral donors include the African Development Bank, the Arab Monetary Fund, the Asian Development Bank, the European Commission, the Inter-American Development Bank, the United Nations, the United Nations Development Program (UNDP), and the World Bank. In FY 2004, external financing accounted for more than a quarter of the IMF's total technical assistance and training activities, with Japan being the most generous donor.

Measures have been undertaken since 1999 to strengthen the effectiveness of IMF technical assistance, particularly through integrating it more closely with surveillance and lending programs; reinforcing coordination with other providers, especially the World Bank; improving modalities of delivery, especially through the establishment of regional centres; strengthening the monitoring and evaluation of technical assistance programs; and promoting the dissemination of information on those programs more widely. A 2005 review of technical assistance by the IMF's Independent Evaluation Office (IEO) also yielded operational recommendations, such as a more medium-term perspective in setting technical assistance priorities. The IMF is considering how to implement the IEO's recommendations.

Standards and Codes

The IMF and World Bank have endorsed internationally recognized standards and codes in 12 areas as important for their work and for which Reports on the Observance of Standards and Codes (ROSCs) are prepared. Standards in the areas of data, fiscal transparency, and monetary and financial policy transparency have been developed by the Fund while others have been developed by other standard setting bodies including the World Bank, the Basel Committee on Banking Supervision, and the Financial Action Task Force (FATF).

ROSCs are prepared and published at the request of the member country by the IMF and/or World Bank in each of the 12 areas. ROSCs covering financial sector standards are usually prepared in the context of the Financial Sector Assessment Program. In some cases, detailed assessments of countries' observance of standards are also published.

An update on the Fund's standards initiative is given in Quarterly Reports on the Assessments of Standards and Codes.

Reports on the Observance of Standards and Codes (ROSCs)

ROSCs summarize the extent to which countries observe certain internationally recognized standards and codes. The IMF has recognized 12 areas and associated standards as useful for the operational work of the Fund and the World Bank. These comprise accounting; auditing; anti-money laundering and countering the financing of terrorism (AML/CFT); banking supervision; corporate governance; data dissemination; fiscal transparency; insolvency and creditor rights; insurance supervision; monetary and financial policy transparency; payments systems; and securities regulation; AML/CFT was added in November 2002. Reports summarizing countries' observance of these standards are prepared and published at the request of the member country. They are used to help sharpen the institutions' policy discussions with national authorities, and in the private sector (including by rating agencies) for risk assessment. Short updates are produced regularly and new reports are produced every few years.

Adopted at the United Nations Monetary and Financial Conference, Bretton Woods, New Hampshire, July 22, 1944.

Entered into force December 27, 1945. Amended effective July 28, 1969, by the modifications approved by the Board of Governors in Resolution No. 23-5, adopted May 31, 1968; amended effective April 1, 1978, by the modifications approved by the Board of Governors in Resolution No. 31-4, adopted April 30, 1976; and amended effective November 11, 1992, by the modifications approved by the Board of Governors in Resolution No. 45-3, adopted June 28, 1990.

Appendix 5

IMF, World Bank and WTO

IMF and WTO

The IMF and the World Bank are sister institutions in the United Nations system. They share the same goal of raising living standards in their member countries. Their approaches to this goal are complementary, with the IMF focusing on ensuring the stability of the international financial system and the World Bank concentrating on long-term economic development and poverty reduction.

The International Monetary Fund and the World Bank were both conceived at an international conference convened in Bretton Woods, New Hampshire, U.S.A. in July 1944. The goal of the conference participants was to establish a framework for economic cooperation and development that would lead to a more stable and prosperous global economy. While this goal has remained central to both institutions, their work has evolved in response to new economic developments and challenges.

The IMF promotes international monetary cooperation and provides policy advice and technical assistance to help countries build and maintain strong economies. The Fund also makes loans and helps countries devise policy programs to solve balance of payments problems—that is, situations where sufficient financing on affordable terms cannot be obtained to meet net international payments. IMF loans are relatively short-term, and funded mainly by the pool of quota contributions provided by its members. IMF staff are primarily economists with wide experience in macroeconomic and financial policies.

The World Bank promotes long-term economic development and poverty reduction by providing technical and financial support to help countries reform particular sectors or implement specific projects—for example, building schools and health centres, providing water and electricity, fighting disease, and protecting the environment. World Bank assistance is generally long-term, and is funded both by member country contributions and through bond issuance. World Bank staff are often specialists in particular issues, sectors, or techniques.

The IMF and World Bank collaborate regularly and at many levels on assistance to member countries and are involved in several joint initiatives. The terms for their cooperation were set out in a concordat in 1989, to ensure effective collaboration in areas where responsibilities overlap. These terms have since been elaborated in guidelines dealing with specific issues, such as public expenditure and loan conditionality.

Regular Collaboration: Collaboration on country assistance is underpinned by regular meetings between the staffs of the IMF and the Bank as well as routine exchanges of information. The two institutions also sometimes conduct country missions in parallel and have staff participate in each other's missions. IMF assessments of a country's general economic situation and policies provide input into the Bank's assessments of potential development projects or reforms. Similarly, Bank advice on structural and sectoral reforms is taken into account by the IMF in its policy advice. The staffs of the two institutions also cooperate on the conditionality involved in their respective lending programs.

The Managing Director of the IMF and the President of the World Bank meet regularly to consult on major issues of the day. They issue joint statements and occasionally write joint articles in the world press, and they have made joint visits to several regions and countries.

Joint Initiatives: During the 1990s, the IMF and World Bank jointly launched two major initiatives to help poor countries. In 1996, the IMF and the World Bank introduced the Heavily Indebted Poor Countries (HIPC) Initiative to reduce the external debt burdens of the most heavily indebted poor countries. In 1999, the IMF and the World Bank initiated the Poverty Reduction Strategy Paper (PRSP) approach—a country-led strategy for linking national policies, donor support, and the development outcomes needed to reduce poverty in low-income countries.

PRSPs underpin the HIPC Initiative and concessional lending by the IMF and World Bank.

In July 2004, the Fund and Bank launched the *Global Monitoring Report (GMR).* This annual report assesses progress on policies and actions needed to achieve the United Nations' Millennium Development Goals (MDGs), which centre on halving poverty between 1990 and 2015. The GMR also considers how well developing countries, developed countries, and the international financial institutions are contributing to the development partnership and strategy to meet the MDGs agreed at a summit in Monterrey in March 2002.

The IMF and World Bank are also working together to make financial sectors in member countries resilient and well-regulated. The Financial Sector Assessment Program (FSAP) was introduced in 1999 to identify the strengths and vulnerabilities of a country's financial system and recommend the appropriate policy responses.

High-level coordination: The Annual Meetings of the Boards of Governors of the IMF and the World Bank provides another forum for Fund-Bank collaboration and cooperation. There, Governors consult with one another and present their countries' views on current issues in international economics and finance. The Boards of Governors make decisions on how current international economic issues should be addressed and approve corresponding resolutions.

A subset of IMF and World Bank Governors also convene during the semi-annual meetings of the Development Committee. This was established in 1974 to advise the Boards of Governors of the IMF and World Bank on critical development issues—including trade and global environmental issues—and on the financial resources required to promote economic development in low-income countries.

Directors sitting on the Executive Boards of the Fund and Bank—which meet at least three times each week at their respective Washington D.C. headquarters—confer and consult with one another regularly. A few countries have a single Executive Director who sits on both Boards.

IMF and World Trade Organization (WTO)

The IMF and the WTO are international organizations with 141 members in common. While the IMF's central focus is on the international monetary and financial system, and the WTO's is on the international trading system, both work together to ensure a sound system for global trade and payments.

The International Monetary Fund (IMF) is an international organization of 184 countries that works to ensure the stability of the international monetary and financial system. The IMF's mandate includes facilitating the expansion and balanced growth of international trade, promoting exchange stability, and providing the opportunity for the orderly correction of countries' balance of payments problems. The IMF was established in 1945.

The World Trade Organization (WTO) is an international organization of 146 countries that deals with the rules of trade between nations. The WTO works to help international trade to flow smoothly, predictably, and freely, and provides countries with a constructive and fair outlet for dealing with disputes over trade issues. The WTO came into being in 1995, succeeding the General Agreement on Tariffs and Trade (GATT) that was established in 1947.

The work of the IMF and the WTO is complementary. A sound international financial system is needed to support vibrant international trade, while smoothly flowing trade helps to reduce the risk of payments imbalances and financial crisis. The two institutions work together to ensure a strong system of international trade and payments that is open to all countries. Such a system is critical for enabling economic growth, raising living standards, and reducing poverty around the globe.

The IMF and the WTO work together on many levels, with the aim of ensuring greater coherence in global economic policymaking. A cooperation agreement between the two organizations, covering various aspects of their relationship, was signed shortly after the creation of the WTO.

Regular Consultation: The IMF has observership status at the WTO, and participates actively in many meetings of WTO committees, working groups, and bodies. The WTO Secretariat attends meetings of the IMF Executive Board or the Board Committee on Liaison with the WTO on matters of common interest. Trade policy issues often feature prominently in Fund surveillance activities and are addressed in the context of IMF-supported programs whenever they give rise to balance of payments problems. Equally, IMF surveillance reports, including assessments of exchange rate policies, are important inputs to the WTO's periodic reports on member countries' trade policies (Trade Policy Reviews).

The WTO is required to consult the IMF when it deals with issues concerning monetary reserves, balance of payments, and foreign exchange arrangements. For example, WTO agreements allow countries to apply trade restrictions in the event of balance of payments difficulties. The WTO's Balance of Payments Committee (BPC) bases its assessments of restrictions on the IMF's determination of a member's balance of payments situation.

Informal consultation between IMF staff and the WTO Secretariat takes place regularly regarding trade policy developments and advice for individual countries. The IMF and WTO also regularly share data and research. For example, in the context of the Doha Development Agenda and in response to a WTO request, the IMF completed studies on the erosion of preferences, trade-related loss of fiscal revenue, export subsidies, balance of payments safeguards, and exchange rate volatility and trade.

Technical Assistance and Training: The IMF, the WTO, and other international organizations and donors often work together to help countries improve their ability to trade. In particular, they have developed the Integrated Framework for Trade-Related Technical Assistance to Least-Developed Countries, with a view to strengthening the capacity of these countries to formulate trade policy, negotiate trade agreements, and tackle production challenges in their domestic economies. In addition, the Integrated Framework seeks to ensure that poorer member countries incorporate appropriate trade reforms into their Poverty Reduction and Strategy Papers (PRSPs), which form the basis for concessional support by the IMF and the World Bank.

Fund Assistance for Trade Liberalization: In an effort to support progress under the WTO's Doha round of trade talks, the IMF established the Trade Integration Mechanism (TIM) in April 2004. The TIM is available to all Fund member countries whose balance of payments positions might suffer, albeit temporarily, as a result of multilateral trade liberalization. It is not a new lending facility, but rather a policy aimed at making Fund resources more predictably available under existing IMF facilities.

High-level Coordination: The Managing Director of the IMF and the Director General of the WTO consult regularly on a range of trade-related issues. For example, during the Asian crisis, the two frequently discussed the impact of currency devaluations on trade and the efforts that both institutions should make to prevent ill-conceived trade policy reactions. And at the May 2003 meeting of the WTO General Council, the heads of the IMF and the World Bank shared their views with WTO national delegations on trade issues and coherence in the work of the three organizations. At the September 2003 WTO Ministerial Meeting in Cancún, the First Deputy Managing Director of the IMF announced plans to introduce the TIM.

Looking forward, it is likely that cooperation and consultation between the IMF and WTO will intensify, given the increased areas of mutual support and overlap between the two institutions. Potential areas of heightened interaction include current and prospective WTO agreements on financial services, trade facilitation, and agriculture (in particular, the cotton sector).

IMF's Trade Integration Mechanism (TIM)

The Trade Integration Mechanism (TIM) was introduced in April 2004 to assist member countries to meet balance of payments shortfalls that might result from multilateral trade liberalization. The TIM is not a special lending facility, but rather a policy designed to make resources more predictably available under existing IMF facilities.

Multilateral trade liberalization has been a major contributor to the world economy's unprecedented growth over the past half century. In tackling remaining restrictions on trade, the Doha Development Agenda of the World Trade Organization (WTO) has the potential to benefit all countries. Yet, while overwhelmingly positive in its impact over time, opening the world trading environment further would require countries to adjust. And under certain circumstances, these adjustments could temporarily reduce export revenues, increase import bills, or cause other shortfalls in the external balance of payments.

Some of the potential adjustment pressures derive from more competitive conditions in a country's export markets. For example, the erosion of tariff preferences could lead to a reduction in the demand for a country's exports because other suppliers can now compete on more equal terms. Similarly, the expiration (in 2005) of quotas under the WTO's textiles agreement could lead to more intense competition in textiles and clothing markets—resulting in higher imports and/or lower exports in some countries. Another possible adjustment pressure relates to cuts in agricultural subsidies in the OECD countries. While of course benefiting the vast number of farmers in the developing world, such measures could nevertheless increase the price of food imports (relative to food exports) in some countries.

According to Fund research, balance of payments shortfalls are unlikely to be large for most countries, and would eventually be dominated by the positive impact of more open trade. Nevertheless, they could be significant in the short run for some countries.

The IMF's Trade Integration Mechanism (TIM) aims to mitigate concerns—particularly in developing countries—about financing such balance of payments shortfalls.

The TIM is not a special facility that will provide new resources under special terms. Financial support for balance of payments difficulties arising from trade-related adjustments is already provided under the Fund's existing lending facilities. Rather, the TIM is a policy designed to increase the predictability of resources that are available under existing facilities.

The TIM is expected to create a modest increase in IMF financing, for two reasons. First, the explicit emphasis on trade adjustments will ensure that their impact is carefully estimated and incorporated into Fund-supported programs. Second, the TIM contains a "deviation feature" which provides countries with a greater degree of certainty that IMF financing will be available to assist with larger-than-anticipated adjustments.

A member country can request consideration under the TIM if it expects a net balance of payments shortfall as a result of measures implemented by other countries that lead to more open market access for goods and services. Such measures would typically be introduced either under a WTO agreement or in some other way that treats all countries on a non-discriminatory basis.

The TIM details how the Fund would provide access to its resources to meet a balance of payments need associated with such trade-related adjustments. In particular, the IMF would:

- stand ready to discuss with countries facing such balance of payments shortfalls, new arrangements within its existing lending facilities (i.e., upper credit tranches, the Extended Fund Facility (EFF), or the Poverty Reduction and Growth Facility (PRGF));
- take into account the anticipated impact of the trade adjustment on the member's balance of payments in determining the appropriate size of access under both new and existing arrangements (the "baseline feature"); and
- be prepared to augment arrangements under simplified procedures if the actual balance of payments effect turns out to be larger than anticipated (the "deviation feature").

The TIM does not cover the implications of "own liberalization" measures—for example, any deterioration in a country's balance of payments that results from a reduction in its own import tariffs. However, the Fund will continue to assist its members in anticipating and managing the implications of domestic reforms that may be associated with Doha Round commitments, including through financing under the Fund's existing policies.

Appendix 6

Social Dimensions of the IMF Policies

The IMF's growing emphasis on social policy issues has emerged from an increased awareness that macroeconomic and structural policies have important social implications, which in turn have ramifications for the domestic ownership of economic reform programs and for promoting sustainable economic growth.

The IMF's mandate is to promote international monetary cooperation, the balanced growth of international trade, and a stable system of exchange rates. Fulfilling this mandate is the IMF's primary contribution to sustainable economic and human development. In pursuing it, however, the IMF likewise recognizes that the size and quality of social spending can affect long-run growth and poverty reduction; that macroeconomic viability must include policies that directly address poverty and social concerns; and that, in order to support these objectives, social sector spending should be focused on improving the education and health status of the poor. This realization reflects two broad trends: the emergence of more open and participatory forms of policy-making involving the IMF with various elements of civil society (academics, religious leaders, business groups, labour unions, and NGOs); and a growing recognition that popular support-or "ownership" for adjustment programs is an essential precondition for their ultimate success.

For low-income member countries, the IMF has placed Poverty Reduction Strategy Papers (PRSPs) at the centre of its efforts (see the Fact Sheets on the PRGF and the HIPC Initiative respectively). PRSPs describe a country's macroeconomic, structural, and social policies, and are designed in collaboration with civil society. As of early 2001, 31 countries had produced PRSPs, with the support of the IMF, World Bank, regional development banks, and donors.

IMF-supported programs have sought to promote universal access to basic social services; they have increased public spending for such services in countries where this spending was low, supported high-quality expenditures in these sectors, and protected or sought real increases in these expenditures during adjustment periods when poor households might lack the ability to pay for basic social services. Through policy discussions and technical assistance, the IMF also contributes to improving transparency in governments' decision making and their capacity to monitor poverty-reducing spending and social developments.

In its work in these areas, IMF staff relies heavily on the expertise of other institutions. These include the World Bank, regional development banks, the United Nations Development Program, the International Labour Office, the World Health Organization, and other UN agencies. In particular, the IMF looks to the World Bank for policy analysis, reform options, and estimates of their budgetary cost, as well as data on social indicators.

This dialogue enables the IMF to ensure that social and sectoral programs aimed at poverty reduction can be accommodated and financed within a supportive, growth-enhancing, macroeconomic and budgetary framework.

One way for governments to create room for poverty-reducing outlays is to cut unproductive spending. For instance, it is heartening to note that the declines in military spending worldwide during the 1990s have been accompanied by increases in social spending in a number of countries. Between 1990 and 1999, for example, military expenditure declined by 1.2 percentage point of GDP in low-income countries with Fund-supported programs, while expenditure on health care and education in these countries rose by 0.8 percentage point of GDP. Nevertheless, in many countries efforts still need to be made to reduce excessive military spending.

A recent review of social spending in a representative sample of 32 low-income countries that received IMF support for the period 1985-99 indicated that these countries have made progress in raising public social expenditures and improving social indicators. This overall progress, however, masks considerable variation in experience across countries. On average, for the entire group of countries, per capita real spending on education and health increased at an annual rate of 3.4 percent and 3.3 percent respectively, although smaller gains in education spending were recorded in Africa. Significant and broad-based gains were achieved in social indicators for education and health, including those associated with the International Development Goals for 2015. On average, and on an annual basis, overall primary school enrolment improved by 0.9 percent; female primary and secondary enrolment by 1.2 percent and 1.3 percent, respectively; infant mortality by 1.8 percent; under-five mortality by 2.2 percent; births attended by skilled staff by 1.7 percent; and contraceptive prevalence by 5.3 percent.

In the short term, some measures needed for economic stability may hurt some of society's most vulnerable groups, while helping other groups. For example, currency devaluations may hurt the urban poor through increasing prices of imported products, while helping low-income smallholders producing export crops in rural areas. In countries where the authorities could foresee that reform measures would have a sizable adverse social impact, the policy mix and sequencing of measures have aimed to take this impact into account within a sustainable macroeconomic framework. For instance, IMF-supported programs have aimed to phase out subsidies for food and other items gradually, rather than all at once (e.g., Indonesia following the financial crisis of 1997). An adverse impact, however, cannot always be avoided, even with an appropriate policy mix and sequencing. For instance, a currency devaluation may be at the heart of a reform program. Thus, a tension may emerge between stabilization and social protection objectives. Social safety nets are a means of easing this tension. About three-fourths of the low-income countries that had Fund-supported programs during 1994-98 included social safety nets in their programs.

Social safety nets can take many forms: Subsidies directed at particular groups or cash compensation in lieu of subsidies; improved distribution of essential commodities, such as medicines; temporary price controls on some essential commodities; severance pay and retraining for public sector employees who have lost their jobs; and employment through public works programs. In most cases, the IMF staff largely relies on the World Bank to take the lead in the design of social safety nets, which are then incorporated into IMF-supported programs.

The IMF is still in the learning process in the social policy area. In many cases, weak administrative structures and lack of appropriate social policy instruments have made it difficult to strengthen public spending on social sectors and implement social safety nets. In addition, IMF staff is often constrained by lack of data, which makes it difficult to assess the effectiveness of poverty-reducing spending.

The IMF has taken concrete initiatives to address the social content of reform programs. For example, staff has improved their collection of data on government social expenditures, and the monitoring of social output indicators in member countries-particularly the heavily indebted and poor countries. Work on the PRSP process is still evolving, and is expected to forge a stronger link between social spending and social indicators, as well as focus attention more closely on how to assist the poor. In addition, the IMF and World Bank are jointly embarking on an initiative to assist HIPCs in establishing the capacity to track poverty-related spending. We are constantly looking at what we have done, how effective we have been, and how we can do better

Bibliography

Bibliography

Books

Acheson, A.L. Keith, Ed.; *"Bretton Woods Revised"* 1972, Macmillan Press, London.

Aufricht, Hans: *"The International Monetary Fund"*, 1964, Stevens and Sons, London.

Bruen, A.I.D., *"IMF: Structure, Working and Management"*, 1990, Deep and Deep Publications, New Delhi.

Das, D.K. Ed. "*International Finance*", 1993, Routledge, London.

De Varies, Margaret Garristen, *"International Monetary Fund 1965-1972"*, 1985, IMF Publications,

Washington, D.C.

De Varies, Margaret Garristen, *"International Monetary Fund 1972- 1978"*, 1985, IMF Publications,

Washington, D.C.

De Varies, Margaret Garristen, *"IMF in a Changing World, 1945-1985"*, 1986, IMF Publications, Washington, D.C.

Dormael, Armand Van, *"Bretton Woods: Birth of Monetary System", 1978*, Macmillan Press, London.

Ferguson, Tyrone: *"Third World and Decision Making in the IMF"*, 1988, Pinter Publishers, London.

Froyen, Richard T., *"Macro-Economics"*, 1983, Macmillan Publishing Co., New York.

Ghai, Dharam, *"The IMF and the South: The Social Impact of Crisis and Adjustment*", 1991, Zea Books Ltd., London.

Goldrin, I., and Winters, L.A., Eds., *"Open Economies: Structural Adjustment and Agriculture"*, 1992, Cambridge Press, Cambridge.

Gupta, S.P., *"Statistical methods"*, 2004, Sultan Chand and Sons, New Delhi.

Horie, Shigee, *"The International Monetary Fund"*, 1964, Macmillan Press, London.

Hutchful, Eboe, *"The IMF and Ghana: The Confidential Record"*, 1987, Zea Books Ltd., London.

Jhingan, M.L., *"Macroeconomic Theory"*, 1986, Konark Publishers, New Delhi.

Jhingan, M.L., *"The Economics of Development and Planning"*, 1986, Konark Publishers, New Delhi.

Khan, A.R. and Hossain, M., *"The Strategy of Development in Bangladesh"*, 1989, Macmillan Press, London.

Khan, A.R., *"Economy of Bangladesh"*, 1972, Macmillan Press, London.

Killick, Tony, *"The IMF and Stabilization"*, 1984, Heinemann Educational Books, London.

Killick, Tony, *"Quest for Economic Stabilization"*, 1984, Heinemann Educational Books, London.

Killick, Tony, *"Adjustment and Financing in Developing Countries"*, 1982, IMF Publications, Washington.

Kindleberger, C.P. and Herrick, Bruce, *"The Economic Development"*, 1958, The McGraw Hills Book Company, New York.

Muns, Joaquin, *"Adjustment, Conditionality and International Financing"*, 1984, IMF Publications, Washington, D.C.

Newbold, Paul: *"Statistics for Business and Economics"*, 1984, prentice Hall, N.J.

Parkin, Machael: *"Macro-Economics"*, 1984, Prentice Hall, N.J.

Pastor, M.J.: *"The International Monetary Fund and Latin America"*, West View Press, Boulder.

Richards, A. and Waterbury, John: *"A Political Economy of the Middle East"*, 1990, West View Press, Boulder.

Sen, Amartya, *"Growth Economics"*, 1970, Penguin Books ltd.

Sodersten, Bo, *"International Economics"*, 1980, Macmillan Publishing Co. London.

Solmon, Lewis C., *"Macro-Economics"*, 1981, Addison Wesley Publishing Company, Phillipines.

Urrutia, Miguel, *"Economics and Social Progress in Latin America"*, 1988, Inter American Development Bank, New York.

Williamson, John, Ed. *"IMF Conditionality"*, 1983, Institute for International Economics, Washington, D.C.

Journals and Periodicals

ADB: *Asian Development Review.*
Bank of Mexico: *Review of Economic Situation in Mexico.*
BIDS: Bangladesh Development Studies
EIU: Country Reports
GOI: Economic Survey
IMF: Balance of Payments Statistics
IMF: Finance and Development
IMF: Government Finance Statistics
IMF: IMF-Survey
IMF: International Financial Statistics
IMF: Occasional Paper
IMF: Staff Paper
IMF: World Economic Outlook
UN: Economic Report on Africa
UN: Economic and Social Survey of Asia and Pacific
UN: Economic Survey of Africa
UN: Economic Survey of Asia and Pacific
UN: Economic Survey of Latin America
UN: National Accounts: Analysis of Main Aggregates
UN: National Accounts Statistics: Main Aggregates and Detailed Tables
UN: Statistical Yearbook
UN: Statistical Yearbook for Asia and Far East
UN: Statistical Yearbook for Latin America
UN: World Development
UN: World Economic Survey

Articles

Agheveli, B. B., Kim, I.S. and Ness, H., "Growth and Adjustment in South Africa", *Finance and Development*, Sept. 1987, Washington, D.C., pp. 12-16.

Apse, Pedro and gurria, J.A., "The State and Economic Development: A Mexican Perspective', *Proceedings of the World Bank Annual Conference on Development Economics, 1992*, The World Bank, (1993), pp.9-14.

Boumgarter, Ulrich, "The Success of Indian Adjustment Programme", *Economic Times*, 20th April, 1994, Bombay, p.5.

Bhatia, R.J., "Adjustment Efforts in Sub-Saharan Africa, 1980-84", *Finance and Development*, Sept 1985, Washington, D.C., pp. 19-22.

Bleger, M.I. and Chu, Ke Young, "Measurement of Fiscal Impacts: Methodological Issues", *IMF Occasional Paper*, No. 59, (June 1988), Washington.

Calvo, G.A; Leiderman, L., and Reinhart, C.M., "Capital Inflows and Real Exchange Rate Appreciation in Latin America: The Role of External Factors", *IMF Staff Paper*, Vol. 40, No. 1 (March 1993).

Chand, S.K. and Til, R.V., "Ghana: Toward Successful Stabilization and Recovery", *Finance and Development*, March 1988, Washington D.C., pp.32-35.

Crockett, Andrew D., "Stabilization Policies in Developing Countries: Some Policy Considerations", *IMF Staff Paper*, Vol. 28, No.1 (March 1981), Washington, D.C.

Donovan, Donal J., "Red Responses Associated with Exchange Rate Action in Selected Upper Credit Tranche Stabilisation Programs", *IMF Staff Paper*, Vol. 28, No. 4 (Dec 1981), Washington, pp.698-727.

Donovan, Donal J., "Macroeconomic Performance and Adjustment Under fund-Supported Programs: The Experience of Seventies", *IMF Staff Paper*, Vol. 29, No. 2 (June 1982), Washington, pp.171-203.

Doroodian, Khosrow, "Macroeconomic Performance and Adjustment under Policies Commonly Supported by the International monetary Fund", *Economic Development and Cultural Change*, Vol. 41, No. 4 (July 1993), The University of Chicago Press, pp.849-861

Edwards, Sebastian and Montiel, P.J., "Devaluation Crises and the Macroeconomic Consequences of Post Adjustment in Developing Countries", *IMF Staff Paper*, vol. 36, no. 4 (Dec 1989), Washington, pp. 895-903.

Frenkel, J.A. and Khan, M.S., "The International Monetary Fund's Adjustment Policies and Economic Development" in Das, D.K., Ed., *International Finance*, 1993, London, pp. 86-100.

Goldrin, I. and Winters, L.A., "Adjustment and the Rural Sector: A Counterfactual Analysis of morocco", *Open Economies: Structural Adjustment and Agriculture*, OECD, 1993, pp.93-145.

Goldstein, Morris;" The Global Effects of Fund Supported Adjustment programs", *IMF Occasional Paper*, No. 42 (March 1986), Washington.

Goldstein, M. and Montiel, P., "Evaluating Fund Stabilization programs with Multicountry Data", *IMF Staff Paper*, Vol. 33 (March 1986), Washington, pp.304-341.

Gotur, Padma, "Bangladesh: Tackling the Problem of Poverty", *Finance and Development*, June 1992, Washington, pp. 38-39.

Guitian, Manuel, "Fund Conditionality: Evolution of Principles and Practices", *IMF Pamphlet Series*, No. 38 (1982), Washington, pp. 1-51.

Gwin, Catherine, "Financing India's Structural Adjustment: The Role of Fund", in Williamson john, Ed. *IMF Conditionality*, Washington, pp. 511- 31.

Harrigan, J. and Mosley, P., "Evaluating the Impact of World Bank Structural Adjustment Lending: 1980-1987", *The Journal of Development Studies*, Vol. 27, no. 3, (April 1991), London, pp. 63-94.

Heller, P.S., Bovenberg, Chu Ke Young and Shome, "The Implications of the Fund Supported Programs for Poverty: Experience in Selected Countries", *IMF Occasional Paper*, No. 58 (May 1988), Washington, pp.1-42.

Hooke, A.W., "The International Monetary Fund: Its Evolution, Organization and Activities", *IMF Pamphlet Series*, No. 37, (1982), Washington.

The IMF Staff, "Fund-Supported Programmes, Fiscal Policy and Income Distribution", *IMF Occasional Paper*, No. 46, (Sept 1986), Washington.

The IMF Staff, "Ghana: Adjustment and Growth, 1983-91", *IMF Occasional Paper*, no. 86 (1991), Washington, pp.1- 65.

Johnson, G.G., "Formulation of Exchange Rate Policies in Adjustment programs", *IMF Occasional Paper*, No. 36 (August 1985), Washington.

Kelly, M.R., 'Fiscal Adjustment and Fund Supported Programs, 1971-80", *IMF Staff Paper*, Vol. 29, No. 4(Dec 1982), Washington, pp.561-602.

Khan, M.S. and Knight, M.D., "Do Fund Supported Adjustment Programs Retard Growth?", *Finance and Development*, (March 1986), Washington, pp.30-32.

Khan, M.S., "The Macroeconomic Effects of Fund Supported Adjustment Programmes", *IMF Staff Paper*, Vol. 37, No. 2 (June 1990), Washington, pp. 195-230.

Khan, M.S. and Knight, M.D., "Fund Supported Adjustment Programs and Economic Growth", *IMF Occasional Paper*, No.41 (Nov 1985), Washington.

Khan, M.S. and Knight, M.D., "Stabilization programs in Developing Countries: A Formal Framework", *IMF Staff Paper*, Vol. 28, No. 1 (March 1981), Washington, pp. 1-53.

Khan, M.S. and Montiel, P.J., "Growth Oriented Adjustment Programs", *IMF Staff Paper*, Vol. 36, no. 2 (June 1989), Washington, pp. 277-305.

Kiguel, M.A. and Liviatan, N., "Progress Report on Heterodox Stabilization Programs", *Finance and Development*, (March 1992), Washington, pp. 22-37.

Krugman, Paul, "Toward a Counterrevolution in Development Theory", *Proceedings of World Bank Annual Conference on Development Economics*, 1992, The World Bank 1993, pp. 15-37.

Kuczynski, Pedro-Pablo, "International Capital Flows to Latin America: What is the Promise?", *Proceedings of World Bank*

Annual Conference on Development Economics, 1992, the World Bank (1993), pp.323-325.

Kumar, Man Mohan S., "The Stabilizing Role of the Compensatory Financing Facility", *IMF Staff Paper*, Vol. 36, no. 4 (Dec 1989), Washington, pp. 771-809.

Loser, C. and Kalter, E., "Mexico: The Strategy to Achieve Sustained Economic Growth", *IMF Occasional Paper*, No.99, Sept. 1992, Washington, pp. 1-13.

Pastor, M.J., "The Effects of IMF Programs in the Third world: Debate and Experience from Latin America", *World Development*, Vol. 15, no. 2 (19870, pp. 249-262.

Polka, Jacques J., "A Marriage between Fund and Bank Models?", *IMF Staff Paper*, Vol. 37, no. 1 (March 1990), Washington, pp. 183-186.

Rahman, S.H., "Structural Adjustment and Macroeconomic Performance in Bangladesh in the 1980s", *The Bangladesh Development Studies*, Vol. XX, No. 2-3, (June-Sept 1992), Dhaka, pp.89-125.

Reichmann, T. and Stillson, R. T., "Experience with Programs of Balance of Payments Adjustment: Stand By Arrangements in the Higher Tranches, 1963-72", *IMF Staff Paper*, Vol. 25, No. 3 9June 1978), Washington, pp.293-309.

Sarkar, Prabijit, "Debt Crisis in Less Developed Countries and the Transfer Debate Once Again", *The Journal of Development Studies*, Vol. 27, No. 4, (July 1991), London, pp.84-101.

Sisson, Charles A., "Fund Supported Programs and Income Distribution in LDCs", *Finance and Development*, March 1986, Washington, pp. 33-36.

Tanzi, Vito, "The Impact of Macroeconomic Policies on the Level of Taxation and the Fiscal Balance in Developing Countries", *IMF Staff Paper*, Vol. 36, No. 3 (Sept 1989), Washington pp. 633-655.

UNCTAD, "Adjustment and Stagnation in Sub-Saharan Africa", *Trade and Development Report*, 1993, UN, pp. 93-102.

Winters, Cecelia Ann, "Unanticipated Capital Flows and the Mexican Economy: An Empirical investigation", *The Journal of Development Studies*, Vol.29.No.3, (April 1993), London, pp.504-517.

Zulu, J.B. and Nsouli, S.M., "Adjustment programs in Africa: The Recent Experience", *IMF Occasional Paper,* No. 4, April 1985, Washington.

Index

Index